LOST LANDMARKS
OF
ORANGE COUNTY

BY CHRIS EPTING

SANTA
MONICA
PRESS

Published by: Santa Monica Press LLC
P.O. Box 850
Solana Beach, CA 92075
1-800-784-9553
www.santamonicapress.com
books@santamonicapress.com

SANTA
MONICA
PRESS

Printed in China

Santa Monica Press books are available at special quantity discounts when
purchased in bulk by corporations, organizations, or groups. Please call our
Special Sales department at 1-800-784-9553.

ISBN-13: 978-1-59580-112-8 (print)
ISBN-13: 978-1-59580-776-2 (ebook)

Publisher's Cataloging-in-Publication data

Names: Epting, Chris, 1961-, author.
Title: Lost landmarks of Orange County / by Chris Epting.
Description: Solana Beach, CA: Santa Monica Press, 2024.
Identifiers: ISBN: 978-1-59580-112-8 (paperback) | 978-1-59580-776-2 (ebook)
Subjects: LCSH Orange County (Calif.)--Description and travel. | Orange County
(Calif.)--History. | Orange County (Calif.)--History, Local. | BISAC TRAVEL
/ United States / West / Pacific (AK, CA, HI, OR, WA) | TRAVEL / Special
Interest / Amusement & Theme Parks | TRAVEL / Special Interest / Roadside
Attractions | HISTORY / United States / State & Local / West (AK, CA, CO, HI,
ID, MT, NV, UT, WY)
Classification: LCC F868.O6 .E 2023 | DDC 979.4/96--dc23

Front cover courtesy of the Orange County Archives
Cover and interior design and production by Future Studio

CONTENTS

Preface 5

INTRODUCTION   The History of Orange County 9

CHAPTER ONE   Early History 13

CHAPTER TWO   Theme Parks, Museums,
                      and Other Attractions 28

CHAPTER THREE   Racetracks 61

CHAPTER FOUR   Eating and Drinking 70

CHAPTER FIVE   Theaters 101

CHAPTER SIX   Bowling, Ice Skating, Miniature Golf,
                      and Skateboarding 121

CHAPTER SEVEN   Music 137

CHAPTER EIGHT   Dairies 180

CHAPTER NINE   Agriculture 191

CHAPTER TEN   Oil 202

CHAPTER ELEVEN   Surfing 207

CHAPTER TWELVE   Military 220

CHAPTER THIRTEEN   Planes and Trains 231

CHAPTER FOURTEEN   Sports 242

CHAPTER FIFTEEN   Weird, Wonderful, and One-of-a-Kind 253

Acknowledgments 300

Photo Credits 300

The author at the site of Frank Lloyd Wright Jr.'s proposed tower at the Westfair shopping center in Huntington Beach.

PREFACE

AS I EMBARK ON this journey through the vanished landscapes of Orange County, California, I am filled with a profound sense of purpose. In the pages of this book, I aim to document the places that no longer exist—restaurants, racetracks, music venues, drive-in movie theaters, theme parks, and more—that have shaped the collective memories of generations. It is a tribute to the rich tapestry of experiences that have made Orange County one of the most vibrant and interesting places in the United States.

Why is it crucial to preserve the remnants of a past that has faded away? Why do we feel a deep-rooted connection to these lost landmarks? The answers lie in the power of memory and the profound impact that shared experiences have on our lives.

Our memories act as portals that transport us to moments frozen in time. They allow us to revisit the laughter, the excitement, the joy, and sometimes even the heartache that unfolded within the walls of these forgotten places. Each demolished restaurant, closed theater, and abandoned music venue holds within it a treasure trove of stories waiting to be told. By documenting these lost landmarks, we ensure that the memories they hold remain alive for future generations.

Studying the past is not merely an exercise in nostalgia; it is a vital tool for understanding the present and shaping the future. As we delve into the history of Orange County's vanished gems, we begin to unravel the threads that have woven together the fabric of our community. We gain insight into the values, dreams, and aspirations of those who came before us, and we find inspiration in their resilience and creativity.

Orange County has always been a place of innovation, reinvention, and boundless possibilities. It is a testament to the shared experiences of its diverse population that the region has flourished. The stories of these lost landmarks reflect the tapestry of cultures, passions, and dreams that have coalesced to create the vibrant mosaic we see today.

In the vast landscape of Orange County's history, there are

iconic destinations that have become synonymous with the region—Disneyland and Knott's Berry Farm, for example. These beloved attractions have left an indelible mark on our collective consciousness. But as we delve deeper into the lost landmarks of Orange County, we uncover a treasure trove of forgotten gems that once graced our landscape.

How many still remember the Buffalo Ranch, where majestic herds roamed freely against a backdrop of rolling hills? Or the thrill of driving through Lion Country Safari, where the untamed beauty of the animal kingdom was just a car's length away? And what about the Japanese Village and Deer Park, a tranquil oasis where visitors could interact with gentle creatures in a serene setting?

These unique and lesser-known destinations held a special place in the hearts of locals and visitors alike. They offered an alternative form of entertainment, a chance to connect with nature, and a window into cultures and experiences beyond our own. Each of these lost landmarks had its own charm, weaving unforgettable memories into the tapestry of Orange County's vibrant history.

These forgotten destinations remind us that the landscape of Orange County's entertainment and leisure has always been evolving. They showcase the bold and innovative spirit that has defined this region, as entrepreneurs sought to capture the imaginations of residents and tourists alike.

In our fast-paced world, where change is inevitable, it is easy to overlook the significance of the past. Yet, by celebrating and preserving the memories of what has been lost, we honor the collective spirit that has defined Orange County. We pay homage to the entrepreneurs who took risks, the artists who ignited our imaginations, and the communities that thrived within these cherished spaces.

Though technically "lost," these landmarks continue to reside in the hearts and minds of those who experienced them. They are the invisible threads that bind us together, reminding us of our shared history and the importance of preserving our cultural heritage.

To provide readers with a comprehensive understanding of each topic, I've structured the book to begin each chapter with an introductory essay. These essays aim to provide historical context, setting the stage for the forthcoming discussions and shedding light on the significance of the places and events that are about to be explored. Throughout my journey of researching and writing this book, I've strived to capture the essence of Orange County's history and the transformations it has undergone. I hope that through these pages, you will gain a deeper appreciation for the region and its evolution over time.

In writing this book, I wanted to bridge the gap between generations and backgrounds. For those who grew up in Orange County, my intention is for the book to act as a time machine, transporting you back to a time filled with innocence and joy. My goal is to awaken dormant memories and spark conversations that connect generations, with parents reminiscing with their children and grandchildren about the places that shaped their own childhoods.

For newcomers to Orange County, the book serves as a window into the region's history and a way to connect with the shared experiences of its long-time residents. It provides a sense of context and belonging, helping you to understand the cultural fabric of your new home and fostering a deeper appreciation for the community you now find yourself to be a part of.

Mason's El Camino Barbecue and Drive-In
Hiway 101 – San Clemente, California – At the South End of Town

Even passing tourists, who may only have a brief encounter with Orange County, can find value in this book. It offers you a glimpse into the region's past, allowing you to see beyond the surface and uncover the layers of history that have shaped the area. It invites you to engage with the local culture, creating a richer and more meaningful experience during your visit.

I have poured my heart and soul into researching and documenting as many significant places as possible. I have strived to capture the essence of each lost landmark, chronicling their stories and preserving their memory within the pages of this book. However, I am aware that despite my best efforts, there may be some noteworthy places that I have unintentionally missed. For this, I humbly apologize. My goal is to provide a comprehensive account of the lost landmarks, but the ever-changing landscape and the vast history of Orange County make it a challenging task to include every single place. I would be truly grateful if you, as a reader, could provide any valuable insights or share any significant places that you believe should be included in future editions of the book. Your feedback is invaluable to me, as it allows me to continuously improve and expand upon the work I have started.

Ultimately, *Lost Landmarks of Orange County* represents a shared longing—a yearning for the places we hold dear, regardless of where we come from. It invites you to reflect on your own personal histories while immersing yourselves in a broader narrative of a community. By capturing the universal essence of nostalgia and intertwining it with the history of Orange County, I have tried to create connections, foster understanding, and celebrate the vibrant tapestry of this beloved region.

Lastly, I would like to express my deepest gratitude to you, the reader, for joining me on this journey through the lost landmarks of Orange County. Whether you grew up in this vibrant region, recently moved here, or are simply visiting, there is so much to gain from exploring these forgotten treasures. Let us cherish and preserve the memories that define us, for they are the threads that connect us to our past and illuminate the path to our future. As we celebrate the lost landmarks of Orange County, we honor the spirit of innovation, creativity, and community that have shaped this remarkable place.

Onward, and thank you for reading.

—CHRIS EPTING

To learn more about these lost landmarks, visit www.thelostland-marks.com, where you will find more great stories along with unique merchandise inspired by many of these iconic, long gone places.

THE HISTORY OF ORANGE COUNTY

ORANGE COUNTY, CALIFORNIA, LOCATED in the southern part of the state, has a rich and diverse history that spans thousands of years. From its indigenous inhabitants to Spanish colonialism, American ranchos, and the rise of the vibrant modern community, Orange County has undergone significant transformations.

The earliest known occupants of the region now known as Orange County were Native American tribes, including the Tongva and Acjachemen peoples. They thrived in the area for thousands of years, living off the abundant natural resources and engaging in trade with neighboring tribes. Their villages were scattered throughout the coastal and inland areas, and their way of life was deeply connected to the land and sea.

In 1769, Spanish explorers led by Gaspar de Portolà arrived in the area. They established a series of missions and presidios along California's coast, including Mission San Juan Capistrano in present-day Orange County. The mission system aimed to convert Native Americans to Christianity and solidify Spanish control over the region. The missions became centers of agriculture, education, and religious activity and left a lasting impact on the local culture.

After Mexico gained independence from Spain in 1821, the missions were secularized, and their lands were distributed among Mexican citizens. Many former mission lands were transformed into large ranchos, which were sprawling estates dedicated to cattle and agricultural production. Rancho Los Alamitos, Rancho Santiago de Santa Ana, and Rancho San Joaquin were among the notable ranchos in Orange County during this period.

In 1848, the Treaty of Guadalupe Hidalgo ended the Mexican-American War, and California became part of the United States. The Gold Rush of 1849 brought an influx of settlers to California, including Orange County. The area's fertile soil, mild climate, and proximity to the coast made it an attractive destination for agricultural development.

The completion of the Southern Pacific Railroad in the late 19th century accelerated the growth of Orange County. Rail connections brought new settlers and facilitated the transportation of agricultural products to markets. The citrus industry in particular flourished, and Orange County gained a reputation as a major citrus-producing region. The region's first incorporated city, Anaheim, was founded in 1870 and became a center of citrus cultivation.

In the early 20th century, the completion of the Pacific Electric Railway's "Red Car" system further enhanced transportation and connectivity within Orange County. The rise of the film industry in nearby Los Angeles also had an indirect impact on the region, as some filmmakers sought scenic locations in Orange County for their productions.

The 1920s, 1930s, and 1940s witnessed significant changes in Orange County. The discovery of oil reserves in the area led to the development of oil fields and refineries, contributing to the region's economic growth. World War II brought a military presence to the county with the establishment of military bases like El Toro Marine Corps Air Station and the Santa Ana Army Air Base. The war also brought a flood of defense workers and servicemen to the area.

In the post-war era, Orange County experienced a population boom and suburbanization. The construction of the Interstate Highway System, including the Santa Ana Freeway (I-5), facilitated commuting and opened up new areas for development. The region's proximity to Los Angeles, combined with its pleasant climate, attracted families seeking a suburban lifestyle. Planned communities like Irvine and Newport Beach emerged, offering well-designed neighborhoods, parks, and amenities.

The 1950s and 1960s marked a period of rapid growth and transformation for Orange County. The aerospace industry, driven by companies like North American Aviation and McDonnell Douglas, established a strong presence in the region. The development of aerospace technology and defense contracts brought high-paying jobs and fueled economic prosperity.

Orange County also experienced cultural and social changes during this time. The establishment of the University of California, Irvine in 1965 contributed to the county's intellectual and educational landscape. The university became a hub for research, innovation, and higher education.

In the 1970s and 1980s, Orange County faced challenges and setbacks. The collapse of the aerospace industry in the late 1980s resulted in significant job losses and economic downturn. Additionally, a financial crisis occurred in 1994 when the county treasurer's office made risky investments that led to bankruptcy. Orange County managed to recover from these setbacks and reestablish itself as a prosperous and resilient community.

The late 20th century and early 21st century witnessed further growth and diversification of Orange County's economy. The tourism industry flourished with the development of world-class resorts and attractions like Disneyland Resort, Knott's Berry Farm, and the Anaheim Convention Center. The county's beautiful coastline, with cities such as Huntington Beach and Laguna Beach, became popular destinations for beachgoers and surfers.

Orange County also became a center for technology and innovation. The emergence of the "Silicon Beach" corridor in South Orange County attracted numerous tech companies, startups, and venture capital firms. The county's strong educational institutions, such as the University of California, Irvine and California State University, Fullerton, provided a skilled workforce and fostered research and development.

In recent years, Orange County has continued to thrive as a vibrant and diverse community. It has embraced cultural diversity and is home to a large Hispanic, Asian, and Middle Eastern population. The county's culinary scene has gained recognition, with a variety of international cuisines and award-winning restaurants.

Orange County's commitment to environmental sustainability is also evident. Efforts have been made to preserve open spaces, protect endangered species, and promote renewable energy. The county's numerous parks, nature reserves, and hiking trails provide opportunities for outdoor recreation and connection with nature.

The history of Orange County is a story of evolution, from its indigenous roots to Spanish colonization, agricultural development, suburbanization, and technological advancements. Despite facing challenges along the way, Orange County has emerged as a prosperous and dynamic region, known for its economic vitality, cultural diversity, and natural beauty. As it continues to evolve, Orange County remains a symbol of the American dream and a testament to the resilience and ingenuity of its residents.

MAP
OF
ORANGE COUNTY
CALIFORNIA
COMPILED BY
S.H.FINLEY
1889.

CHAPTER ONE

EARLY HISTORY

ORANGE COUNTY, WITH ITS rich historical tapestry, holds a treasure trove of landmarks that bear witness to the county's earliest history. While the passage of time has seen many of these landmarks disappear, their significance has not been forgotten. Today, many lost landmarks have been identified and commemorated through the placement of historic plaques and markers. These tangible remnants of the past serve as poignant reminders of the stories and events that shaped Orange County.

Carbondale
Located 1.2 miles east of Santiago Canyon Road
Santiago Canyon

The site of Carbondale holds a fascinating history. In 1881, following the acquisition of the Santa Clara Coal Mine by the Southern Pacific, a thriving mining camp emerged on the flats of this area. This bustling camp boasted various amenities, including a hotel, saloons, shacks, a store, and even a post office. Carbondale became a vibrant community, driven by the mining activities in the region. But the prosperity of Carbondale was short-lived. Just three years later, in 1884, the Santa Clara Coal Mine depleted its resources, and the mining operations came to an end. With the closure of the mine, Carbondale quickly faded away, leaving behind no visible trace of its existence.

The story of Carbondale serves as a reminder of the transient nature of many mining towns and the rise and fall of communities closely tied to extractive industries. While Carbondale may no longer physically exist, its brief but significant presence in the annals of history adds to the tapestry of the region's past.

Coast Live Oak Marker
25151 Serrano Road and Winding Way
Lake Forest

Here is a timeline of key events related to the area listed on the plaque found here by the actual historic live oak tree stump.

1769: The Portola Expedition enters the region that would later become Orange County.

1821: California comes under Mexican rule.

1842: Rancho Canada de los Alisos is granted to Don Jose Serrano, which would later become the site of Heritage Hill Historical Park.

1850: California achieves statehood.

1862: A severe drought devastates the local cattle industry.

1864: The first record of the Don Jose Adobe, an adobe structure that would become a notable landmark.

1888: Railroad service expands into Aliso City, which is now known as El Toro.

1889: Orange County is established.

1890: The El Toro Grammar School is constructed.

1891: St. George Episcopal Mission is constructed.

1908: The Harvey Bennett Ranch House is built.

1932: Extensive restoration work is carried out on the Don Jose Serrano Adobe.

1974: The site of Heritage Hill Park is deeded to Orange County.

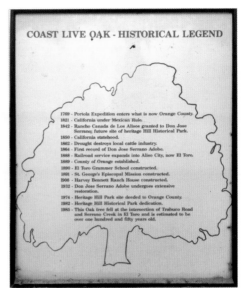

1982: Heritage Hill Historic Park is officially dedicated.

1985: An oak tree estimated to be over 150 years old falls at the intersection of Trabuco Road and Serrano Creek in El Toro.

De Anza Campsite
North Cottonwood Street
Orange

On September 22, 1779, Juan Bautista de Anza led a group of more than 200 emigrants and soldiers from the presidio at Tubac, Mexico, on a journey to establish the settlement of San Francisco. After enduring many difficult miles of travel, the party arrived at the San Gabriel Mission on January 4, 1776. It was at this point that they received news that the San Diego mission had been burned by Native Americans, and Father Luis Jayme had been murdered. In response to the Indian rebellion, Anza and a portion of his escort were immediately dispatched to San Diego to aid in suppressing the uprising.

The Anza relief party established its first camp near the present location on January 7, 1776. The specific location is not mentioned in the information provided, but it would have been somewhere in the vicinity of the San Gabriel Mission.

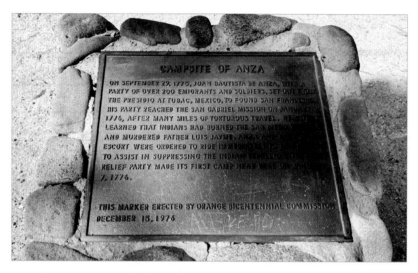

This event marked a significant moment in the Anza Expedition, as it highlighted the challenges and dangers faced by the Spanish settlers and missionaries in their efforts to establish and maintain missions in Alta California. The journey led by Juan Bautista de Anza played a crucial role in the expansion of Spanish colonization and the establishment of San Francisco as a new settlement.

Early School
Intersection of Santa Ana Canyon Road and Imperial Highway, specifically on the right side when traveling west on Santa Ana Canyon
Anaheim

The boulder here stands as a testament to the historical significance of the location it marks. It signifies the site of one of the earliest public schools in the county, built in 1867. The establishment of this school was a notable milestone in the educational development of the area.

The first teacher at this school was Jennie Swift, whose dedication and commitment to education helped lay the foundation for learning in the community. Her contributions were instrumental in shaping the early educational experiences of the local students. Following Jennie Swift, William M. McFadden took on the role of teaching at this school from 1869 to 1879. His tenure marked a significant period of education and growth for the students who attended the school during that time. The marker here serves as a tangible reminder of the school's historical importance and the transformative impact it had on the community.

First Site of the Olive Mill
16780 E. Buena Vista Avenue
Orange

The three-story flour and feed mill, originally established by Thomas Dillin and his sons, commenced operations on November 1, 1882. The mill was powered by a turbine that utilized the flow of Santa Ana River irrigation water, which descended to the valley

below. This mill played a vital role in the early economy of Orange County.

Unfortunately, on September 29, 1889, a devastating fire engulfed the mill, resulting in its destruction. Given its importance to the local economy, the mill was subsequently rebuilt. The second iteration of the mill was situated in the southwest corner of the park, although the specific park is not mentioned in the information provided.

The reconstructed mill continued functioning at this site until 1932, serving the community's needs for flour and feed production. Throughout its existence, the mill played a significant

role in supporting the agricultural activities and economy of early Orange County.

The mill's reliance on the Santa Ana River for its power supply underscores the importance of water resources in the region's development during that time period. The milling industry was a crucial component of the agricultural infrastructure, processing grains and providing essential products for both local consumption and trade. The mill's presence contributed to the growth and prosperity of early Orange County.

Grijalva Adobe Site
1087 South Rancho Santiago Boulevard
Orange

The Grijalva Adobe holds a significant place in the history of Orange County. Juan Pablo Grijalva, a Spanish soldier, arrived in California as part of the Anza Expedition in 1776. It was on a hill in the region that he constructed one of the earliest adobe structures in what is now Orange County.

In 1801, Juan Pablo Grijalva petitioned for the use of the land that would later become known as the Rancho Santiago de Santa Ana. This land grant was a significant development, as it provided Grijalva with legal recognition and rights to the vast territory.

Juan Pablo Grijalva's ownership of the land was short-lived, as he passed away in 1806.

Following his death, his son-in-law, Jose Antonio Yorba, and his grandson, Juan Pablo Peralta, filed a petition to gain control of the Rancho Santiago de Santa Ana in 1810. Their petition proved successful, granting them the rights to the land and its resources.

The Grijalva Adobe and the subsequent ownership of the land by Yorba and Peralta played a crucial role in the early development of Orange County. The adobe structure served as a testament to the region's Spanish colonial heritage and the resilience of early settlers in California. The Rancho Santiago de Santa Ana became a prominent landholding in the area, contributing to the agricultural and economic growth of the region. Over time, the landscape transformed as the rancho expanded, and subsequent generations built upon the foundation laid by Juan Pablo Grijalva.

The marker here at the site of the Grijalva Adobe represents the enduring legacy of the early settlers and the establishment of Orange County's rich cultural and agricultural heritage.

"Katella"
Anaheim Garden Walk shopping center
400 Disney Way
Anaheim

Kate and Ella Rea, the daughters of the Rea family, held a significant role as early settlers of Anaheim. Their contribution to the community was so profound that the family decided to name their ranch after them—hence the birth of "Katella Ranch." This designation not only honored the sisters but also served as a testament to their presence and influence in the area.

As time went on, the wagon track in Anaheim gained recognition and popularity. In recognition of Kate and Ella's impact, the track was eventually named after them, becoming known as Katella Avenue. This renaming further solidified the sisters' place in Anaheim's history and served as a lasting tribute to their legacy. To this day, their remarkable story continues to be remembered and celebrated. A plaque commemorating Kate and Ella's contributions can be found here, acting as a reminder of the profound impact they had on the early settlement of Anaheim and the subsequent development of the area. The tale of Kate and Ella Rea and their connection to "Katella Ranch" and Katella Avenue exemplifies the significance of personal legacies and the enduring power of local history. Their names have become woven into the fabric of Anaheim, leaving an indelible mark that resonates with residents and visitors alike.

La Cristianita
415 Avenida Granada
San Clemente

La Cristianita is a historic site located in San Clemente, California. It holds significance as the location where the first Christian baptism in Alta California took place. The baptism was conducted by Padre Francisco Gómez, a member of the Portolá Expedition, in the year 1769. The site is situated approximately two miles inland from the point where this marker is located in San Clemente. The baptismal ceremony marked an important moment in the history of early Spanish colonization and the spread of Christianity in California. La Cristianita serves as a reminder of this significant event and its historical importance.

La Habra Birthplace
Intersection of South Euclid Street and East Habra Boulevard
La Habra

The first post office in La Habra was established in 1896, and the settlement was officially named "La Habra" at that time. The post office was in a corner of Coys Store, which was situated at the corner along El Camino Viejo, an old road that connected the missions in the area. Due to its location, the corner became a significant trading point in the fertile La Habra Valley. A marker here identifies the spot.

Northam Ranch House
Yorktown and Main Streets
Huntington Beach

The marker at the site of the old Northam Ranch House commemorates the historical significance of the property in the history of Huntington Beach. Here's a description of the marker:

Located uphill from the marker once stood the Northam Ranch House, which played a pivotal role in the history of Huntington Beach. The property was originally part of Rancho Las Bolsas, a vast Spanish land grant. In 1896, rancher and land dealer Robert J. Northam purchased the 1,400 acres surrounding this hillcrest.

Robert J. Northam, often referred to as "Diamond Bob" due to his expensive tastes, was a prominent figure in the region during the turn of the twentieth century. Using a mule team, Northam relocated at least one home to the property in 1897. The final structure was in an L-shape and combined elements of the Neoclassical and Queen Anne architectural styles.

Northam resided in the ranch house for less than a decade, and in 1905, the property was acquired by the Huntington Beach Company. This company played a significant role in capitalizing on the local oil boom and subsequently transforming the once-isolated community into a major city.

The marker highlights the historical importance of the Northam Ranch House and its association with Robert J. Northam, the development of Huntington Beach, and the growth of the region in the early 20th century. It serves to preserve the memory of this pivotal landmark and its significance in the local history of Huntington Beach.

Old Irvine Blacksmith Shop
14952 Sand Canyon Avenue
Irvine

The old Irvine blacksmith shop holds a significant place in the history of Orange County. Constructed between 1915 and 1916, it stands as a tangible piece of the region's past. During this era, Orange County was predominantly covered in orange groves and fields, and the blacksmith shop played a crucial role in supporting the agricultural activities of the Irvine Ranch, the Irvine Bean and Grain Growers Association, and the East Grove Agricultural shipping center. The shop provided essential services for the maintenance and repair of farm equipment and machinery used in the cultivation and shipment of crops such as lima beans and California oranges.

For 70 years, the building served its original purpose as a blacksmith shop, catering to the needs of farmers and ranchers in the area. The historical significance of the blacksmith shop is evident through the branded marks on the wall behind the forge. These

brands, representing various Orange County cattle ranches, offer a glimpse into the region's rich ranching heritage. Architecturally, the building is a classic representation of a western structure with its iconic false front, making it one of the few remaining examples of this style in Southern California. It stands as an archetype of the western blacksmith shop, symbolizing the history and culture of the region.

During World War II, the blacksmith shop played a crucial role in supporting the war effort by aiding in the harvesting of lima beans. As the United States was engaged in the war, the demand for food supplies, including legumes like lima beans, increased significantly to feed the troops and support the home front. Today, the old blacksmith shop has been repurposed and transformed into the Knowlwood Restaurant. This transformation represents the evolution of the American West, which grew through the expansion of the railroad and the development of agriculture.

Sack Storage Warehouse
14988 Sand Canyon Avenue
Irvine

The 1895 Sack Storage Warehouse holds great significance in the local history of Orange County. The building is listed on the

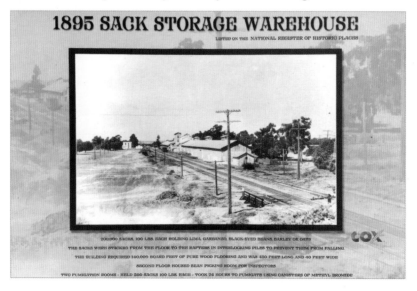

National Register of Historic Places, recognizing its cultural value. The marker here begins by highlighting the immense volume of beans and grains handled at the packing house. It states that a staggering 200,000 sacks were used to store the produce. Each sack weighed 100 pounds and contained lima beans, garbanzo beans, black-eyed beans, barley, or oats. To ensure stability and prevent the sacks from falling, they were carefully stacked from the floor to the rafters in interlocking piles.

The building itself is described as requiring 140,000 board feet of pure wood flooring, indicating its substantial size. It stretched 450 feet in length and was 40 feet wide, providing ample space for the packing and storage operations.

The marker also mentions specific areas within the packing house. On the second floor, there was a dedicated bean picking room where inspectors would examine and select the beans. This room served as a quality control area to ensure that only the best beans were packed and shipped.

Santa Ana Birthplace
Broadway and Main Streets
Santa Ana

Santa Ana has a rich history that is intertwined with the visionary actions of its founder, William H. Spurgeon. In the mid-19th century, as Spurgeon rode through the area on horseback, he came across a sycamore tree that caught his attention. Intrigued by the picturesque surroundings of the mustard fields, he decided to transform the landscape into a thriving community. Impressed by the potential of the land, Spurgeon purchased 74.2 acres for a mere $595. With an entrepreneurial spirit and a clear vision in mind, he set out to develop a village that would become the foundation of what is now Santa Ana. Spurgeon's determination led him to plow down the mustard fields and construct a 24-block village that would serve as the town's nucleus.

One notable architectural gem that stands as a testament to Spurgeon's legacy is the stone courthouse built on property he sold to the county. Situated on an entire city block, this courthouse boasted a tower that rose higher than any other building in the town at the time. Remarkably, the courthouse has endured the test

of time and stands proudly to this day, a symbol of Santa Ana's history and progress.

Spurgeon's contributions to the community extended beyond the physical infrastructure. In addition to being the town's founder and builder, he also served as the local postmaster. In an era when mail delivery was a crucial service, Spurgeon took on the responsibility of managing the town's mail, storing it in a humble wooden shoebox.

While the passage of time has brought changes to Santa Ana, it is important to note that some remnants of its past still remain. Although the famous sycamore tree that Spurgeon climbed is no longer standing, its significance is commemorated by a plaque in the area. This plaque serves as a reminder of the city's origins and the vision of its founder.

Silverado Birthplace
Silverado Canyon Road (next to the fire station)
Silverado Canyon

Silverado was founded in 1878 after the discovery of silver in the area. The mining boom period, which lasted from 1878 to 1881, saw a significant influx of miners who came to Silverado in search of silver.

During this time, Silverado quickly developed into a thriving community. It was served by a daily stagecoach service connecting it to Los Angeles and Santa Ana, which facilitated transportation and trade in the area. The town experienced a vibrant and colorful existence as miners and their families settled there, establishing homes, businesses, and other essential services to support the mining industry.

The discovery of silver in Silverado attracted attention and led to a period of rapid growth and prosperity. However, like many mining boom towns, the fortunes of Silverado were short-lived. The silver deposits eventually dwindled, and by the early 1880s, the boom subsided, causing a decline in mining activities and a subsequent decrease in population.

Although the mining boom era of Silverado was relatively short, the town's history as a mining community has left a lasting legacy. Today, Silverado is a small unincorporated community nestled in the canyons of the Santa Ana Mountains, still retaining some of its historical charm and offering glimpses of its mining past. A marker here traces the history.

CHAPTER TWO

THEME PARKS, MUSEUMS, AND OTHER ATTRACTIONS

THEME PARKS HAVE PLAYED a significant role in the growth and development of Orange County. The region's rise as a prominent tourist destination can be largely attributed to the success and popularity of iconic parks like Disneyland and Knott's Berry Farm. These parks have not only shaped the local economy but have also become cultural touchstones for both residents and visitors.

Disneyland, which opened its doors in 1955, was the brainchild of Walt Disney and quickly became a symbol of American imagination and entertainment. It was the first ever theme park of its kind, offering a revolutionary form of family entertainment. Disneyland's success prompted a surge of tourism in Orange County, attracting visitors from all over the world and inspiring the establishment of numerous hotels, restaurants, and other businesses to cater to the growing number of tourists.

Similarly, Knott's Berry Farm—which was initially a small berry farm and restaurant—evolved into a theme park in the 1950s. It gained popularity for its unique western-themed attractions and entertainment. Knott's Berry Farm contributed to the county's tourism industry by providing a different experience from Disneyland, attracting visitors seeking a more rustic and nostalgic atmosphere.

While Disneyland and Knott's Berry Farm have remained enduring symbols of Orange County's theme park culture, it is essential to recognize the numerous other parks and attractions that have come and gone over the years. Many parks that were once popular destinations, such as Lion Country Safari and Japanese Village and Deer Park, no longer exist today. Although these parks and attractions may have faded into history, they hold significant historical and cultural value.

Remembering the parks and attractions that have disappeared is crucial for several reasons. Firstly, it allows us to acknowledge the evolving nature of the entertainment industry and the changing tastes and preferences of visitors. The rise and fall of various parks highlight the dynamic nature of the tourism landscape and the need for continuous innovation to stay relevant.

Secondly, remembering the bygone parks preserves the memories and experiences of past generations. These parks were once cherished destinations for families and individuals, and their stories help to connect different generations and create a sense of shared heritage. With that, let's go!

Balboa Fun Zone
600 E. Bay Avenue
Newport Beach

It all started back in 1936, when a boatyard owner named Al Anderson decided to shake things up and bring some excitement to the Balboa peninsula. So, Anderson rolled up his sleeves and got to work. In no time, a marvelous Ferris wheel and a whimsical merry-go-round were erected on the property. And that was just the beginning! Soon enough, kiddie rides and an arcade joined the party, transforming the Balboa Fun Zone into a haven for families seeking good old-fashioned entertainment.

But here's a fun fact: even before the Fun Zone came to be, the Balboa auto ferry was already making waves! Can you believe it started its service back in 1919? And get this—it's still up and running today, faithfully shuttling cars between Balboa Island and the Balboa peninsula. With capacity for up to three cars per trip, it's a lifeline for those looking to explore both sides of the harbor. Just be prepared for a bit of a wait during the bustling summer months. But fear not, the ferry's turnaround time is relatively speedy since the journey across the harbor is delightfully short.

Now, fast forward to the present day. Despite changes in ownership over the years, the Balboa Fun Zone has stood the test of time. It's a beacon of nostalgia, beckoning visitors of all ages to bask in the sun, feel the salty sea breeze on their cheeks, and enjoy a dose of good old-fashioned fun.

So, if you're yearning for a taste of the past, a place where laughter and joy fill the air, head on over to the Balboa Fun Zone. It's a treasure trove of Southern California history, and it's waiting

FUN ZONE, BAY FRONT, BALBOA,

to make your day a memorable one. It's important to note that the Balboa Fun Zone, while still open for business, has seen some changes over the years. It's a bit bittersweet, I must say. Some of

the beloved attractions that once made it truly special have vanished like a magician's disappearing act.

Gone is the famed carousel, with its beautifully painted horses and whimsical music. The laughter and squeals of delight that once filled its surroundings now echo only in memories. And remember that thrilling, slightly spooky dark ride that sent shivers down your spine? Well, it's no longer there to transport you into a world of mystery and excitement.

Even the bumper cars, those joyfully chaotic collisions of fun, have bid their farewell. It's a shame, really, as they were a staple of the Balboa Fun Zone experience for so many years. It seems that time and changing tastes have taken their toll, and these attractions have become a part of the Fun Zone's nostalgic past.

In the midst of these changes, there is still a glimmer of hope. The Ferris wheel, that iconic symbol of the Fun Zone, still stands tall, offering breathtaking views of the surrounding beauty. It's a reminder of the laughter and joy that once filled this place, even if some of the other attractions have gone astray.

While it's true that the Balboa Fun Zone may not be the same as it once was, with some of its most cherished features missing, there is still plenty to enjoy. It may be a shadow of its former self, but it's a shadow that still holds a touch of magic and a hint of the enjoyment that once made it shine.

Buffalo Ranch
Corner of MacArthur Boulevard and Bonita Canyon Drive
Newport Beach

Buffalo Ranch opened in 1955 and was located in what is now Newport Beach. It sat on 115 acres of land and was operated by Gene

Clark, an ex-building contractor from Kansas (and grandson of renowned Indian chief Geronimo), who leased the land from the Irvine Company. This was the first instance where the Irvine Company allowed an outside business onto its land. The ranch initially started with a herd of 72 buffalo, and over time, the number of buffalo on the ranch grew. To enhance the authenticity of the experience and provide cultural entertainment for the tourists, several Indian families from Kansas were invited to live in the area and work at the ranch. These families would perform various tribal dances for the visitors.

In late 1959/early 1960, Buffalo Ranch was shut down due to rising land costs. At the same time, a nearby site had been chosen for the University of California, Irvine campus, and the Irvine Company had hired the campus' architect, William Pereira, to plan the city of Irvine around it. Pereira, who considered himself a "barn freak" and enjoyed renovating them, took the vacant Buffalo Ranch barn and converted it into his on-site planning office. As the project grew, Pereira added additional buildings to the site, which he renamed "Urbanus Square." It was here that much of the cities of Irvine and Newport Beach were planned, as well as many of Pereira's projects outside the Los Angeles area (such as the Geisel Library in San Diego).

Bison Road, which still exists today, was originally constructed as an access road to Buffalo Ranch. It serves as a connection between Jamboree Road and MacArthur Road in Newport Beach. At Bonita Canyon and McArthur, a large bronze statue of a buffalo stands with a plaque placed in front of it honoring the site's history. Part of the barn, including the silo that Pereira had converted into a 360-degree survey platform for his planning efforts, was moved to Centennial Farm at the Orange County Fair.

California Alligator Farm
7971 Beach Boulevard
Buena Park

The Los Angeles Alligator Farm, originally located in the Lincoln Heights neighborhood of Los Angeles, was a renowned and popular tourist attraction from 1907 until 1953. The farm captured the fascination of locals and visitors alike with its impressive collection of reptiles, with a particular emphasis on crocodilians.

In 1953, the Los Angeles Alligator Farm relocated to Buena Park, just across from Knott's Berry Farm, and was renamed the California Alligator Farm. The new location spanned across a larger area, allowing for further expansion of the park and its exhibits.

The California Alligator Farm continued its tradition of hosting captivating alligator and snake shows, drawing in crowds of tourists and locals.

The attraction provided visitors with a unique and immersive experience. The park featured a jungle-like setting, complete with lush vegetation and carefully designed enclosures to mimic the natural habitats of the reptiles. It housed over 100 species of reptiles, representing all five orders, making it a comprehensive reptile sanctuary.

One of the main highlights was the daily alligator and snake shows. During the summer months, these shows took place on a daily basis, while in the off-season, they were held weekly. The shows provided thrilling entertainment for visitors, showcasing the raw power and agility of these creatures through carefully choreographed performances.

Over the years, attendance at the California Alligator Farm began to decline. The changing preferences of visitors and the emergence of new entertainment options contributed to the drop in attendance. In 1984, the decision was made to shut down the park.

Following the closure of the California Alligator Farm, the animals found new homes. The reptiles were relocated to a private estate in Florida, where they could continue to receive proper care and attention. Today, there is a Claim Jumper restaurant at the site.

The Japanese Village and Deer Park
6122 Knott Avenue
Buena Park

The Japanese Village and Deer Park opened in 1967 in Buena Park and offered a Japanese-themed experience for visitors. The park featured traditional Japanese buildings, shows, and an environment where deer roamed freely, drawing inspiration from

Nara Park in Japan. The entrance to the park was marked by a torii gate, a traditional Japanese gate often seen at Shinto shrines.

The Japanese Village and Deer Park gained some attention in the entertainment industry as it was featured in two episodes of the CBS-TV detective drama *Mannix*. The episodes "Overkill" (1971, Season 4, Episode 24) and "Enter Tami Okada" (1974, Season 8, Episode 8) filmed extensive sequences at the park, showcasing various exhibits and animals. One of the scenes even featured a trainer riding two dolphins in tandem.

Unfortunately, the park closed its doors in 1975, just five years after it was sold to Great Southwest Co., a subsidiary of Six Flags. The park's owners faced financial difficulties, and as a result, they resorted to euthanizing some of the deer in the park by giving them lethal injections. The owners claimed that the deer had tuberculosis, but authorities intervened and put an end to the practice after nearly 200 deer had been euthanized.

After the closure of the Japanese Village and Deer Park, a second amusement park called Enchanted Village opened on the same site on June 18, 1976. Animal trainer Ralph Helfer was a partner in the park and served as its chairperson. One of the notable attractions at Enchanted Village was Oliver, a chimpanzee known for his human-like behavior.

During its operation, Enchanted Village featured a signature stunt and animal show that incorporated themes and storylines from the 1977 film *The Island of Dr. Moreau*. This show aimed to entertain visitors with a combination of trained animals and theatrical elements. The park itself had a South Pacific Tiki theme, covering an area of 32 acres. It included appeals such as trained animal shows, a traditional Polynesian show, and a few ride attractions. Enchanted Village also made a brief appearance in the

1977 film *Curse of the Black Widow*. Despite its relatively short existence, the park closed in the fall of 1977, bringing an end to its operations. Today, it's an industrial park.

Joy Zone
900 Ocean Avenue
Seal Beach

Seal Beach, incorporated in 1915, has a rich history intertwined with seaside entertainment and early Hollywood. In 1916, the city's seaside amusement park, the Joy Zone, opened to the public. It featured one of the longest wooden piers on the Pacific Coast and a prominent attraction called the Derby Roller Coaster.

The Joy Zone aimed to recreate the lively atmosphere of popular amusement parks like Coney Island. It offered a variety of attractions, including carnival games, fair food, a bathhouse, a dance hall, and the Jewel City Café. The visionary behind the Joy Zone, Philip A. Stanton, hoped to establish Seal Beach as the "Coney Island of the Pacific." The amusement park quickly gained popularity, attracting up to 20,000 visitors each week during its peak.

Seal Beach's vibrant entertainment scene also captured the attention of early Hollywood. Silent film stars such as Fatty Arbuckle and Buster Keaton were known to visit the amusement park. Additionally, film studios sought to shoot "beach comedies" in and around the pier, taking advantage of the scenic location.

One notable film production that utilized Seal Beach was Cecil B. DeMille's 1923 version of *The Ten Commandments*. According to *The Orange County Tribune*, the beach was used as a set for the

iconic scene portraying the parting of the Red Sea. This is just one example of Seal Beach being used as a filming location during the early days of Hollywood.

Seal Beach's Joy Zone and its connection to the film industry contributed to the city's cultural and historical significance. While the amusement park is no longer in operation, its legacy and the allure it held for both locals and visitors remain an important part of Seal Beach's history. However, like many other coastal towns during the early 20th century, Seal Beach experienced its share of illicit activities. The prohibition era in the 1920s created a demand for smuggled alcohol, and Seal Beach's proximity to Anaheim Landing made it a convenient drop-off point for bootleggers. During this time, gambling and prostitution also found their way into the town.

However, the landscape changed with the onset of the Great Depression. The amusement park was closed down after the Derby Roller Coaster burnt down. The park then fell into disrepair, and the economic downturn affected the viability of illegal activities such as gambling and prostitution.

The end of prohibition in the 1930s removed the need for smuggled alcohol, impacting the illicit alcohol market. As the 1950s rolled around, Seal Beach experienced a shift in its demographics. Families began moving into the city, and the focus shifted towards more family-oriented and community friendly activities. With the changing times and the influx of families, the vice-friendly politics of the past gradually changed. Efforts were made to clean up the town and prioritize a more wholesome environment. Seal Beach transformed into a residential community with a focus on family life, shedding its association with gambling, prostitution, and other illicit activities.

Jungle Island
Directly across Beach Boulevard from Knott's Berry Farm
Buena Park

Jungle Island, once part of Knott's Berry Farm, was a fascinating and enchanting park-within-a-park that held a tale of unrealized dreams and forgotten wonders. Originally envisioned as the South Seas Island Boat Ride, the park underwent a remarkable transformation, shifting its theme from a Tiki paradise to the rugged allure of the Old West. But, despite stunning concept art and design work, the South Seas Island Boat Ride project never came to fruition.

Instead, the boat troughs found an unexpected purpose as the short-lived Overland Trail Ride pathway. This pathway showcased animated woodland animals and pioneer wagons, providing visitors with a glimpse into the adventurous spirit of the pioneers. It

was a unique and charming attraction, albeit one that didn't have a long lifespan.

Adjacent to the Overland Trail Ride, Jungle Island emerged as a promising endeavor. Led by Forrest L. Morrow Sr., a talented landscaper and folk artist, Jungle Island became a haven for Morrow's whimsical creations known as Wood-imals. These imaginative creatures were crafted from twisted tree branches and stumps, transforming the island into a magical realm where young adventurers could roam freely and embark on exciting escapades.

The dense and jungle-like atmosphere of Jungle Island added to its allure, immersing visitors in a world teeming with creativity and imagination. As they explored the island, children could encounter a menagerie of Wood-imals, each one a unique and awe-inspiring creation. From towering tree creatures to mischievous woodland critters, the Wood-imals breathed life into the park and sparked the imaginations of those who visited.

Jungle Island offered more than just the chance to admire Morrow's remarkable craftsmanship. It was a playground where children could let their imaginations run wild, pretending to be intrepid explorers navigating untamed jungles and encountering extraordinary creatures. The park provided a space for young adventurers to create their own stories and embark on thrilling adventures, fostering a sense of wonder and excitement.

Sadly, like the South Seas Island Boat Ride and the Overland Trail Ride, Jungle Island's existence was relatively short-lived. A shift in leadership marked the beginning of the end for Jungle Island. In the early 1980s, Knott's Berry Farm, under new CEO management, decided to transform the cherished jungle into a natural area. This decision signaled a departure from the imaginative realm that Jungle Island had created, and it ultimately led to the park's demise.

The creation of Jungle Island aimed to offer California residents and travelers a unique experience that differentiated from the existing theme parks in the area. But despite its initial success, financial challenges posed a constant threat to the park's existence. Its whimsical charm and captivating Wood-imals enchanted visitors for a time, but eventually, the park closed its doors, leaving behind memories of a forgotten oasis of imagination and creativity.

Today, remnants of Jungle Island can still be found, although the property is under private ownership and does not permit visitors. These remnants serve as a reminder of the once-vibrant park and the dreams and wonders it once held. While Jungle Island may have faded into history, its legacy lives on in the memories of those fortunate enough to have experienced its magic during its existence.

Lion Country Safari

26001 Pintado

Irvine

On June 16, 1970, Lion Country Safari opened its doors to the public in Irvine. Despite facing tough competition from popular attractions like Disneyland, Knott's Berry Farm, and the beach, Lion Country Safari had certain advantages such as a favorable climate, a large local population, and a significant tourist base.

But what truly set Lion Country Safari apart was an unexpected star attraction that arrived in February 1971: an elderly and nearly toothless lion named Frasier who the park acquired from a Mexican circus. Frasier's advanced age and physical condition made him an unlikely candidate for stardom. His tongue dangled from one side of his mouth, and he had difficulty walking. Yet, the lionesses in the park saw him differently.

To everyone's surprise, Frasier became extremely popular among the lionesses, leading to a population boom of lion cubs at the park. Despite his less-than-impressive appearance to humans, Frasier's charm and prowess made him a symbol of virility and strength in the eyes of the lionesses. His distinctive features and endearing personality also made him a beloved figure among visitors. Frasier's influence extended beyond the park's boundaries. His sorry visage adorned various park souvenirs, including t-shirts, further enhancing his fame. Such was his impact that a 1973 feature film titled *Frasier the Sensuous Lion* was made, depicting his

remarkable story. The movie, rated PG, captivated audiences with Frasier's unique journey and the significant role he played in Lion Country Safari's success.

Unfortunately, Frasier's life came to an end in June 1972, when he was between 17 and 20 years old (which is equivalent to an impressive 85 to 100 years in human terms). His legacy continued to live on, as he had sired an astonishing 35 cubs during his time at the park. Frasier's story remains a testament to the unforeseen impact an unlikely star can have, captivating hearts and inspiring the imagination of both visitors and filmmakers alike.

In 1978, Bubbles the hippo made news with her escape from Lion Country Safari. Her escape and subsequent adventures captured the attention of many people at the time.

After digging under her fence, Bubbles managed to find refuge in a nearby drainage pit, where she stayed for approximately 19 days. Eventually, she left the pit and made her way up a nearby hill, where a ranger encountered her. In an attempt to safely capture her, the ranger shot her with two tranquilizer darts. Regrettably, the tranquilizer had an adverse effect on Bubbles, causing her to stop breathing shortly after being shot. Despite efforts to revive her, she was pronounced dead. Her passing was a somber moment for those involved and those following the story. Today, Bubbles' skull and bones can be found stored in the Natural History Museum in Los Angeles.

In November 1984, Lion Country Safari, which had operated for over 14 years, closed its doors permanently. The closure was due to various factors, including changing public interests, increased competition from other attractions, and perhaps financial challenges.

The site of the former Lion Country Safari did not remain vacant for long. In 1986, just two years after the closure, the area was transformed into the Wild Rivers water park. The former Safari Camp, which had once housed various safari-themed attractions, was repurposed to become part of the new water park. Wild Rivers

water park offered a different kind of entertainment compared to Lion Country Safari. Instead of showcasing wildlife and safari experiences, it provided water-based attractions and activities for visitors to enjoy. The park featured water slides, pools, and other water-themed attractions, attracting families and thrill-seekers looking for a refreshing and fun experience. Today, it's all been developed into housing communities

LOST DISNEYLAND LANDMARKS

As one of the most iconic and beloved amusement parks in the world, Disneyland has always been known for its constant evolution and innovation. In order to keep its magic alive and maintain its appeal to visitors, Disneyland is always looking to grow and adapt to changing times. Consequently, this means that certain attractions, which may have once been popular and cherished, can outlive their usefulness or appeal and must be retired from the park. It is in this process of change that these attractions become lost landmarks.

When an attraction reaches the end of its lifespan in Disneyland, it can often become a lost disappear altogether. Sometimes, though, remnants and traces of retired attractions can still be found in the park, serving as nostalgic reminders of the past. Elements of retired attractions may be repurposed or integrated into new experiences, allowing guests to catch glimpses or references to the original attraction. These nods to the past help preserve the legacy of these lost landmarks, ensuring that their memory lives on in the hearts of Disneyland enthusiasts. There are also instances, however, where retired attractions disappear completely from the park. This might be due to the need for space to accommodate new developments, or because the attraction has become outdated and no longer aligns with the park's vision. When this happens, the lost landmarks fade away, leaving behind only memories and photographs.

All that said, here's a list of attractions that were once present at Disneyland but are no longer available:

1. **Adventure Thru Inner Space:** Located in Tomorrowland, this attraction took guests on a journey through the "Mighty Microscope" to explore the inner workings of the human body. It operated from 1967 to 1985.
2. **America Sings:** Opened in 1974, America Sings was a musical revue featuring animatronic characters that celebrated American history through song. It closed in 1988 and was replaced by Innoventions.

3. **The Art of Animation:** This exhibit, located in Tomorrowland, showcased the process of Disney animation and gave guests a behind-the-scenes look at how animated films were created. It operated from 1958 to 1966 and was replaced by the Tomorrowland Terrace restaurant.
4. **The Carousel of Progress:** Originally created for the 1964 New York World's Fair, this attraction was relocated to Disneyland in 1967 and operated there until 1973. It showcased the progress of technology and daily life through the 20th century. The Carousel of Progress was moved to Walt

Disney World's Magic Kingdom in Florida, where it still operates today.

5. **Country Bear Jamboree:** This attraction, located in Frontierland, featured a cast of singing animatronic bears. It opened in 1972 and closed in 2001 to make way for The Many Adventures of Winnie the Pooh.

6. **The Disneyland Alweg Monorail System:** Originally opening in 1959 as the first daily operating monorail in the Western Hemisphere, the Disneyland Monorail System underwent several updates and changes over the years. The original Mark I trains were retired in 1961, and the Mark II trains operated until 1987 when they were replaced by the current Mark V trains.

7. **The Disney Gallery:** Originally located in New Orleans Square, the Disney Gallery was an art gallery that showcased original artwork and Disney memorabilia. It operated from 1987 to 2007 and was later relocated to Main Street, where it became the Disneyland Dream Suite.

8. **The Disneyland Hotel Marina:** The Disneyland Hotel once had its own marina, allowing guests to rent small watercraft such as pedal boats and canoes to enjoy the adjacent waterway. The marina closed in the late 1990s due to changes in the hotel's expansion plans.

9. The Flying Saucers: This attraction was located in Tomorrowland from 1961 to 1966 and featured a large field of individual flying saucers that guests could ride. The attraction faced technical difficulties and was eventually replaced by the Tomorrowland Speedway.

10. The House of the Future: Located in Tomorrowland from 1957 to 1967, this attraction presented a vision of futuristic living with innovative technologies and designs. It was one of the first fully plastic houses ever constructed.

11. **The Indian Village:** Found in Frontierland from 1956 to 1971, the Indian Village showcased Native American culture with displays of traditional dwellings, crafts, and performances.

12. **The Mickey Mouse Club Theater:** This theater, which opened in 1955, showcased Mickey Mouse cartoons and other Disney animated shorts. It later transformed into the Fantasyland Theater, which has hosted various live shows and productions over the years.

13. **The Mike Fink Keel Boats:** The Mike Fink Keel Boats operated from 1955 to 1997 and allowed guests to take a scenic ride on the Rivers of America aboard replicas of 19th-century keelboats. The attraction closed to make way for the expansion of New Orleans Square.

14. **Mine Train Through Nature's Wonderland:** This attraction, located in Frontierland, opened in 1960 and took guests on a scenic journey through various wilderness settings, including deserts, forests, and rivers. It closed in 1977 and was replaced by Big Thunder Mountain Railroad.

15. **Motor Boat Cruise:** Operating from 1957 to 1993, the Motor Boat Cruise allowed guests to pilot small motorboats around the waterways of Tomorrowland. It provided a leisurely and interactive experience but was eventually closed to make way for other attractions.

16. **The PeopleMover:** The PeopleMover was a slow-moving transportation system that took guests on a tour of Tomorrowland. It operated from 1967 to 1995. The track still exists, but the attraction was replaced by Rocket Rods, which operated from 1998 to 2000.

17. **The Phantom Boats:** This attraction, open from 1955 to 1956, allowed guests to pilot small motorboats around a waterway. Due to operational challenges, low capacity, and maintenance issues, it was closed and replaced by the Submarine Voyage.

18. **Rainbow Caverns Mine Train:** Found in Frontierland from 1956 to 1959, this attraction took guests on a train ride through a series of colorful caverns. It was later reimagined and became the Mine Train Through Nature's

Wonderland.

19. **Rocket to the Moon/Mission to Mars:** Originally opening as Rocket to the Moon in 1955, this attraction was transformed into Mission to Mars in 1975. It simulated a space voyage to the moon and Mars, but it closed in 1992 and later became Redd Rockett's Pizza Port.

20. **Skyway to Fantasyland:** Operating from 1956 to 1994, the Skyway was an aerial gondola transportation system that took guests between Tomorrowland and Fantasyland. It provided a unique view of the park but was eventually closed due to maintenance costs.

21. **Skyway to Tomorrowland:** Similar to the Fantasyland Skyway, this attraction operated from 1956 to 1994 and provided an aerial journey from Tomorrowland to Fantasyland. It offered unique views of the park but was eventually closed due to maintenance costs.

22. **The Submarine Voyage:** Operating from 1959 to 1998 as the Submarine Voyage, this attraction took guests on a simulated underwater journey through vibrant landscapes and encounters with marine life. It was later reimagined as the Finding Nemo Submarine Voyage in 2007.

23. **The Swiss Family Treehouse:** Based on the film *Swiss Family Robinson*, this walk-through attraction opened in 1962 and allowed guests to explore a treehouse filled with interactive scenes and props. It was transformed into Tarzan's Treehouse in 1999.

24. **The Tahitian Terrace:** This restaurant, located in Adventureland, offered a Polynesian-themed dining experience with live entertainment. It operated from 1962 to 1993 and was replaced by Aladdin's Oasis.

25. **The Viewliner:** Operating from 1957 to 1958, the Viewliner was a small-scale train ride located in Tomorrowland. It featured two miniature trains that circled a portion of the park. The attraction had a short lifespan and closed due to operational challenges.

LOST KNOTT'S BERRY FARM LANDMARKS

In a similar vein to Disneyland, Knott's Berry Farm also finds itself in a constant state of evolution and transformation to remain relevant and popular for its guests. As one of the oldest and most beloved theme parks in the United States, Knott's Berry Farm has a rich history of attractions that have delighted generations of visitors. To keep up with changing times and evolving guest expectations, Knott's Berry Farm must update and, at times, replace its attractions, leading to the creation of lost landmarks within the park.

Knott's Berry Farm has always strived to provide unique and thrilling experiences to its guests. This requires the park to continuously explore new concepts, technologies, and trends in the entertainment industry. As new and innovative attractions are introduced, older ones may start to lose their appeal and become outdated. In order to maintain the park's popularity and cater to the expectations of modern visitors, Knott's Berry Farm must make the difficult decision to update or replace these attractions.

Similar to Disneyland, the retirement of attractions at Knott's Berry Farm can result in the creation of lost landmarks within the park. Some retired attractions may still leave their mark, either through repurposed elements or nostalgic references. For instance, familiar characters or themes from former attractions may be incorporated into new experiences, allowing guests to reminisce about the past while enjoying the present. This allows the park to honor its history and preserve the memory of these lost landmarks, even as they give way to new adventures.

But just as with Disneyland, there are instances where former attractions at Knott's Berry Farm disappear entirely. This may occur when an attraction has become obsolete or when the park requires the space for new developments. When this happens, the lost landmarks of Knott's Berry Farm vanish, leaving behind only memories and stories shared by those who experienced them.

The retirement of attractions and the creation of lost landmarks is a natural part of the theme park industry. It is a testament to the commitment of parks like Knott's Berry Farm to provide fresh and exciting experiences for their guests. By updating and replacing attractions, Knott's Berry Farm ensures that visitors can always find something new and captivating when they return to the park. While the park has introduced new attractions, there have been several rides and attractions that are no longer found at Knott's Berry Farm. Here are a few notable examples:

1. **Bigfoot Rapids:** Bigfoot Rapids was a river rafting ride that operated from 1988 to 2018. Guests boarded large circular rafts and navigated through rapids and waterfalls. The ride was replaced by Calico River Rapids, which opened in 2019 with a new storyline and updated theming.

2. **Boomerang:** Boomerang was a shuttle roller coaster that

operated from 1990 to 2020. It featured multiple inversions and sent riders through a series of high-speed forward and backward loops. In 2020, the ride was removed to make way for a new attraction called Knott's Bear-y Tales: Return to the Fair.

3. **The Haunted Shack:** The Haunted Shack was a walk-through attraction that featured optical illusions and interactive elements. It operated from 1954 to 2000. The building that housed the attraction was later converted into the Mystery Lodge, a live theater show.

4. **Kingdom of the Dinosaurs:** Kingdom of the Dinosaurs was an indoor dark ride that took guests on a time-traveling journey to the age of dinosaurs. It featured animatronic dinosaurs and various special effects. The attraction operated from 1987 to 2004 and was later replaced by Voyage to the Iron Reef, a 4D interactive dark ride.

5. **Kingdom of the Sea Aquarium:** Kingdom of the Sea Aquarium was an aquarium and marine-life attraction that operated from 1968 to 1993. It housed various aquatic animals, including sharks, dolphins, and penguins. The space later became the location for other attractions, such as Perilous Plunge.

6. **Knott's Bear-y Tales:** Knott's Bear-y Tales was a dark ride that debuted in 1975. Guests embarked on a journey through whimsical scenes featuring animatronic bears and other characters. The ride closed in 1986 but made a

brief return in 2019 as "Knott's Bear-y Tales: Return to the Fair," a 4D interactive dark ride during the park's Boysenberry Festival.

7. **Mystery Lodge:** Mystery Lodge was a live theater show that opened in 1994. It combined storytelling, special effects, and holographic projections to immerse guests in Native American folklore. The show closed in 2018 and was replaced by an interactive dark ride called "Wander of the Wilderness."

8. **Perilous Plunge:** Perilous Plunge was a massive water flume ride that opened in 2000. It was one of the tallest and steepest water rides in the world, featuring a 115-foot drop at a near-vertical angle. Due to maintenance issues and low ridership, the ride closed in 2012 and was eventually dismantled.

9. **Roaring '20s Corkscrew:** The Roaring '20s Corkscrew was a classic roller coaster that operated from 1975 to 1989. It featured two inversions and was one of the first modern steel roller coasters on the West Coast. It was eventually replaced by Boomerang.

10. **Sky Cabin:** Sky Cabin was a rotating observation tower that provided panoramic views of the park and surrounding area. It operated from 1976 to 2019. The ride was closed for renovations in 2010 but never reopened. In 2019, it was re-themed and reopened as K.T. Tower, a drop tower attraction.

11. **The Sky Jump:** The Sky Jump was a free-fall tower ride that operated from 1976 to 1989. It allowed guests to experience the sensation of parachuting from a great height. The area where the Sky Jump was located is now home to the Supreme Scream drop tower.

12. **The Timber Mountain Log Ride:** The Timber Mountain Log Ride is another classic attraction that opened in 1969. It is a log flume ride that takes guests on a journey through a forest and a mountain-themed setting. It features animatronic characters and a thrilling drop. The log ride has undergone refurbishments over the years but remains a popular attraction.

13. **Wacky Soap Box Racers:** Wacky Soap Box Racers was a unique ride where guests could design and race their own soapbox cars down a track. It operated from 1986 to 1996 and provided a fun and interactive experience. The area where Wacky Soap Box Racers was located is now home to the Boardwalk area of the park.

14. **Windjammer Surf Racers:** Windjammer Surf Racers was a dueling roller coaster that operated from 1997 to 2000. The ride featured two tracks with riders racing against each other. But it faced numerous technical issues and was plagued with downtime. After several attempts to fix the problems, the ride was permanently closed and later removed.

The Movieland of the Air Museum
Orange County Airport
18601 Airport Way
Santa Ana

The Movieland of the Air Museum, located at Orange County Airport in Santa Ana, opened its doors to the public on December 14, 1963. This museum was the realization of a shared vision held by renowned movie pilots Paul Mantz and Frank Tallman. Together, they curated an impressive collection of aircraft and movie memorabilia, which they proudly showcased to visitors for the first time.

Spanning across a five-acre complex, the museum featured over 50 rare airplanes. These aircraft were displayed both inside a large hangar and in an outdoor area. Among the notable planes were World War I Nieuports, Spads, as well as World War II Corsairs and Mustangs. Additionally, the museum boasted an extensive collection of aviation armaments, uniforms, logbooks, movie posters, medals, trophies, and other valuable mementos.

Mantz and Tallman were highly regarded and accomplished movie pilots, having made significant contributions to aviation in the film industry. Their expertise and passion for aviation were evident in the carefully curated collection at the Movieland of the Air Museum. It offered visitors a unique opportunity to explore the history of aviation and its intersection with the world of cinema.

As visitors entered the Movieland of the Air Museum through its main entrance, they were greeted by a captivating sight—a missile pointed towards the sky, serving as a striking centerpiece. The museum's hangar was filled with a dozen or more aircraft lining its sides, each carefully positioned to create an immersive experience. Thoughtfully crafted dioramas were placed behind the aircraft, representing specific time periods or films in which the planes had been featured.

Inside the hangar, visitors could explore displays adorned with hundreds of photographs, most of which captured moments from Mantz and Tallman's various movie projects. These photographs were accompanied by press clippings, movie posters, and informative details about each aircraft. The majority of the aircraft showcased indoors were fabric-covered antiques, ranging from Frank Tallman's Bleriot to the Spirit of St. Louis replica constructed by Paul Mantz for the 1957 film. Notably, a place of honor was dedicated to NX1204, one of Mantz's P-51C Mustang racers. The Movieland of the Air Museum provided an engaging and educational experience for visitors, allowing them to appreciate the history of aviation and its connection to the world of cinema.

After the unfortunate death of Paul Mantz in July 1965, the Movieland of the Air Museum faced a setback. To settle some lawsuits and address matters related to the Mantz estate, Frank Tallman, Mantz's partner, was compelled to sell 45 aircraft and numerous displays to a group of investors from Nebraska in February 1966. It was initially anticipated that the aircraft would be resold and subsequently removed from the museum, and some planes were sold off during this period.

The majority of the sold aircraft remained on display at the museum until May 1968. At that time, the renowned Tallmantz Auction took place. Interestingly, it was not Tallman himself who conducted the auction; instead, it was the Nebraska investors who sold off the collection. Following the auction, the sold aircraft were swiftly removed from the museum, prompting Tallman to temporarily close the facility as new aircraft were prepared for display.

In 1969, the Movieland of the Air Museum reopened its doors to the public. A significant portion of the museum's outdoor area, as well as the Tallmantz ramp, were occupied by B-25 aircraft from the film *Catch-22*. The museum closed in 1985.

The Movieland Wax Museum
7711 Beach Boulevard
Buena Park

The Movieland Wax Museum, founded in 1962 by Allen H. Parkinson, was a beloved attraction located in Buena Park. Inspired by his visit to the famous Madame Tussauds wax museum in London, Parkinson sought to create a similar experience in the United States. The museum quickly became a popular destination for movie enthusiasts and tourists alike.

The grand opening of the Movieland Wax Museum was a star-studded event, with renowned silent film actress Mary Pickford in attendance. Pickford, one of the most influential figures in early Hollywood, dedicated the museum, adding a touch of glamour and prestige to the occasion.

Parkinson enlisted the talents of sculptor Antonio Ballester Vilaseca to create lifelike figures of various celebrities. Vilaseca was responsible for crafting the wax likenesses of numerous Hollywood icons, including Clark Gable, Leslie Howard, David Niven, Natalie Wood, and Charlton Heston. The attention to detail and craftsmanship in these figures made them highly prized and contributed to the museum's success.

During its heyday, the Movieland Wax Museum became renowned for its special events and celebrity involvement. Many actors and actresses attended the unveiling of their wax counterparts and generously donated costumes to be worn by their likenesses. This added authenticity and allowed visitors to feel even closer to their favorite movie stars.

But, after 43 years in operation and welcoming approximately 10 million visitors, the Movieland Wax Museum closed its doors in 2005. Its closure was due to a combination of factors, including changing tourism trends and the rise of digital entertainment experiences. The following year, an auction was held to sell off many of the wax figures and sets that had enchanted visitors for decades.

Sadly, in 2016, the original Movieland Wax Museum building was torn down, marking the end of an era. Today, the former Starlite Gift Shop, which once stood in front of the museum, has been replaced by a Starbucks.

Movieworld: Cars of the Stars and Planes of Fame Museum
6929 Orangethorpe Avenue
Buena Park

Jim Brucker, a former farmer, had a passion for collecting cars and amassed over 700 of them by 1970. He saw an opportunity to rent these cars to movie makers for their films and established a business called Oxnard's Movie Land Cars of the Stars and Picture Car Company in Los Angeles. This venture allowed filmmakers to access a wide variety of antique and classic cars for their productions.

In 1970, Brucker and his son Jimmy opened another establishment called Movieworld: Cars of the Stars and Planes of Fame Museum in Buena Park. This museum was a spectacular place that not only showcased the collection of cars and planes but also featured motion picture props, posters, and other memorabilia from Hollywood's history.

To enhance the artistic direction of the museum, the Bruckers hired Ed Roth as their artistic director. Ed Roth was a renowned custom car artist known for his unique and imaginative designs. Through Roth, the Bruckers were introduced to another famous custom car artist, Robert Williams, who also contributed to the museum's displays.

Von Dutch, another notable figure in the custom car and motorcycle scene, was drawn to Movieworld as well. He parked his bus, which served as both his home and workshop, at the museum for many years.

Movieworld: Cars of the Stars and Planes of Fame Museum became a prominent attraction that celebrated the history of Hollywood and showcased an extensive collection of cars, planes, props, and memorabilia. It closed in 1979 and everything was auctioned off in 1993.

Old MacDonald's Farm
27741 Crown Valley Parkway
Mission Viejo

Let's travel back to a time when the rolling hills of Mission Viejo echoed with the laughter of children and the gentle bleating of farm animals. It was a petting zoo like no other, a slice of rural paradise in the heart of Southern California.

In the early days, this enchanting farm found its humble beginnings at Knott's Berry Farm, a beloved amusement park in Buena Park. With its location near the seal pool and the site of the carousel, Old MacDonald's Farm opened its gates in January 1955. From the moment visitors stepped foot on this hallowed ground, they were transported to a world of joy and discovery.

The farm was lovingly tended to by its devoted operators, Fulton and Kay Shaw. They poured their hearts and souls into creating a haven where children could connect with nature and animals. For years, families flocked to Old MacDonald's Farm, eager to experience the magic that awaited them. But alas, as time passed, the Shaws felt a call to new horizons. In early 1969, they bid farewell to Knott's Berry Farm and set their sights on Mission Viejo. There, in

August of that same year, Old MacDonald's Farm was reborn, like a phoenix rising from the ashes.

Every great tale has its share of challenges, and so it was with Old MacDonald's Farm. A dispute arose between the Shaws and Knott's Berry Farm, who had continued to use the cherished name "Old MacDonald's Farm" for their own petting zoo. In the end, a compromise was reached, and the Knott's version was renamed "The Animal Farm." Despite the setbacks, the spirit of Old MacDonald's Farm remained resilient. Generations of wide-eyed children and their families continued to visit, forging memories that would last a lifetime. But as the winds of change swept through the land, the farm faced its ultimate fate. Sometime around 1980, Old MacDonald's Farm closed its gates for the final time. The vibrant tapestry of joy and laughter that once adorned the hills of Mission Viejo faded away, leaving behind only cherished memories. The land that once housed this magical place now wears a different face, transformed into the bustling Kaleidoscope shopping center.

Western Trails Museum
7862 Speer Avenue
Huntington Beach

Marion Speer, a passionate collector of Native American and Old West artifacts, established the Western Trails Museum in 1936. His love for these historical items led him to create a space to showcase his extensive collection to the public. Speer built a building next to his house in Huntington Beach, on a street that was later named for him.

In 1941, Speer expanded the museum by completing a 600 square-foot addition. The museum quickly became a popular destination for school groups and the general public, who flocked to see his remarkable collection of 12,000 arrowheads, mineral specimens, fossils, guns, tools, and other captivating artifacts.

After nearly 20 years of running the museum, Speer made a significant decision in 1956. At the age of 72, he generously donated his entire collection to Knott's Berry Farm, where he continued to serve as the curator. The Western Trails Museum found its new home just south of the saloon in Ghost Town, within the grounds of Knott's Berry Farm.

Marion Speer remained dedicated to preserving the history and heritage of the American West until his retirement in 1969. At the age of 84, he stepped down from his position as the curator. His tireless efforts and expertise had made the Western Trails Museum a cherished attraction for visitors from far and wide.

Sadly, Speer passed away in 1978 at the age of 93. His legacy lives on through the Western Trails Museum, where his passion for Native American and Old West artifacts continues to captivate and educate visitors to this day.

CHAPTER THREE

RACETRACKS

LET'S TAKE A WILD ride through the vibrant racing scene of Orange County in the 1940s, '50s, '60s, '70s, and '80s! See, during this era, Orange County was more than just a sunny paradise, filled with palm trees and pristine beaches. It was a haven for speed enthusiasts, a place where racing dreams took flight on wheels of thunder. And at the heart of it all were the racetracks that dotted the county, breathing life into the adrenaline-fueled passions of both professionals and amateurs alike.

There were professional tracks—hallowed grounds where the motoring legends of the time pushed their fine-tuned machines to the limit, captivating audiences with their daredevil skills. There were also amateur dirt tracks which played a vital role in shaping Orange County's racing legacy. These grassroots venues, often carved out of the county's abundant open spaces, were where the local daredevils and aspiring racers honed their skills and chased their dreams.

Motocross, that exhilarating blend of off-road racing and airborne acrobatics, found a fertile playground in Orange County's backyard. Kids with a thirst for adventure and a love for two wheels could hit the dirt tracks, soar over jumps, and get their hearts pumping with the thrill of motocross. These tracks became the birthplace of champions, where future legends like Jeremy McGrath and Ricky Johnson first tasted victory.

But let's not forget the sheer abundance of open space that Orange County boasted back then. It was a different time, when the county still wore its rural charm proudly. Wide expanses of untouched land stretched out as far as the eye could see, providing ample room for the racing community to carve out their own patches of paradise. The availability of open space was a catalyst, allowing these venues to sprout up and flourish, providing a canvas for racing dreams to become a reality. Back then, Orange County was a land of speed, where the roar of engines echoed through the canyons, and the smell of gasoline infused the air with excitement. Let's revisit some of those lost racing landmarks.

Huntington Beach Speedway
Near Atlanta Avenue and Beach Boulevard
Huntington Beach

In the post-war era of 1946, as the allure of speed and entertainment swept through the nation, Tom Talbert had a vision. He saw the potential for a local business that would captivate the community, and purchased approximately 60 acres of land near Beach Boulevard and Atlanta Avenue to build this business on. Inspired by his belief in the passion for racing, he set out to create the "finest midget car racetrack on the West Coast." Thus, Huntington Beach Speedway was born—a place where speed, spectacle, and the roar of engines would come to life.

In late 1946, Huntington Beach Speedway opened its gates to an eager crowd of 3,500 racing enthusiasts. The oval track, which was 1/5 of a mile long, was modeled after the renowned Gilmore Stadium in Hollywood. It promised a thrilling experience like no other. As midget cars zipped around the oval leaving trails of excitement in their wake, fans were drawn into a world of adrenaline-fueled competition. The inaugural race marked the beginning of a new era in motorsports, as Huntington Beach Speedway quickly established itself as a premier destination for racing aficionados.

As the years went by, Huntington Beach Speedway evolved to accommodate a wide range of racing disciplines and thrilling spectacles. The roar of motorcycles replaced the hum of midget cars, adding a new dimension to the venue's racing repertoire. Spectators reveled in the daring maneuvers and lightning fast speeds

that graced the track, their cheers echoing through the stands. The Speedway even witnessed unconventional events such as auto polo, where Model T Fords competed in a thrilling twist on the sport. Jalopy races also gained popularity, further diversifying the entertainment offered to the passionate crowds.

July 3, 1947 marked a pivotal moment in the history of Huntington Beach Speedway. On that day, a staggering 14,000 spectators flocked to the venue, creating an atmosphere of electric energy and anticipation. It was the largest crowd the Speedway had ever seen, a testament to the enduring appeal of the sport and the venue's reputation as a hub of excitement. As the years passed, the advent of television began to impact attendance, leading to dwindling crowds. The once thriving Speedway struggled to maintain its fan base, and in May 1958, Tom Talbert made the difficult decision to close its doors.

Throughout its existence, Huntington Beach Speedway underwent various name changes, adopting monikers such as Beach Speedway, Talbert Stadium, Huntington Beach Stadium, and American Legion Stadium. Nevertheless, regardless of the name on its gates, the Speedway left an indelible mark on the hearts of racing enthusiasts and the history of the community. It served as a testament to the passion for speed and entertainment, a place where dreams were pursued and victories celebrated.

Orange County International Raceway
Adjacent to the I-5 Freeway
Irvine

Orange County International Raceway (OCIR) was a popular racing facility located in Irvine. It featured a combination of a 1/4-mile

drag strip, a two-mile road course, and a motocross track. The race-way was situated near the Interstate 5 (I-5) Santa Ana Freeway, making it easily accessible to race fans. OCIR opened its doors on August 5, 1967, and quickly became a prominent venue for various motorsport events. The founders of OCIR had a vision of hosting a wide range of races, including sports car, motorcycle, midget, and stock car competitions, alongside National Hot Rod Association (NHRA) sanctioned drag racing events.

The track construction incorporated several features to en-hance the spectator experience. These included extensive land-scaping, permanent restrooms, concession stands, reserved seats with backs, and drinking fountains placed throughout the facility. The introduction of these amenities set OCIR apart from other drag race venues in the region. Additionally, OCIR was notable for being the first drag racing facility in the sport to feature an electric scoreboard. This technology allowed for a more accurate, real-time display of race results, enhancing the overall viewing experience for spectators.

One of the most significant contributions associated with OCIR was the establishment of the Bob Bondurant School of High Performance Driving. Founded at the track in 1968, the school provided professional driving instruction and training for individuals interested in improving their driving skills, particularly in high performance vehicles. The school's presence at OCIR further

elevated the raceway's reputation and attracted motorsport enthusiasts from various backgrounds. Orange County International Raceway was not only renowned for its cutting-edge design and modern facilities but also for the opportunities it provided for both racing and education in the world of motorsports.

For approximately 16 years, OCIR attracted enthusiastic crowds and hosted numerous exciting races. Due to various factors, including rising land values and increasing urban development in the surrounding area, OCIR was eventually forced to close its doors on October 30, 1983.

Despite its closure, Orange County International Raceway holds a significant place in the history of motorsports in Southern California. It remains a fond memory for many racing enthusiasts who experienced the thrill of racing at this iconic venue.

Saddleback Motocross Park
Santiago Canyon Road near the Eastern Transportation Corridor
Orange

Located in rolling hills near the beach and within close proximity to major motocross manufacturers, the Saddleback motocross track

became a hub for the motocross industry. The track's accessibility allowed aspiring riders to connect with industry professionals and potentially secure opportunities to become factory stars.

Riders who frequented Saddleback understood the ever-changing nature of the track. In the morning, the dirt would be saturated with mud, making it a formidable challenge for riders as their bikes would accumulate extra weight. But, as the day progressed, the track would dry out, offering excellent traction and ideal berms for exhilarating racing. By the second moto, the track would transform into a dusty, blue groove surface, resembling racing on asphalt.

For many, Saddleback represented more than just a motocross track. It was a way of life and a defining factor of one's identity within the motocross community. The track's unique location and its significance in the motocross world made it a special place for both riders and fans alike. Saddleback's uniqueness and iconic status can be attributed to several distinctive features of the track:

1. **Banzai Hill and Webco:** Banzai Hill and Webco were integral parts of Saddleback's iconic culture. Banzai Hill was a treacherous uphill jump that required skill, bravery, and a fearless attitude. Riders had to gather enough speed and momentum to

conquer the steep incline and make a successful jump. Webco, on the other hand, was a challenging downhill section with deep ruts and jumps, demanding precise control and technique.

2. **The Magoo-Hannah Double Jumps:** The double jumps named after legendary riders "Magoo" (Marty Smith) and "Hannah" (Bob Hannah) were renowned features of Saddleback. These jumps were considered extremely difficult and required exceptional skill, timing, and fearlessness to successfully clear.

3. **The Start Hill:** The Start Hill at Saddleback was renowned as the world's best natural dyno. It provided a challenging and thrilling start to races, testing the horsepower and acceleration of the bikes. The steep incline of the Start Hill separated the riders right from the beginning, setting the stage for intense competition.

4. **Suicide Mountain:** This was another noteworthy obstacle on the track, known for its steepness and the risk it posed to riders who attempted to conquer it.

5. **The Tree Turn:** The Tree Turn at Saddleback was one of the most photographed corners in motocross history. This

particular section was characterized by a tight turn located near a prominent tree, creating a visually striking and challenging element of the track. The Tree Turn demanded precise cornering technique and emphasized the importance of line selection and bike control.

These elements of Saddleback combined to create a track that not only challenged riders' skills and bravery but also became an integral part of motocross history. The track's unique features and the legends associated with them contributed to its status as an iconic motocross venue.

During its operational years, 1967–1984, Saddleback Motocross Park served as a focal point for motocross enthusiasts, riders, and industry professionals in the region. Its challenging track, iconic features, and proximity to major motocross manufacturers contributed to its status as a premier motocross venue. Saddleback Motocross Park's legacy extends beyond its role as a motocross track. It holds a special place in Orange County's history as a cultural landmark and symbol of the area's association with motocross and extreme sports. The track's impact on the local community, tourism, and economy cannot be understated. Even after its closure in 1984, Saddleback continues to hold a special significance in the hearts of motocross enthusiasts and remains an important part of Orange County's history.

The Santa Ana Drags
19300 Ike Jones Road
Santa Ana

The Santa Ana Drags was the first drag strip in the United States, and thus holds a special place in the history of drag racing. Despite its humble beginnings, it quickly became a hub for racing enthusiasts and produced some legendary pioneers in the sport. One fun aspect of the Santa Ana Drags was its incredibly low startup cost. With just $1,000, the founder, C.J. "Pappy" Hart managed to create a racing venue that would go on to make a significant impact on the world of drag racing. It's a testament to his resourcefulness and passion for the sport.

The Santa Ana Drags provided a platform for both casual par-

ticipants and serious racers to showcase their skills and passion for speed. The strip became a melting pot of automotive enthusiasts, creating an atmosphere of excitement and camaraderie. Another interesting feature of the strip was the inclusion of timing clocks. These clocks allowed racers to receive accurate times for each run, adding a professional touch to the racing experience. It must have been thrilling for the participants to see their times displayed, fueling their competitive spirit.

The strip served as a breeding ground for talent, and many well-known drag racers of the time honed their skills and made their mark at this iconic landmark. The Santa Ana Drags laid the foundation for the sport and set the stage for the countless drag strips that followed. Its humble origins, affordable entry fees, timing clocks, and basic amenities all contributed to making it a special place for racers and fans alike. Now the land that once was the drag strip is home to the Lyon Air Museum, founded by the late developer and Air Force veteran Gen. William Lyon.

CHAPTER FOUR

EATING AND DRINKING

THE RESTAURANT CULTURE IN Orange County has played a signif-icant role in shaping the culinary landscape of the region over the years. From vibrant neighborhood eateries to iconic establishments, these restaurants have left a lasting impression on the local commu-nity. While many of these beloved old places have been replaced or closed down, they continue to hold a special place in the memories of Orange County residents.

Orange County has long been a melting pot of diverse cultures, and its restaurant and bar scene reflects this rich tapestry. Over the years, immigrants from various parts of the world have brought their culinary traditions and flavors to the region, resulting in a vibrant and eclectic food culture. Neighborhood restaurants in particular have been instrumental in showcasing these culinary traditions and be-coming gathering places for locals.

These old neighborhood restaurants were more than just places to eat; they were social hubs where friends and families would gather to share meals and create lasting memories. Many of these estab-lishments were family-owned, with generations of the same family running the business for years and years. The owners would often greet regular customers by name, creating a sense of familiarity and community. As the years have passed, the gastronomic landscape of Orange County has evolved, with new restaurants and dining trends emerging. While this evolution is exciting, it is also bittersweet for those who remember the old neighborhood eateries that have dis-appeared. These establishments represented a simpler time, a place where people could connect over a shared love for good food and good company.

Arnold's Farm House
6601 Manchester Boulevard
Buena Park

The story of Arnold's Farm House began in 1956, when it emerged as a proud successor to an old farm house that had graced the same spot since the early 1900s. The restaurant's rich history seeped through its walls, exuding a rustic allure that beckoned hungry souls from all walks of life. But what truly set Arnold's apart was its magnificent neon windmill that spun with joy, drawing in exhausted families seeking respite after a thrilling day at Knott's Berry Farm.

Arnold's Farm House was part of a culinary empire crafted by a family with an impeccable taste for good food. They not only owned this beloved establishment but also presided over The Buttery, a traditional, upscale restaurant located just across the street. The family's dedication to providing diverse dining experiences was evident in both venues, catering to different palates and moods.

In 1988, the restaurant's fate was sealed, and it succumbed to the mighty wrecking ball. The once-bustling home of delectable meals, laughter, and cherished memories gave way to make room for progress. Today, a car dealership sits in the very spot where Arnold's Farm House once stood.

Belisle's
12001 Harbor Boulevard
Garden Grove

In the heart of Garden Grove, there stood a legendary restaurant that captured the hearts and taste buds of Orange County. This cherished establishment was none other than Belisle's, a true lost landmark and one of the most beloved dining spots in the region's history.

Harvey and Charlotte Belisle, a delightful couple brimming with culinary passion, embarked on their gastronomic journey shortly before Disneyland opened its magical gates just up the street. From the moment Belisle's welcomed its first guests, it became synonymous with delectable delights and warm hospitality.

The restaurant boasted a menu that was nothing short of extraordinary. One of their most famous creations was their giant volcano mountain strawberry pies. Picture, if you will, a heavenly eruption of luscious strawberries within a flaky crust, topped with billows of whipped cream. Each slice was a masterpiece, a tantalizing treat that left guests in awe of its sheer deliciousness.

But the delights didn't stop there. Belisle's was renowned for its mouthwatering catfish and hush puppies, a Southern-inspired symphony of flavors that transported customers

to diners in the bayous of Louisiana. The catfish, perfectly seasoned and fried to a golden crisp, and the hush puppies, little mor-
sels of cornmeal heaven, danced together on the plate, creating a
harmony of taste that was simply irresistible.

Belisle's had those who craved a taste of barbecue covered, too.
Their barbecued beef ribs were a carnivorous delight, tender and
succulent, smothered in a flavorful sauce that had just the right
amount of tang. With each mouthful, patrons reveled in the fin-
ger-licking goodness that could only be found at Belisle's.

And let's not forget their homemade meatloaf, a comforting
classic that warmed both hearts and bellies. This humble dish, lovingly prepared with a secret blend of spices and savory goodness,
satisfied even the most discerning meatloaf connoisseurs. It was a
testament to the Belisle's dedication to serving honest, home-style
cooking that made you feel like part of the family.

To wash it all down, Belisle's offered a delightful selection
of fresh churned homemade ice cream. From velvety vanilla to
dreamy chocolate, their ice cream was a sweet symphony of flavors that provided the perfect ending to a memorable meal. Each
spoonful was like a taste of pure happiness, leaving smiles on the
faces of young and old alike.

From 1955 until 1995, Belisle's stood as a beacon of culinary
excellence. Its charming, offbeat slogan, "Home made pies. We
dake 'em baily." drew in customers from all corners of the globe. It
was more than just a restaurant; it was a small-town haven, a fami-
ly-run gem that embraced every visitor with open arms.

Sadly, the passage of time brought change, and Belisle's was
torn down by the Garden Grove redevelopment agency in the mid-
1990s. But while the physical building may be gone, the memories
of Belisle's and the culinary magic it created remain everlasting.

Bob and Jeans Café
20612 E. Chapman Avenue
Orange Park Acres

Bob and Jeans Café was a cherished gem of Orange Park Acres, and
holds a special place in the hearts of its former patrons. Located
near the intersection of Chapman Avenue and Newport Avenue,
this little taco joint served as a beloved gathering spot for locals in

what was then East Orange, California. Though its doors closed in the early 1980s to make way for progress and development, the memories and nostalgia associated with Bob and Jeans Café continue to endure.

With its quaint and unassuming exterior, the café exuded a welcoming atmosphere that drew people in from all walks of life. Inside, the aroma of sizzling meats and tantalizing spices filled the air, enticing customers to indulge in the delicious flavors the café had to offer. From mouthwatering tacos to hearty burritos, each dish was carefully prepared with love and attention to detail.

What truly set Bob and Jeans Café apart, however, was not just its delectable menu, but its sense of community. The café became a hub where friends, families, and neighbors could gather, sharing stories and laughter over a satisfying meal. The warm and friendly staff made it feel like a home away from home, leaving an indelible mark on the hearts of everyone who walked through its doors.

As time passed and Orange County experienced rapid growth, Bob and Jeans Café sadly succumbed to the wave of development. The building is gone today, but the memories live on.

Café Frankenstein
860 S. Pacific Coast Highway
Laguna Beach

The Café Frankenstein was a notable coffee house in Laguna Beach during the late 1950s to early 1960s. It gained a reputation as a gathering place for the counterculture and alternative art communities of the time. Located at 860 South Pacific Coast Highway, it attracted a diverse clientele, including beatniks, surfers, folk musicians, teenagers, and other unconventional individuals.

During its operation, Café Frankenstein was considered controversial and was seen as a "den of iniquity" by some members of the semi-conservative Orange County art community. It was rumored to be involved in activities such as drug use and other forms

of debauchery. In response to these rumors and suspicions, two undercover police officers frequented the café for two years in an attempt to catch individuals involved in illegal activities. According to the last owner, Michael Schley, the undercover officers ended up becoming supporters of Café Frankenstein rather than making any arrests. This suggests that the café may not have been as nefarious as it was portrayed, and the officers may have discovered that the rumors were unfounded or exaggerated.

Café Frankenstein played a significant role in the alternative cultural scene of Laguna Beach during the late 1950s and early 1960s. It provided a space for creative expression and attracted a diverse community of artists, musicians, and free-spirited individuals. Some of those who were involved in running the café and contributed to its unique atmosphere were Burt Shonberg, Doug Myres, and George Clayton Johnson.

Burt Shonberg, known as an artist, created a stained-glass window featuring Frankenstein and painted cubist mural art for the club. His artistic contributions added to the visual aesthetics and ambiance of Café Frankenstein. Shonberg was also known for his mural work in other establishments such as Hollywood's Purple Onion, Cosmo Alley, the Bastille, the Seven Chef's, and Pandora's Box. Additionally, he created advertising art for various venues, including Sandalsville on Fairfax Avenue, and for local surf movie events organized by Don Brown. Shonberg's artistry extended to album covers as well, including the cover for Arthur Lee & Love's 1969 LP *Out Here.*

Alongside the artistic elements, Café Frankenstein had a bookstore inside that specialized in banned books. This suggests that the café embraced countercultural and alternative literature, providing a space for individuals interested in exploring ideas outside of mainstream society. Additionally, there was a sandal shop located at the back of the café, which added to the eclectic nature of the establishment. It offered patrons the opportunity to purchase or explore unique footwear options, aligning with the bohemian spirit of the café.

Sid Soffer managed Café Frankenstein from 1958 to 1959 before starting his own beat café called Sid's Blue Beet in Newport Beach. This highlights the interconnectedness of the beat and countercultural scenes during that era. The involvement of Burt Shonberg, Doug Myres, George Clayton Johnson, and Sid Soffer contributed to the distinct character and appeal of Café Frankenstein, making it a significant part of the artistic and alternative scene in Laguna Beach during the late 1950s and early 1960s.

Chez Cary
571 South Main Street
Orange

The Chez Cary restaurant in Orange was a truly exceptional dining establishment during its time. With its founder Cary Muller at the helm, it aimed to provide a high-quality and luxurious experience for its discerning clientele. The restaurant's Main Street location made it a notable destination in Orange County during the 1970s.

From the elegant decor with gleaming crystal, flickering candles, and exquisite china to the gourmet cuisine prepared at the table, the restaurant aimed to provide a memorable dining experience. It positioned itself as one of the great restaurants of the

Dinner

Suggestions

by

Chez Cary

*One of the Great Restaurants
of the Western World*

571 SOUTH MAIN STREET/ORANGE, CALIFORNIA/TELEPHONE 542-3595

Western world, empha-
sizing its commitment to
maintaining the highest
standards of quality.

The Chez Cary went
above and beyond in
terms of service and
pampering. The chairs
were lush velvet wing-
back chairs, designed for
comfort and elegance.
The restaurant even
provided footstools for
ladies, ensuring their
comfort throughout the
meal. Strolling musicians
added to the ambiance,
creating an atmosphere
reminiscent of classic
Hollywood movies. The
restaurant's commitment
to tableside service, which included flaming, carving, and tossing,
indicated its dedication to interactive and theatrical dining. It allowed guests to witness the preparation and presentation of their
food firsthand, adding an element of excitement and spectacle to
the meal.

For cigar enthusiasts, the Chez Cary offered a personalized
touch. A cigar cart would come to your table, allowing guests to select their preferred cigars. Additionally, the matchbooks provided
were personalized with the guest's name, adding an extra touch of
individuality and attention to detail. The restaurant closed in 1990.

Christian's Hut
3121 W. Coast Highway
Newport Beach

Christian's Hut, a Tahitian-style restaurant and bar, was a popular
destination for the Hollywood elite in the late 1930s. Located on

the bayfront where the Newport Towers complex now stands, the establishment was owned by Art La Shelle, whose brother Joe La Shelle was a renowned Hollywood cinematographer. Joe La Shelle won an Oscar for his work. One of his notable films was Alfred Hitchcock's *The Birds*.

Christian's Hut gained a reputation for its excellent oriental style cuisine, attracting celebrities such as Red Skelton, Johnny Weissmuller, Fred Mac Murray, and Howard Hughes, among others. One of the restaurant's unique features was a large outdoor cooking pit, where much of the food was prepared. Another intriguing aspect of Christian's Hut was how they achieved a crispy, charred exterior and a rare interior for their filet mignon. It was a mystery to many patrons, but a regular customer was once informed confidentially about the secret technique. Allegedly, the steak was first frozen, then seared on a white-hot grill before being dropped into a deep fryer. This method seemingly resulted in the desired texture and flavor. The legacy of Christian's Hut as a gathering spot for the Hollywood elite and its unique culinary secrets added to its appeal during its time of operation.

The downstairs bar area of Christian's Hut had a sand floor that extended all the way to the water, allowing patrons to beach their boats. This unique feature likely added to the tropical and beachside ambiance of the establishment. The dining room, on the other hand, was situated upstairs, providing a separate space for guests to enjoy their meals. Marshall, the maître d', had a distinctive habit of kissing the hand of every woman entering the restaurant. This charming gesture earned him the nickname "Francois." It seems Marshall was known for his attentive and gallant demeanor toward female patrons.

Marshall's daughter, Delores, was a beauty queen who went on to marry George Perlin, the owner of the Richfield Station at the corner of Adams Street and Balboa Boulevard. George, known by the nickname "Beast" due to his abundant body hair, and Delores were affectionately referred to as "Beauty and the Beast" after their marriage.

Unfortunately, Christian's Hut met a tragic fate as it burned down in 1963, bringing an end to its era as a popular gathering place for locals and celebrities alike.

CHRISTIAN'S HUT
BALBOA, CALIFORNIA

The End Café
1 Main Street
Huntington Beach

Perched at the very edge of the Huntington Beach pier, there stood a whimsical haven known as the End Café. From the year 1977 until the early 1990s, this legendary establishment captured the hearts and taste buds of locals and visitors alike. With its enchanting atmosphere and delectable offerings, it became an irreplaceable treasure in the history of Huntington Beach.

The man behind this iconic establishment was John Gustafson, who was fueled by an unwavering passion for culinary delights and a deep love for his community. While other restaurants on the pier served simple fare like hot soup, chilled fisherman's delights, and hearty hotdogs, the End Café went above and beyond, offering a menu brimming with creativity and flavor.

Despite facing numerous challenges, Gustafson's determination and perseverance kept the End Café alive. Even the mighty storms that swept through Huntington Beach not once, but twice, couldn't dampen his spirits. With every tempest that threatened to crumble the café, Gustafson rebuilt it with unwavering resolve, refusing to let his dream be washed away into the vast ocean.

The End Café became a symbol of resilience, a testament to the indomitable human spirit. It stood as a beacon of hope and a

gathering place for locals and tourists seeking solace, delicious food, and a touch of magic. The whimsical décor, adorned with seashells, twinkling lights, and colors that mirrored the ocean's dance, invited patrons to escape the ordinary and revel in an extraordinary experience.

As the years passed, the End Café earned its place in the hearts of the community. It was a place where memories were made, friendships kindled, and love stories blossomed. The café resonated with laughter, joy, and the sound of clinking glasses, creating a tapestry of moments that would forever be etched in the annals of Huntington Beach history.

Eventually, the End Café bid its farewell, making way for a new chapter on the pier. A Ruby's restaurant graced the hallowed spot, continuing the tradition of culinary delights and seaside charm. But like the ebb and flow of the tides, even Ruby's had its time, recently closing its doors, leaving behind a void at the end of the iconic pier.

GAY BARS IN LAGUNA BEACH

In the lively and open-minded city of Laguna Beach, there existed a beachfront community that embraced diversity and celebrated the freedom to be oneself. This picturesque coastal town possessed a rich history of lost landmarks involving gay bars, with Main Beach serving as the focal point for these vibrant establishments.

One of the most prominent icons in Laguna Beach's gay nightlife scene was the Coast Inn, a charming beachside inn that had been a popular destination since the early 1900s. In the early 1960s, the inn's owner, affectionately known as "Pappy" Smith, passed away, leaving his son Carl to take the reins of its management. Carl, recognizing the changing times and the growing demand for LGBTQ+ spaces, decided to embrace the vibrant gay community that had found solace and acceptance within Laguna Beach's welcoming embrace.

Under Carl's stewardship, the Coast Inn became a haven for the LGBTQ+ community. Its most famous establishment, the Boom Boom Room, located within the inn, swiftly became

an iconic gay bar. With its inviting atmosphere, pulsating
music, and lively dance floor,
the Boom Boom Room quickly
became a cherished gathering
place for both locals and visitors alike.

Meanwhile, just a stone's
throw away from the Coast
Inn, Main Beach flourished. It
was here that another legendary gay bar, Dantes, became a
beloved fixture in the community. Known for its welcoming ambiance and thrilling
entertainment, Dantes was a
true beacon of acceptance. It

was not uncommon for the bar to place immense orders, such
as 500 cases of Budweiser, to cater to the large crowds that
flocked to Main Beach during holiday weekends.

As time passed and the city evolved, changes were inevitable. Main Beach underwent a transformation, with the
construction of Main Beach Park. While this provided a wonderful recreational space for the community, it also meant
that Dantes had to close its doors, leaving behind a legacy of
cherished memories.

Despite the loss of Dantes, the spirit of acceptance and
openness continued to thrive in Laguna Beach. The torch of
LGBTQ+ nightlife was carried forward by a smaller, but no less
significant, establishment called the Bounce. Owned by Kelly
Boyd, who understood the importance of preserving this vibrant part of the city's history as a gay man himself, the Bounce
became a sanctuary for the LGBTQ+ community. The owner of
the Bounce, recognizing the enduring pride and resilience of
the gay community, made it his mission to ensure that the establishment continued to evolve and improve. The bar became
a place where people from all walks of life could come together, celebrate their identities, and forge lasting friendships. As

the years passed, the Bounce grew in popularity and became a symbol of progress and inclusivity. The city of Laguna Beach, known for its open-mindedness and acceptance, rallied behind the bar, recognizing its value as a safe space for the LGBTQ+ community. With ongoing improvements and a commitment to fostering a sense of unity and belonging, the Bounce proudly carried the torch of its predecessors, honoring the legacy of lost landmarks and preserving the vibrant spirit of Laguna Beach's gay nightlife.

As the crowds flocked to the shores of Laguna Beach, seeking both sun-soaked relaxation and a vibrant social scene, they discovered two hidden gems: the Little Shrimp and West Street Beach, located south of Camel's Point in the enchanting South Laguna. These destinations, with their breathtaking coastal views and welcoming atmosphere, became a magnet for those in search of a place where they could be their authentic selves.

Legend has it that Michael Michaels, the charismatic owner of the Little Shrimp, recognized the potential for expanding the gay nightlife scene in Laguna Beach. Seeing the growing demand and the limited capacity of his own establishment, he approached Carl Smith, the proprietor of the Coast Inn, and his wife with a proposition during a dinner gathering. Michaels suggested that the South Seas bar at the Coast Inn be transformed into a gay bar, as it had the space to accommodate larger crowds compared to the Little Shrimp.

Intrigued by the idea and recognizing the opportunity to further embrace the LGBTQ+ community, Carl Smith took Michaels' advice to heart. He saw the potential of creating a dedicated space where the gay community could gather and

celebrate their identities freely. With Michaels' encourage-
ment, Carl hired a gentleman named Reggie as the main bar-
tender for the South Seas bar. Reggie, a former press agent for
the iconic Judy Garland, possessed a deep understanding of
the power of word-of-mouth publicity.

Reggie cleverly spread the word that the South Seas bar
was undergoing an exciting transformation, turning into a
gay-friendly establishment. With his background in public
relations and a network of connections, he ensured that the
news reached far and wide, generating a buzz of anticipation
among both locals and visitors.

The summer holiday weekend arrived, and the South Seas
bar at the Coast Inn was ready to unveil its new identity. As
the doors swung open, a surge of energy coursed through the
air, and a diverse crowd filled the space. The atmosphere was
charged with excitement, as people from all walks of life came
together to revel in the newfound freedom of expression.

Word of the South Seas' transformation spread like wildfire, drawing in patrons who were eager to experience this vibrant addition to Laguna Beach's gay nightlife scene. The bar
quickly became a hub of celebration, where laughter, music,
and camaraderie intertwined.

Over time, the South Seas bar at the Coast Inn solidified
its place as a beloved landmark in Laguna Beach's LGBTQ+
history. It became a symbol of acceptance, a testament to the
power of community, and a cherished memory for those who
experienced its magic.

As the years unfolded, the South Seas bar evolved alongside the changing times. It continued to host countless social
gatherings, providing a sanctuary for love, acceptance, and
self-expression. Its legacy lives on as a testament to the courage and vision of those who believed in creating spaces where
everyone could feel seen, valued, and celebrated.

Thus, the story of lost landmarks involving gay bars in
Laguna Beach serves as proof of the city's enduring spirit of
acceptance and the unwavering determination of its LGBTQ+
community to create spaces where everyone can be celebrated for who they are.

Karam's
Corner of Main Street and Balboa Boulevard
Balboa Island
Newport Beach

Karam's restaurant, located in Newport, was known for being the epitome of fine dining in its heyday. The establishment boasted a luxurious atmosphere, complete with valets dressed in full tuxedos. In 1953, Karam's hosted a fundraiser for George Hoag, who aimed to initiate efforts to build a new hospital in the area. The event turned out to be quite successful, raising $100 per person, which would be equivalent to around $1,000 in today's currency. The fundraiser seated 125 people and was attended by influential individuals from the community.

Interestingly, there were rumors of a "private party" held at Karam's from 2 A.M. TO 4:30 A.M., which reportedly generated even more funds for the hospital. It is said that this additional event contributed an extra $5,000 to the cause. The bar remained open during this time, allowing guests to continue their contributions while enjoying drinks and socializing. The fundraiser organized by Karam's for George Hoag's hospital project showcased the restaurant's commitment to supporting the community and its charitable endeavors. The event attracted prominent figures, including half of the city council and the police chief, who attended without charge. Generous donations of provisions, food, and drinks from various sources further enhanced the success of the fundraiser. Today at the location is a pizza place.

La Palma Chicken Pie Shop
928 N. Euclid Street
Anaheim

La Palma Chicken Pie Shop, located in Anaheim, holds a special place in the hearts of many as one of the most beloved and iconic restaurants in Orange County. Established in 1955, it quickly gained popularity after Otto and Angie Hasselbarth took over the restaurant in 1972.

The Hasselbarths' dedication and hard work contributed to the

restaurant's success and loyal fan base. Otto in particular played a significant role in its daily operations. He would arrive at La Palma Chicken Pie Shop as early as 4 A.M. to handle all the baking, ensuring that the famous flaky chicken pot pies and other delectable treats were freshly made. After completing his morning tasks, Otto would go home for a short nap before returning around 1:30 P.M. to continue working until the restaurant's 8 P.M. closing time.

The restaurant's signature dish, the flaky chicken pot pie, was a major draw for customers. Made with a golden crust and filled with tender chicken and flavorful gravy, it became a beloved staple among visitors. Additionally, La Palma Chicken Pie Shop was known for serving a delicious German chocolate cake that delighted dessert enthusiasts.

Sadly, in 2016, La Palma Chicken Pie Shop closed its doors following Otto's passing. The restaurant's closure marked the end of an era and left a void in the community. A piece of its history was preserved when the iconic neon sign, which had become a symbol of the establishment, was saved and acquired by the Museum of Neon Art in Glendale.

Latka's Golden Glove Tavern Site
5061 Warner Avenue
Huntington Beach

Latka's Golden Glove Tavern was a legendary local bar that opened its doors in 1975 in Huntington Beach. It quickly became a popular spot for boxing enthusiasts and locals alike, thanks to its unique history and the charismatic presence of its owner, George Latka.

George Latka, a former professional boxer, was the driving force behind the tavern. He had achieved considerable success in his boxing career, with only six losses in 55 professional fights. His exceptional record and his unique approach to the sport earned him the nickname "the boxing professor." What set George apart was not only his boxing skills but also his academic achievements. He was the first professional fighter to earn a college degree, having graduated from UCLA in 1944.

Besides his success in the ring, George also made a name for himself as a boxing referee and judge. In fact, he had the distinction of participating in the world's first televised fight in 1940. This exposure in the early days of television helped solidify his reputation in the boxing community.

Later in his career, George ventured into the world of acting, with one of his most notable roles being in the 1980s film *Raging Bull*. In the movie, he portrayed the referee for the Jake LaMotta/Marcel Cerdan world title fight, further cementing his connection to the sport.

With his extensive knowledge and experience, George Latka created an atmosphere in Latka's Golden Glove Tavern that was unparalleled. The bar itself was adorned with boxing memorabilia, including gloves, photos, and championship belts, creating a unique ambiance. Patrons were surrounded by the rich history of the sport as they enjoyed their drinks and engaged in lively conversations.

One of the highlights of visiting the tavern was having the opportunity to hear George's captivating stories. He would regale customers with tales of his own boxing career, behind-the-scenes anecdotes from his time as a referee and judge, and fascinating accounts of the golden age of boxing. His storytelling ability and infectious enthusiasm made every visit to Latka's Golden Glove Tavern an unforgettable experience.

For about 20 years, Latka's Golden Glove Tavern remained a beloved establishment in Huntington Beach. It was a place where boxing aficionados, sports enthusiasts, and locals could gather to share their love for the sport and engage with George Latka's larger-than-life personality. Unfortunately, the tavern eventually closed its doors in the early 1990s, leaving behind a legacy of boxing history and cherished memories.

Neptune's
Huntington Beach Pier
Huntington Beach

Ella Christensen, known affectionately as the "queen of the pier," left an indelible mark on the Huntington Beach pier for over three decades. Her dedication and contributions to the community earned her the admiration and respect of locals and visitors alike. Ella's story begins in the early 1950s when she managed the tackle shop on the pier. But it was her role as the proprietor of the legendary Neptune's that solidified her place in Huntington Beach history.

Neptune's, a small snack shop that also served beer, became an iconic gathering spot where countless locals would come to watch the sun set over the Pacific Ocean. Ella's warm hospitality and the relaxed atmosphere of Neptune's created a sense of community and camaraderie among its patrons. The snack shop became synonymous with Huntington Beach's laid-back beach culture, and Ella was at the heart of it all.

Throughout the 1980s, Neptune's continued to thrive as one of the most beloved haunts in Orange County. The pier faced major storm damage in 1988, leading to its temporary closure. Unfortunately, this closure also marked the end of Neptune's, leaving behind a void in the hearts of those who cherished the memories made there.

In addition to Neptune's, Ella also ran another establishment on the pier called Captain's Galley. While it had its own following, it was Neptune's that people remember Ella best for. Its loss left behind one of the most longed-for landmarks in Orange County, a place where Ella's spirit and the sense of community she fostered continue to be missed. Ella Christensen's legacy as the "queen of the pier" lives on, etched in the memories of those who experienced the magic of Neptune's. Her dedication to creating a welcoming space where people could come together and enjoy the beauty of Huntington Beach has left an enduring impact.

Nixon's Restaurant
1501 W. Commonwealth Avenue
Fullerton

Richard Nixon, the 37th President of the United States, has a significant Orange County history. He was born in Yorba Linda. His family home, which is still standing today, is located next to the Richard Nixon Presidential Library and Museum.

During his presidency, Nixon also resided in what was known as the Western White House in San Clemente. The Western White House served as Nixon's primary residence outside of Washington, D.C. It was a coastal estate where the president conducted official business and hosted international dignitaries.

Richard Nixon's brother, Donald Nixon, also had a unique connection to Orange County. He opened a chain of five restaurants called Nixon's, one of which was located in Fullerton. These restaurants were known for their striking mid-century modern architectural design.

The Fullerton Nixon's restaurant in particular featured a dramatic butterfly roof, floor-to-ceiling windows, a vertical fin, and minimalist features, making it a notable example of mid-century modern architecture. The restaurant had a large seating capacity of 425 people and offered various menu options. One of the most notable items on the Fullerton Nixon's menu was the triple-decker "Nixon Burger."

However, the Fullerton Nixon's restaurant closed its doors in 1957. The site where the restaurant once stood is now occupied by a medical practices facility. Despite the closure of the restaurant, the architectural legacy of Nixon's restaurants and their unique design elements continue to be appreciated by enthusiasts of mid-century modern architecture.

Original Knowlwood Restaurant
Corner of La Palma Avenue and Imperial Highway
Anaheim Hills

This iconic restaurant's history is deeply intertwined with the Knowlton family. Roy and Faye Knowlton, along with their partner Gene Wood, founded the chain in 1957. Originally named

Orangewood Ranch, the restaurant quickly gained popularity for its delicious sandwiches, hearty burgers, creamy shakes, and comforting cups of coffee. In 1962, the name was changed to Knowlwood, and the Knowlton family bought out Gene Wood the following year, solidifying their ownership of the establishment. Over the years, Knowlwood Restaurant grew into a beloved local institution, known for its classic American comfort food and friendly atmosphere.

Generations of Orange County residents have fond memories of dining at the Knowlwood Restaurant. Families would gather for weekend meals, friends would meet up for lunch, and couples would enjoy date nights within its cozy confines. The restaurant's walls were adorned with vintage photographs and memorabilia, showcasing the rich history of the area and the establishment itself.

Knowlwood became synonymous with quality food, warm hospitality, and a sense of community. Patrons would often engage in lively conversations with the friendly staff, creating a welcoming and familiar atmosphere. The restaurant's menu featured a variety of classic American dishes, including their famous burgers cooked to order, crispy onion rings, and homemade pies that were the perfect sweet ending to a satisfying meal.

The closure of the original Knowlwood Restaurant in Anaheim Hills on February 2, 2012 marked the end of an era for Orange County residents. It was not just a place to eat; it was a place where memories were made, traditions were established, and connections were forged. The loss of this iconic establishment left a void in the hearts of many who had grown up frequenting its tables.

Fortunately, the Old Town Irvine location continues to serve as a reminder of the legacy of Knowlwood Restaurant. It stands as a testament to the enduring spirit of family-owned businesses and the importance of preserving cherished traditions.

Pinnacle Peak Steakhouse
9100 Trask Avenue
Garden Grove

In Garden Grove in the 1970s and '80s, Pinnacle Peak Steakhouse was more than just a place to satisfy your carnivorous cravings. It was a haven for tie-wearing enthusiasts and fashion rebels alike. Yes, you heard it right—this quirky joint had a unique tradition that left unsuspecting patrons both amused and slightly more casual in their attire. The walls of the restaurant were adorned with a vast collection of neckties, but not just any ordinary neckties. These were the remnants of unsuspecting guests who had fallen victim to the restaurant's playful tradition.

It went something like this: as you sat down at your table, blissfully unaware of the impending sartorial challenge, a sneaky server would approach you with scissors in hand. With a wicked grin, they would politely request your necktie, explaining that it was the restaurant's custom to snip off the ties of their patrons. Some bravely surrendered their fashion accessory, while others clung to their ties with a mix of defiance and amusement. But there was no escaping the fate that awaited them.

The walls of Pinnacle Peak Steakhouse were a testament to this quirky tradition. Each tie, neatly snipped and carefully pinned, told a story of a daring customer who left a piece of themselves behind. From vibrant paisleys to retro polka dots, the ties formed a kaleidoscope of fashion statements frozen in time. Patrons would return years later, searching for their forgotten ties, relishing the memories that the restaurant had become a part of.

But Pinnacle Peak Steakhouse was more than just a tie-slicing haven. It was a culinary paradise where succulent steaks reigned supreme. The aroma of sizzling meat would greet you as you entered, teasing your taste buds and setting the stage for a truly unforgettable dining experience. Mouthwatering cuts of prime beef, cooked to perfection, were the star of the menu. From tender filet mignon to juicy rib eyes, every bite was a symphony of flavors that left you yearning for more. The atmosphere of the restaurant was just as delightful as the food itself. The wait staff, clad in cowboy hats and boots, exuded a warm and friendly charm that made you feel right at home. The walls were adorned with vintage photographs and memorabilia, transporting you back to a simpler time where the wild west and hearty appetites reigned supreme.

As time marched forward, Pinnacle Peak Steakhouse closed its doors, leaving behind a legacy that would forever be etched in the hearts of those who had the pleasure of dining there.

The Reuben E. Lee
151 East Coast Highway
Newport Beach

Amidst the luxurious yachts and majestic sailing vessels of Newport Harbor, an unexpected sight once captivated the attention of onlookers. The Reuben E. Lee, a Mississippi River-style steamer, stood proudly off Bayside Drive, opposite Linda Isle. For over four decades, this unique landmark defied convention and left an indelible mark on the harbor's landscape. Constructed by the renowned Reuben's Steakhouse chain, the ship transcended its maritime surroundings, offering a dining experience that transported guests to the vibrant culture of the Deep South. With its delectable cuisine, lively entertainment, and evocative ambiance, the Reuben E. Lee became an icon of Newport Harbor, forever etching its name in the annals of maritime history.

In 1964, the Reuben E. Lee embarked on its maiden voyage as a dining establishment, beckoning patrons to indulge in an unforgettable culinary adventure. Situated at 151 East Coast Highway, the riverboat-style eatery was a delightful departure from the traditional fare found along the coast. Specializing in succulent steaks and delectable seafood, the restaurant's menu mirrored the rich flavors of the Mississippi River and New Orleans' vibrant cuisine. Each dish transported diners to the heart of the Deep South, tantalizing taste buds and igniting a passion for culinary exploration.

Stepping aboard the Reuben E. Lee was akin to stepping into a portal, transcending the boundaries of time and space. The ship's interior was a meticulously crafted homage to the Gulf states, recreating the ambiance and charm of a bygone era. The warm melodies of jazz music permeated the air, inviting guests to sway to the rhythm and lose themselves in the enchantment of the moment. The ship's vibrant atmosphere, replete with dancing and laughter, fostered a sense of camaraderie among diners, transforming strangers into friends as they reveled in the spirit of the Deep South.

While the Reuben E. Lee may have appeared out of place amidst the opulence of the harbor, its uniqueness became its greatest asset. The ship's distinctive presence drew the gaze of passersby, inviting them to uncover the hidden treasures within its hull. In a sea of grand yachts and majestic sailing vessels, the Mississippi River-style steamer stood as a symbol of individuality and creative

expression. The Reuben E. Lee's divergence from the norm captivated the imagination and left a mark on the hearts of all who beheld it.

After three decades of culinary excellence, the Reuben E. Lee
closed its doors as a dining establishment, marking the end of an
era. The ship found a new home at the Newport Harbor Nautical
Museum, where it was rechristened The Pride of Newport. As part
of the museum's collection, the riverboat continued to capture
the imagination of visitors, combining maritime history with the

allure of the Deep South. It stood as a testament to the ship's legacy, serving as a reminder of its vibrant past.

But fate had a different plan for the Reuben E. Lee. When the Newport Harbor Nautical Museum relocated to the Fun Zone, the ship found itself adrift, devoid of purpose. The once-bustling decks and joyous echoes fell silent, leaving the vessel empty and yearning for new adventures. Despite efforts to find new tenants or buyers, the ship languished in solitude, its grandeur gradually fading into obscurity.

In 2007, with no viable options on the horizon, the Reuben E. Lee faced an unfortunate fate. The ship, once a beacon of delight and inspiration, was sold for scrap and dismantled, marking the end of its illustrious journey. This bittersweet conclusion brought an end to an era, leaving behind memories of laughter, culinary delights, and the enchantment of a bygone time. The once vibrant riverboat was reduced to fragments, its history scattered like whispers on the wind.

Though the physical vessel may have vanished, the spirit of the Reuben E. Lee endures. The Mississippi River-style steamer, with its distinctive presence and cultural immersion, left a lasting mark on Newport Harbor's history.

The Ritz
2801 West Coast Highway
Newport Beach

The original Ritz restaurant holds a significant place in the culinary history of Newport Beach. Established by Hans Prager in 1977, the upscale eatery quickly gained a reputation for its unique ambiance and distinctive features, including the red-lipped waitresses and the popularity of three-martini lunches.

The Ritz restaurant initially opened near the Newport Pier in 1977, attracting locals and visitors alike with its fine dining offerings and lively atmosphere. In 1982, the restaurant underwent a move to a more upscale location in the Newport Center, a chic area of Newport Beach. This relocation allowed The Ritz to cater to a more affluent clientele and solidify its position as a premier dining establishment in the region.

Under Hans Prager's management, The Ritz flourished, becoming known for its elegant decor, high-quality cuisine, and the distinct image of the waitresses sporting red lipstick. The concept of three-martini lunches, whereby businessmen would indulge in day-drinking, became a symbol of indulgence, and also became synonymous with The Ritz.

Unfortunately, in 2014, The Ritz restaurant closed its doors after the site manager, the Irvine Company, declined to renew the lease. This marked the end of an era for the iconic establishment, leaving behind fond memories and a void in the Newport Beach dining scene. The Ritz restaurant's long history in Newport Beach showcased its ability to adapt to changing times while maintaining its distinctive charm. It played a significant role in shaping the culinary landscape of the area and was celebrated for its upscale ambiance and unique character.

Sam's Seafood
16278 Pacific Coast Highway
Sunset Beach

In Sunset Beach, a Tiki-inspired structure stood as a beloved landmark for over half a century. Many knew it as Sam's Seafood restaurant—a place where memories were crafted, flavors were savored, and the essence of coastal living thrived.

The story of Sam's Seafood began in 1923 when two Greek immigrant brothers, Sam and George Arvanitis, opened a humble bait shop in nearby Seal Beach. Little did they know that their entrepreneurial spirit would lay the foundation for an iconic establishment that would transcend generations. From its humble beginnings as a bait shop, Sam's Seafood evolved into a thriving fish market, catering to the discerning tastes of local residents. As

the 1940s unfolded, the Arvanitis brothers recognized the growing demand for a dining experience that showcased the abundance of the ocean's bounty. They transformed their establishment into a restaurant, and thus began the enduring legacy of Sam's Seafood.

It was the neon blue swordfish sign that adorned the facade of Sam's Seafood that truly captured the imagination of locals and visitors alike. The iconic swordfish became synonymous with the restaurant, gracing postcards, matchbooks, coasters, and countless other mementos. Over time, the restaurant underwent several name changes, from Sam's Seafood Spa to Sam's Seafood Grotto, each iteration building upon the legacy of its predecessors.

In the early hours of a fateful February morning in 1959, tragedy struck as fire engulfed the beloved Sam's Seafood restaurant. The community mourned the loss of a cherished establishment, fearing that the memories and vibrant spirit it held would be forever lost to the ashes. But the indomitable spirit of the Arvanitis family prevailed. Rising from the ruins, they embarked on a mission to recreate the magic of Sam's Seafood, breathing new life into their vision with a spectacular Tiki-themed design. The new building, adorned with Polynesian-inspired motifs within a Hawaiian Village, caught the attention of customers.

This incarnation of Sam's Seafood became a beacon of enchantment, cultivating an atmosphere where the allure of the tropics mingled with the coastal charm of Sunset Beach. It was within these hallowed walls that some of the most legendary tales were born, forever etching Sam's Seafood into the archives of Orange County's collective memory. Stories abound of luminaries gracing the halls of Sam's Seafood. The likes of Lucille Ball and Desi Arnaz were said to have indulged in the culinary delights offered within its Tiki-inspired oasis. A treasured photograph captures surfing legend Duke Kahanamoku proudly displaying a trophy alongside the Katsaris family, who took over ownership after the Arvanitis family, all adorned in vibrant aloha shirts—a testament to the enduring allure of this iconic establishment.

In the vibrant tapestry of Sam's Seafood's history, one particular moment stands out—a black-and-white photograph capturing Bradley Nowell, the frontman of Sublime and former Surfside resident, performing at Sam's just a year before his untimely passing. The image not only immortalizes a talented musician but also serves as a testament to the cultural significance of Sam's Seafood, a place where artistry and community converged.

In 2008, the torch was passed, and Sam's Seafood transformed into Don's the Beachcomber, yet the spirit of the classic place endured. The neon blue swordfish sign, a beacon of nostalgia, continued to illuminate the night sky, keeping the memories of Sam's Seafood alive for all who passed by. Today, the establishment bears the name "Don's," a gentle reminder of its storied past, while still honoring the heritage it carries.

As the future of the building remains uncertain amidst talks of redevelopment in the area, the kitschy, classic Tiki restaurant structure stands as a resilient testament to the enduring spirit of Sam's Seafood. It serves as a reminder of the countless memories created within its walls and the cultural heritage it represents.

Villa Sweden
552 Main Street
Huntington Beach

If you were fortunate enough to experience Huntington Beach in the latter half of the 20th century, then surely the Villa Sweden holds a special place in your heart. Located downtown, the Villa Sweden was a true gem, renowned for its wholesome all-you-can-eat

spread and reasonable prices. It was a place where families and friends gathered to indulge in a delightful feast of Swedish cuisine.

Stepping inside the Villa Sweden was like entering a culinary wonderland. The aroma of Swedish meatballs wafted through the air, tempting your taste buds and making your stomach rumble with anticipation. And of course there was the dark limpa bread, which had a distinct flavor unlike anything else and paired perfectly with the savory dishes on offer. And let's not forget about the desserts! While many of their selections had a Swedish touch, they also offered dishes that would have fit right in at any Midwestern family potluck. From cabbage rolls to carrot-raisin salad, their menu was a delightful fusion of flavors.

The story of the Villa Sweden began when the Backlund family immigrated to America from Sweden in 1951. With their culinary expertise and a desire to share their culture with the community, they opened the doors of the restaurant in 1961. For decades, the Villa Sweden became a beloved gathering spot for locals and visitors alike, a place where memories were made and appetites were satisfied.

Villa Sweden closed in the 1980s, but the building that once housed this culinary treasure still remains.

Wimpi's
5th Street and Pacific Coast Highway
Huntington Beach

Wimpi's was a beloved fast food joint in downtown Huntington Beach back in the 1970s and 1980s. It gained a reputation for serving delicious burgers, fries, chili cheese fries, and root beer floats, which became popular choices for surfers after a day of riding the waves. Wimpi's menu also featured items like peanut butter shakes, strips and cheese, and mocha shakes, which added to its appeal.

The fast food joint became an icon among locals and visitors alike, particularly surfers who frequented the area. In the 1980s, downtown Huntington Beach underwent a redevelopment process, which unfortunately led to the closure of Wimpi's. As urban planning and revitalization efforts took place, some older establishments, including Wimpi's, were forced to close their doors to make way for new developments and businesses.

CHAPTER FIVE

THEATERS

AS YOU MAY REMEMBER, drive-in movie theaters were once a beloved and popular form of entertainment throughout Orange County. These outdoor theaters allowed moviegoers to watch films from the comfort of their cars, creating a unique and nostalgic experience. As car culture grew in the state, drive-ins became even more popular, offering convenience and a sense of freedom for movie enthusiasts.

During the 1950s and 1960s, the charm and innocence of drive-in movie theaters symbolized the post-war era and the rise of suburban lifestyles. Orange County, with its expanding suburban communities and car-oriented culture, embraced drive-ins as a form of leisure and entertainment. Families, couples, and friends would pile into their cars, park in front of a large outdoor screen, and enjoy movies under the open sky.

Drive-in theaters also played a significant role in the social lives of teenagers during this time. They provided a sense of privacy and independence for young couples on their first dates. Teenagers could escape the watchful eyes of parents and enjoy a movie together in the privacy of their own car. The drive-in experience became synonymous with youthful romance, creating lasting memories for many.

The decline of drive-in theaters began in the late 1960s and continued through the 1970s and beyond. Several factors contributed to their disappearance from the landscape, not only in Orange County but across the country. One primary reason was the increasing value of land. As urban areas expanded and land became more valuable for commercial and residential development, drive-in theaters faced pressure to sell their properties for more profitable ventures.

Additionally, the advent of multiplex cinemas and home entertainment systems, such as VCRs and later DVD players, provided more convenient and diverse movie-watching options. The rise of indoor movie theaters with multiple screens and the ability to show a variety of films simultaneously diminished the appeal of drive-ins, as well as single-screen theaters.

While the loss of these historic movie theaters is undoubtedly disheartening, it is worth noting that efforts have been made to preserve and restore some of Orange County's historic theaters. The Fox Fullerton Theatre, formerly known as the Fox West Coast Theater, was saved from demolition and underwent an extensive renovation. Today, it stands as a cultural center, hosting live performances and special events, while still maintaining its historic charm. Similarly, the Yost Theater in Santa Ana, originally built as a vaudeville theater in 1912, has been restored to its former glory. The theater now serves as a venue for live music, comedy shows, and community events, preserving its place in Orange County's cultural history.

Similarly, the Lido Theatre in Newport Beach, built in 1938, has preserved its art deco-style architecture and is a beloved local landmark. These surviving theaters serve as a testament to the enduring allure of traditional movie-going experiences. They offer a glimpse into the past and remind us of the importance of preserving our cultural heritage. Efforts to restore and revitalize these theaters not only benefit the local community but also provide an opportunity for new generations to appreciate the history and charm of these iconic establishments. Now, on to the theaters that were not as lucky . . .

Anaheim Drive-In
1500 Lemon Street
Anaheim

The Anaheim Drive-In movie theater, a prominent landmark in Orange County's entertainment scene, made its grand debut just two weeks after the opening of Disneyland on August 3, 1955. The inaugural film showcased at this iconic drive-in was *An Annapolis Story,* marking the beginning of a long-standing tradition of outdoor cinema.

Constructed at a cost of $350,000, the Anaheim Drive-In quickly became a beloved destination for movie enthusiasts across the county. With a staggering capacity to accommodate up to 2,000 vehicles, it provided a spacious and immersive movie-watching experience under the open sky. Patrons would park their cars in designated spots, tune in to a specific radio frequency for the movie's audio, and enjoy the magic of cinema from the comfort of their own vehicles.

The theater complex also boasted a snack bar that could

accommodate up to 500 film-goers, offering a variety of delectable treats to enhance the movie-watching experience. From popcorn and candy to refreshing beverages, the snack bar provided a delightful selection of concessions to satisfy every moviegoer's cravings.

In the 1980s, recognizing the growing demand for more screens, the Anaheim Drive-In expanded its offerings by adding two additional screens. This expansion allowed for a greater variety of films to be screened simultaneously, catering to a wider audience and further solidifying its status as a premier entertainment destination in the region.

As the years went by, the drive-in theater faced various challenges. Eventually, it transformed into a swap meet, hosting a bustling market where visitors could browse through a diverse array of goods. But on March 26, 1990, the Anaheim Drive-In bid farewell to its cinematic legacy, showing its last movie as a traditional theater.

Following the closure, there were plans to develop theaters on the site, with AMC Theaters initially considering an expansion of their nearby multiplex into a 20-screen stadium. Those plans were later abandoned. Instead, Pacific Theaters took the opportunity to repurpose the land and built a shopping center, breathing new life into the once vibrant site. The transformation marked the end of an era for the Anaheim Drive-In Movie Theater, leaving behind cherished memories and a significant chapter in Orange County's entertainment history.

Balboa Theater
707 E. Balboa Boulevard
Newport Beach

Another iconic theater that once graced Orange County was the Balboa Theater in Newport Beach. Built in 1928, it was known for its Art Deco design and stunning neon marquee. The Balboa Theater showcased both movies and live performances and was a beloved entertainment venue for locals and visitors. Unfortunately, due to declining attendance and financial challenges, the Balboa Theater closed in 1992 and was subsequently demolished, leaving behind a void in the local cultural landscape.

The Broadway Theatre
416 N. Broadway
Santa Ana

The Broadway Theatre in Santa Ana was a significant venue in Orange County. It opened its doors on June 2, 1926. The inaugural performance featured Ernest Torrence in *The Rainmaker*. The theater was designed for Ed Yost by architects Carl Boller and A. Godfrey Bailey. It boasted a large organ, which was played by organist Bartley Sims during its opening.

By 1950, the theater was operated by Cabart Theaters Corp. Unfortunately, on February 25, 1952, a fire broke out and caused significant damage to the theater. It was rebuilt and reopened on March 16, 1955, under the name New Broadway Theatre. The first film screened at the reopening was *Battle Cry*, starring Van Heflin. Regrettably, the New Broadway Theatre closed its doors in 1987. A devastating fire in 1989 further damaged the theater, leading to its eventual demolition in the following year, 1990.

Buena Park Drive-In Complex
6612 Lincoln Avenue
Buena Park

The Buena Park Drive-In was a notable drive-in theater complex that existed for several decades. Its history is intertwined with two separate drive-in theaters that were eventually merged into one.

The first drive-in theater at this location was known as the China-car Drive-In, which opened on May 5, 1949. It was a popular entertainment venue where moviegoers could enjoy films from the comfort of their cars. In 1953, the China-car Drive-In was renamed the Lincoln Drive-In.

Another drive-in theater called the Buena Park Drive-In was opened adjacent to the Lincoln Drive-In on April 22, 1970. This new addition expanded the entertainment offerings in the area. Operated by Pacific Theaters, both the Lincoln and Buena Park Drive-Ins coexisted side by side.

The Buena Park Drive-In gained popularity and recognition as a premier drive-in theater experience. On its opening night, it showcased the iconic science fiction film *2001: A Space Odyssey*, which added to its appeal.

In June 1984, in response to increasing demand, a third screen was added to the Buena Park Drive-In complex. This expansion allowed for a greater selection of films to be shown simultaneously, enhancing the overall movie-watching experience for the audience.

After operating for over 44 years, the Buena Park Drive-In complex ultimately closed its doors on July 5, 1993. The property was subsequently demolished in 1996. Today, the site where the drive-in once stood has been transformed into a large housing development.

Cinedome
3001 W. Chapman Avenue
Orange

The Cinedome theater complex was renowned and highly regarded in Orange County. It gained a reputation as one of the premier theaters in the area, particularly known for its exceptional 70 mm presentations during the 1970s, 1980s, and 1990s.

The Cinedome opened its doors in June 1969 with two screens, offering moviegoers a state-of-the-art cinematic experience. Its modern design and advanced technology set it apart from other theaters at the time. The inclusion of 70 mm screenings made it a sought-after venue for film enthusiasts who appreciated the larger format and enhanced visual and audio quality.

The theater complex continued to expand over the years to meet the growing demand for its services. In November 1974, two more screens were added, further diversifying the film offerings and accommodating a wider range of movie selections. Responding to its popularity, the Cinedome expanded yet again in 1977, adding two additional screens.

The complex continued to evolve, with another two screens

being added in 1986, and three more screens in 1992. This expansion allowed the Cinedome to showcase an even greater variety of films simultaneously, catering to the diverse interests of its audience.

As one of the most popular theater complexes in Orange County, the Cinedome attracted movie lovers from far and wide. Its commitment to providing top-notch cinematic experiences, solidified its status as a premier destination for film enthusiasts.

Despite its popularity, the Cinedome theater complex closed its doors in January 1999. Subsequently, the complex was torn down, marking the end of an era for this iconic Orange County theater.

Fountain Valley Drive-In
18141 Brookhurst Street
Fountain Valley

The Fountain Valley Drive-In was a beloved drive-in movie theater that opened its doors on July 12, 1967 with a screening of Walt Disney's classic film, *Snow White and the Seven Dwarfs*. Known for its family-friendly atmosphere, the drive-in quickly became a popular entertainment destination for moviegoers in the area.

The Fountain Valley Drive-In gained popularity over the years, attracting both locals and visitors from nearby areas. It became known as a place where families could gather for an evening of entertainment, enjoying the magic of cinema under the open sky. The drive-in provided a nostalgic and relaxed atmosphere, creating cherished memories for many.

The Fountain Valley Drive-In sadly closed its doors in October 1984. Following its closure, the site was repurposed, and today it is occupied by the Orange Coast Memorial Medical Center.

Fox West Coast Theatre
308 N. Main Street
Santa Ana

The Fox West Coast Theatre holds a special place in architectural history as the 100th theater designed by the renowned Boller Brothers. Constructed by Charles E. Walker, the theater was built on the site of the old Princess Theatre. The project was completed at an impressive speed, with three shifts working around the clock to bring the vision to life. The construction cost amounted to $250,000, a significant investment at the time.

When it first opened its doors in January 1924, the Fox West Coast Theatre boasted a seating capacity of 1,355. The main floor accommodated 800 seats, while there were 55 loges and 500 seats in the balcony. To ensure the structural integrity of the balcony, it was tested with a weight of 25 tons of cement. The inaugural film played at the theater was *Two Wagons, Both Covered*, starring the beloved actor Will Rogers.

One notable feature of the theater was the installation of a Wurlitzer pipe organ, which added to the grandeur and provided musical accompaniment to the films.

In September 1925, West Coast Theatres assumed ownership

of the venue, while Charles E. Walker continued as the resident manager. Over the years, the theater underwent several name changes, starting as the New Walker Theatre. It was later known as the Fox Walker Theatre, then the West Coast Walker Theatre, and finally settled on the name Fox West Coast Theatre.

The Fox West Coast Theatre played a significant role in the cultural and entertainment scene of its time. It showcased a wide range of films and hosted various live performances, making it a popular destination for the local community. The theater's elegant design and architectural features, combined with its state-of-the-art technology, created a memorable and immersive experience for the audience.

As the years went by, the Fox West Coast Theatre continued to be a prominent landmark in the city, representing a golden era of cinema. Like many historic theaters, it eventually faced challenges with the rise of multiplex cinemas and changing audience preferences.

As the 1980s approached, the theater faced a decline and fell into a state of disrepair. It ceased operating as a movie theater and was left neglected. Fortunately, in 1991, the Christian Tabernacle recognized the historical and cultural significance of the building and purchased it for $750,000. They dedicated an additional $50,000 toward its restoration. A church member named Pete Montanez, who was also a general contractor, played an instrumental role in the theater's restoration. Despite the challenge of having lost his right forearm in an accident, Montanez generously donated his time and expertise, investing two years and contributing $200,000 worth of labor to bring the theater back to its former glory. The efforts put forth by the Christian Tabernacle and the dedication of Pete Montanez resulted in a successful restoration of the Fox West Coast Theatre. Their commitment to preserving the historical integrity of the building, despite the challenges they faced, is commendable.

In recognition of its architectural and historical significance, the theater was placed on the National Register of Historic Places in 1982. This designation serves as a testament to the theater's cultural value and ensures its protection for future generations to appreciate and enjoy. Today, the Fox West Coast Theatre stands as a restored landmark, symbolizing the rich history and architectural legacy of its time. It serves as a reminder of the importance of preserving our cultural heritage and the transformative power of restoration efforts.

Highway 39 Drive-In
7901 Trask Avenue
Westminster

The Highway 39 Drive-In opened its doors on June 29, 1955 and went on to become a popular destination for moviegoers seeking a unique and immersive cinematic experience.

The drive-in theater boasted an impressive 1,600 car capacity, making it one of the largest drive-ins in the West at the time. Its colossal screen, nearly ten stories high, provided a captivating visual backdrop for movie enthusiasts. The theater's opening night featured James Stewart in *Strategic Air Command* and George Montgomery in *Robbers' Roost*, setting the stage for many memorable movie screenings to come.

Highway 39 Drive-In's expansive snack bar, which was operat-

ed by Pacific Theatres, set it apart from other drive-ins. Six times larger than the average snack bar, it featured a counter space that extended almost a quarter block long. This allowed moviegoers to indulge in a wide variety of refreshments while enjoying their favorite films under the stars.

Over the years, the Highway 39 Drive-In evolved to meet the changing demands of its audience. On June 15, 1979, it transformed into a four-screen theater, expanding the entertainment options available to patrons. This adaptation allowed for the simultaneous screening of multiple movies, catering to diverse tastes and preferences.

Like many drive-in theaters across the United States, the Highway 39 Drive-In faced challenges as the years went by. The rise of multiplex cinemas, changing viewing habits, and the increasing value of the land on which the drive-in was situated contributed to its eventual closure. On March 31, 1997, after 56 years of operation, the Highway 39 Drive-In ceased operations, marking the end of an era in Orange County's drive-in theater history.

The Mesa Theatre
1890 Newport Boulevard
Costa Mesa

In the years following World War II, there were multiple attempts to construct a movie theater in Costa Mesa. However, building controls imposed during the post-war period posed a significant obstacle.

According to articles from that era in the *Costa Mesa Globe Herald*, local officials and citizens made efforts to overcome these building controls. They lobbied Congressmen and even the President of the United States in order to facilitate the construction of a theater in the town. Eventually, a town-wide ballot was held, and the citizens voted in favor of having a theater.

After the building controls were lifted, the Mesa Theater was constructed and officially opened on November 4, 1948. The theater was built by Mason Siler, who was also the operator of the historic Lido and Balboa theaters in Newport Beach. The architectural design of the Mesa Theater was in the Streamline style, and it was created by A. Dwight Gibbs, the same architect responsible for

the Carthay Circle Theatre in Los Angeles.

The Mesa Theater was an impressive structure, built at a cost of $175,000. It boasted 925 luxury seats and offered additional amenities such as a crying room (for cranky kids) and a smoking room. The theater became a popular venue for moviegoers in Costa Mesa, providing them with a modern and enjoyable cinematic experience.

After operating as an independent theater for several decades, the Mesa Theatre was acquired by Edwards Theatres in 1981, becoming the 16th location of the Edwards chain in Orange County. However, by 1997, the theater had transitioned into a second-run house, showing movies that had already been released in first-run theaters. This business model proved to be economically unfeasible, and as a result, Edwards Theatres made the decision to close the Mesa Theatre. In its final years of operation, the Mesa Theatre offered admission at a price of $1 for a double feature, which was not much higher than the original admission price of 60 cents back in 1948.

Unfortunately, the Mesa Theatre was demolished in 1998. Subsequently, a Borders Books store was constructed on the site where the theater once stood. Today, it's a supermarket.

The Miramar Theatre

150 W. Avenida Pico
San Clemente

The Miramar Theatre opened on May 12, 1938. It was notable for having a bowling alley constructed and opened at the rear of the theater in 1946. The entrance to the bowling alley was situated at 150 W. Avenida Pico. The theater itself featured a prominent 44-foot-high tower above its entrance, showcasing the Spanish Colonial architectural style.

Unfortunately, the Miramar Theatre closed its doors in 1992, and there have been concerns regarding its potential demolition following its sale to a local developer. While the new owner has expressed intentions to preserve certain key architectural elements, such as the Spanish Colonial tower, preservationists are skeptical about the theater's overall fate. It is unlikely that the building, which was 64 years old at the time of its closure, would retain its historical significance if only a few original elements were saved. The Miramar Theatre is currently listed as a historic property by the city. Its future use is being considered for a restaurant, retail, office space, or senior housing.

The Niguel Theatre

32844 Crown Valley Parkway
Dana Point

The Niguel Theatre was a single-screen movie theater located near the borders of Dana Point and Laguna Beach, adjacent to the Pacific Coast Highway. It opened on June 9, 1965 with the film *Mirage,* starring Gregory Peck. The theater had a Spanish theme and was originally owned by the family of actor James Cagney, who was an early investor in Dana Point real estate.

In the late 1970s, the Niguel Theatre was sold to Pacific Theatres. However, it closed down in 1980. After the closure of the theater, the building was razed, and the property was redeveloped into a high-end strip mall called Monarch Bay Plaza.

Today, Monarch Bay Plaza stands on the site where the Niguel Theatre once stood, offering various upscale retail stores, restaurants, and other businesses. The theater's closure marked the end

of an era for moviegoers in the area, but the redevelopment transformed the property into a different kind of commercial space.

Orange Drive-In
291 N. State College Boulevard
Orange

The Orange Drive-In holds a significant place in the history of Southern California's drive-in culture. Opening its doors on June 19, 1941, it quickly became a popular destination for moviegoers in the area. Situated amidst the picturesque orange groves, the theater was located on Highway 101 and Placentia Avenue. Initially, it was simply known as "Drive-In," as seen in movie advertisements in the Santa Ana Army Air Base newspaper.

During this time, Los Angeles had only a few drive-ins, with the Pico Drive-In being the first in the city. The Orange Drive-In provided a unique and novel entertainment experience, particularly for the thousands of soldiers stationed at the nearby Santa Ana Army Air Base. Many of these soldiers, hailing from different states, were introduced to the early Southern California drive-in culture through their visits to the Orange Drive-In.

In 1955, Disneyland opened just two miles away from the Orange Drive-In. This marked a significant change in the surrounding area, as Highway 101 was replaced by the Santa Ana Freeway, and Placentia Avenue was transformed into State College Boulevard. The drive-in continued to thrive and adapt to the changing times.

From 1955 to 1961, the Orange Drive-In took on an additional role as a venue for Sunday morning services. Dr. Robert Schuller, a prominent televangelist and founder of the Crystal Cathedral, held his weekly services here. He would preach to the congregation of cars from the roof of the snack bar, creating a unique and unconventional worship experience.

Throughout the

1970s, Orange County boasted a total of 11 drive-in theaters, including the Orange Drive-In. Many of these theaters, including the Orange Drive-In, were managed by Pacific Theatres, a well-known theater chain in the region.

As the years passed, the drive-in theater industry faced numerous challenges, including the rise of multiplex cinemas and changing audience preferences. Unfortunately, the Orange Drive-In eventually closed its doors, marking the end of an era in Orange County's entertainment landscape.

The Red Lantern Theatre
134 S. Brea Boulevard
Brea

The Red Lantern Theatre, later renamed the Brea Theatre, was a significant establishment in Orange County. It opened on March 6, 1922, at a cost of $25,000. With a seating capacity of 600, it was the largest theater in Orange County at the time. The theater's lessee was L.A. Schlessinger, who was also responsible for constructing the County's first movie theater, the West End Theater in Santa Ana, back in 1915.

The theater was described as "Orange County's most beautiful and most original picture and vaudeville palace" in a simple advertisement published in the *Fullerton Daily Tribune*. The opening attraction at the Red Lantern Theatre was a film called *A Game Chicken,* starring Bebe Daniels. Additionally, the theater featured a Robert Morton organ with two manuals and four ranks, which provided musical accompaniment during screenings.

During the 1930s, the theater underwent a name change and became known as the Brea Theatre. According to the Brea Historical Society, the manager during this time was a man named Robert Gumm. Interestingly, Robert Gumm's niece was Frances Gumm, who later became renowned as Judy Garland.

In the early 1950s, the Brea Theatre, which had always operated independently, received a modern facade and marquee, updating its appearance to suit the era's design trends. By the time it closed around 1976 it was operating as an adult movie theater. It was then used as church before it and most of the downtown area was demolished in 1987.

Stadium Eight Drive-In
1501 W. Katella Avenue
Orange

The Stadium Eight Drive-In holds a significant place in Orange County's drive-in theater history as the last drive-in to be built in the area. Opening its gates on May 27, 1970, it proudly held the title of "the only four-screen drive-in in the entire west," adding a touch of innovation to the local cinematic landscape.

The theater complex featured a unique circular design, with a centralized projection booth situated on top of a spacious snack bar. This arrangement allowed for efficient projection and simultaneous screening of movies on all four screens. Visitors could indulge in a variety of snacks and refreshments while enjoying their movie experience, making the Stadium Eight Drive-In a complete entertainment destination.

On its final night of operation, September 12, 1986, the theater bid its farewell with a nostalgic gesture. Admission prices were reduced to the 1970 rates of $2.25 per person, inviting moviegoers to relive the magic of the 1970s with a lineup of films that included classics such as *The Exorcist* and *Saturday Night Fever*. This special event served as a fitting tribute to the theater's history and the era it represented.

Today, a modern indoor theater stadium with an impressive 25 screens stands at the location of the Stadium Eight Drive-In.

Surf Theater
121 Fifth Street
Huntington Beach

Scott's Theatre, later known as the Roxy Theatre and the Surf Theater, holds a special place in the hearts of many as a beloved local landmark in Huntington Beach. Its rich history and diverse programming made it a popular destination for moviegoers and patrons of various civic events. The theater's ability to adapt to the changing tastes of its audience is a testament to its enduring legacy.

Originally opened on May 20, 1925 as Scott's Theatre, it debuted with the film *5th Avenue Models* starring Mary Philbin. Over the years, the theater underwent several name changes, reflecting the evolving times and cultural shifts. In 1937, it was renamed the Roxy Theatre, and in June 1941, it adopted the name Surf Theater, which became synonymous with its identity.

The Surf Theater became renowned not only for showcasing first-run surf films but also for hosting a wide range of cinematic experiences. It was a venue where locals gathered to watch popular movies, from classic westerns to comedies featuring Abbott and Costello. The theater also became a hub for midnight movies, offering a unique late-night viewing experience for film enthusiasts.

One of the most cherished aspects of the Surf Theater was the owner's interaction with the audience. Former patrons fondly recall the owner's playful engagement during shows, throwing candy, Frisbees, and other items to the delighted crowd. These personal touches created a sense of community and made the theater experience even more memorable.

The Surf Theater not only provided entertainment but also served as a gathering place for civic events. Its versatile space allowed for various community functions, further solidifying its role as a local landmark and a cultural hub.

Despite its popularity and cherished memories, the Surf Theater faced its own challenges. It closed its doors in October 1979 and was eventually razed around 1989, marking the end of an era for the iconic venue. The demolition of the theater left behind a void in the community, as generations of moviegoers and patrons mourned the loss of a place that held so many cherished memories.

Warner Drive-In
7361 Warner Avenue
Huntington Beach

The Warner Drive-In was a popular drive-in theater that entertained moviegoers for several decades. Opening its doors on June 29, 1961, the drive-in premiered with two films: *The Wackiest Ship in the Army* and *They Came to Cordova*.

The Warner Drive-In quickly became a beloved entertainment destination in Huntington Beach. With the capacity to hold 600 cars, it provided ample space for movie enthusiasts to enjoy a wide range of films from the comfort of their vehicles. The drive-in experience offered a unique and relaxed atmosphere, where families, friends, and couples could enjoy movies under the stars.

Throughout its years of operation, the Warner Drive-In remained a popular destination for the local community. Its convenient location in Huntington Beach made it easily accessible to residents and visitors alike, contributing to its success.

Unfortunately, after serving as a prominent entertainment hub for over two decades, the Warner Drive-In closed its doors in October 1984. The site underwent a transformation, and today it is occupied by retail stores.

CHAPTER SIX

BOWLING, ICE SKATING, MINIATURE GOLF, AND SKATEBOARDING

CHILDREN WHO GREW UP in Orange County in the 1960s, '70s, and '80s were fortunate to have access to a plethora of fun and affordable options for family-friendly activities. Whether it was bowling, ice skating, miniature golf, or skateboarding, there were numerous places where kids could spend their time and create lasting memories. Over the years, many of these beloved landmarks have sadly disappeared, leaving behind a nostalgic longing for the carefree days of yesteryear.

Bowling alleys were also a hub of excitement and friendly competition for both kids and adults. These lively venues offered the perfect blend of entertainment and camaraderie. Children would eagerly don vintage bowling shoes and select their favorite bowling ball, striving for that satisfying sound of pins crashing.

Ice skating was a popular activity for families and friends to enjoy together. Orange County was home to various ice rinks, where children could lace up their skates and glide across the smooth, glistening surface. The sound of laughter and the chilly air filled these rinks as kids twirled, spun, and attempted their first wobbly steps on the ice.

Miniature golf was another cherished pastime for children in Orange County. These whimsical and imaginative courses offered a delightful blend of challenges and amusement. Kids would navigate through colorful obstacles, putting their skills to the test while basking in the company of family and friends.

Skateboarding truly was and remains an iconic past time in Orange County. Skateboard culture help to define Orange County and skate parks are still as popular today as ever.

Let's revisit some of these beloved lost landmarks!

BOWLING

Anaheim Bowl
1925 West Lincoln Boulevard
Anaheim

Anaheim Bowl was an incredible bowling alley that left a lasting impression on the community. Built in the late 1950s, it quickly became a popular destination for both bowling enthusiasts and casual bowlers.

What made Anaheim Bowl truly unique was its eye-catching Googie entrance, designed by architect Pat De Rosa. The entrance featured a striking white sculpture comprised of interlocking parabolas that intersected a wavelike canopy. This distinct architectural style was characteristic of mid-20th century futurism and added to the allure of the bowling center.

Inside Anaheim Bowl, visitors were greeted by an impressive sight: 52 Brunswick lanes, offering ample space for bowlers to enjoy their favorite sport. As the years went by, Anaheim Bowl kept up with the times and embraced technological advancements. In the 1970s, the center introduced automatic scoring systems, which streamlined the game and made it more accessible to players.

Beyond its bowling lanes, Anaheim Bowl also boasted a restaurant and lounge area known as the Chariot Room. This provided visitors with a place to relax, socialize, and enjoy a meal or drinks after a fun-filled bowling session. The Chariot Room added to the overall experience and sense of community that Anaheim Bowl provided.

Unfortunately, despite its rich history and unique architecture, Anaheim Bowl is no longer standing. It is a reminder of a bygone era when bowling alleys were more than just places to play a sport—they were community hubs and vibrant social spaces.

Brunswick Orange Bowl
2375 N. Tustin Street
Orange

The Brunswick Orange Bowl was a popular bowling alley that provided a fun and entertaining experience for bowlers of all ages.

The bowling alley offered a well-maintained facility with multiple lanes, comfortable seating, and a lively atmosphere. It was a favorite destination for both casual bowlers and league players in the Orange County area. From the early 1970s through the late 2000s, the Brunswick Orange Bowl represented a true neighborhood bowling alley where many birthday parties were hosted and local league bowling was quite popular. Unfortunately, it is no longer in operation, and a restaurant now exists at the location.

Fullerton Bowl
110 Commonwealth Avenue
Fullerton

Fullerton Bowl was another cherished local bowling alley that offered a classic bowling experience with a vintage ambiance. The alley had a range of amenities, including well-kept lanes, a snack bar, and an arcade area. Fullerton Bowl was a popular venue for parties, leagues, and casual outings. It closed down in the early 2000s.

Fullerton Lanes
1501 South Harvard
Fullerton

Fullerton Lanes was a popular bowling alley in Fullerton that provided entertainment and recreation for the local community. It boasted a well-maintained facility with numerous lanes, comfortable seating, and a friendly staff. Fullerton Lanes was known for its welcoming atmosphere and affordable prices, making it a go-to destination for bowlers of all skill levels. The bowling alley closed in the early 2000s.

Holiday Lanes
2015 West 1st Street
Santa Ana

Holiday Lanes was a well-known bowling alley located in Santa Ana. It served as a gathering place for both recreational bowlers and serious league players. The bowling alley featured a modern facility with state-of-the-art lanes, automatic scoring systems, and a vibrant atmosphere. It hosted various events and leagues, making it a hub for the local bowling community. Sadly, Holiday Lanes is no longer in operation, but its legacy lives on in the memories of those who enjoyed its facilities.

Huntington Lanes
19582 Beach Boulevard
Huntington Beach

Huntington Lanes was a popular bowling alley in Orange County. Owned and operated by John Quinliven, it opened its doors in 1961 and remained a favorite destination for local bowlers for several decades.

Huntington Lanes provided a fun and recreational environment for both casual bowlers and serious league players. It had 32 Brunswick lanes, each made with polished maple. Lunches were especially popular at the bowling center's Top Hat Lounge. The establishment attracted a loyal following of bowlers who appreciated the friendly atmosphere and professional staff.

Over the years, Huntington Lanes hosted numerous bowling leagues, tournaments, and events, contributing to the vibrant bowling community in Orange County. It served as a social gathering place where friends and families could come together to enjoy the sport and create lasting memories. It closed down in the late 1990s and a hospital occupies the site today.

Kona Lanes
2699 Harbor Boulevard
Costa Mesa

In Costa Mesa, there stood a bowling center unlike any other. Its name was Kona Lanes—a magical place that opened its doors to the world in 1958, and over the next 45 years became a cherished destination for bowlers and enthusiasts alike. But alas, all good things

must come to an end, and in 2003, Kona Lanes bid farewell, leaving behind a legacy that would forever be etched in the hearts of its patrons.

Kona Lanes was more than just a bowling center; it was a portal to another realm, a glimpse into the future. As visitors approached, their eyes were immediately drawn to the mesmerizing roadside sign, proudly announcing Kona Lanes in bold, glowing letters. But that was just the beginning of the enchantment that awaited within.

Stepping through the doors, one was transported into a world of wonder and excitement. The interior boasted 40 wood-floor bowling lanes, each beckoning players to test their skills and aim for those elusive strikes. Laughter and friendly competition filled the air as bowlers cheered and celebrated their victories.

Beyond the lanes, the bowling center held even more treasures. A game room enticed thrill-seekers with its array of arcade machines, inviting challenges and high scores. A lounge provided a cozy retreat for those seeking respite and camaraderie, where stories were shared and memories were made. And let's not forget the coffee shop, which, over time, transformed into a delightful Mexican diner, tantalizing taste buds with savory flavors and spicy delights.

But what truly set Kona Lanes apart was its captivating design, a testament to the era of Googie architecture. Embracing the spirit of Polynesian-inspired Tiki styling, the building was a spectacle to behold. Neon lights cascaded in vibrant hues, casting an ethereal glow upon the night. Exaggerated rooflines soared into the sky, as if reaching for the stars themselves. Kona Lanes embodied the spirit of its time, a fusion of modernity and exoticism that captured the imagination of all who beheld it.

Yet, as the years passed, the winds of change blew, and Kona Lanes faced its final days. In 2003, with heavy hearts, it closed its doors, bidding farewell to generations of bowlers who had found joy within its walls. It was a bittersweet moment, for Kona Lanes was not merely a bowling center; it was a relic of an era, a testament to a bygone time.

Amidst the sorrow of its departure, fragments of Kona Lanes found new life. Much of its equipment found new homes, preserving the spirit of the center in the hands of avid bowlers. And the iconic sign was lovingly salvaged and sent to Cincinnati, finding a new home in the American Sign Museum, where it still shines brightly, a tribute to the legacy of Kona Lanes.

In 2010, the land was rezoned, paving the way for the construction of senior citizens' apartments and commercial development.

Orange Bowl
839 West Chapman
Orange

The Orange Bowl in Orange was another beloved bowling alley that is no longer in operation. It provided a classic bowling experience with a retro vibe. The alley had a friendly staff, well-kept lanes, and a range of amenities such as a pro shop and snack bar. It was a popular spot for families, friends, and bowling enthusiasts to enjoy a fun-filled day or evening of bowling. It was open from the 1960s until the early 2000s.

Tustin Lanes
1091 Old Tustin Boulevard
Tustin

In 2015, the city of Tustin bid farewell to a cherished establishment that had been an integral part of its community for nearly four decades. Tustin Lanes, a family-owned bowling alley, closed its doors after 38 years of providing a welcoming space for leagues, tournaments, and casual bowlers alike. Despite the rise of trendy bowling centers with modern technology and upscale amenities, Tustin Lanes stood out for its affordability and neighborhood charm. Its closure marked a significant loss to the city, which was not just losing a bowling alley, but also a place that had become an important thread in the fabric of Tustin's social life.

Tustin Lanes was more than just a bowling alley; it was a gathering place where friendships were forged, rivalries were kindled, and memories were made. For leagues and tournaments, it served as a hub of excitement and friendly competition. Bowlers of all ages and skill levels flocked to Tustin Lanes to engage in a sport that offered both recreation and camaraderie. The alley's welcoming atmosphere fostered a sense of community, as regular patrons developed lasting bonds and newcomers were warmly embraced.

While other bowling centers sprung up in the area, boasting flashy technology and high-end cocktails, Tustin Lanes remained steadfast in its commitment to affordability and accessibility. As casual bowling began to lose its popularity, Tustin Lanes stayed true to its roots, catering to a diverse clientele that appreciated both the sport and the affordability it offered. In an era of increasing entertainment costs, the bowling alley provided a budget-friendly option for families, friends, and local organizations to gather and enjoy a timeless pastime.

The closure of Tustin Lanes was a stark reminder of the changing dynamics of the bowling industry. As casual bowling declined in popularity, many traditional bowling alleys struggled to adapt to the evolving demands of consumers. Tustin Lanes became a victim of this industry-wide decline, facing the challenge of competing with more modern and upscale bowling establishments. The decision to replace the beloved alley with a home supply hardware store further emphasized the shifting priorities of the local economy.

ICE SKATING

Ice Capades Chalet Skating Rink
1065 Brea Mall
Brea

The Ice Capades Chalet Skating Rink at the Brea Mall in Brea, California was an incredibly fun place for kids in the 1970s and 1980s. It was the perfect spot for children to experience the joy of ice skating and create lasting memories.

The Ice Capades Chalet Skating Rink was a popular destination, especially during the winter months. The rink was beautifully decorated, with twinkling lights and festive decorations that added to the overall enchanting atmosphere. The moment kids stepped onto the ice, they were transported to a magical winter wonderland.

Children of all ages and skill levels could participate in ice skating at the rink. For beginners, there were helpful instructors available to provide lessons and assist with getting the hang of gliding on the ice. These instructors were patient and encouraging, making it

a comfortable learning environment for young skaters.

One of the most exciting aspects of the Ice Capades Chalet Skating Rink was the occasional appearance of professional ice skaters. Talented figure skaters would sometimes visit the rink to perform dazzling routines, showcasing their skills and inspiring the young skaters. These performances were truly mesmerizing and left a lasting impression on the kids who had the opportunity to witness them.

In addition to regular ice skating sessions, the rink also hosted special events and themed sessions. There were disco nights where skaters could groove to the latest hits while enjoying the thrill of gliding on ice. There were also themed sessions during holidays like Halloween or Christmas, where skaters could dress up in costumes and skate to festive music.

The Ice Capades Chalet Skating Rink was more than just a place to skate—it was a social hub for kids in the community. Many friendships were made on the ice as children bonded over their shared love for skating. Birthdays were often celebrated at the rink, with kids inviting their friends for a fun-filled day of ice skating and laughter.

The rink itself was well-maintained and provided a safe environment for kids to enjoy their skating adventures. Skates were available for rent, ensuring that everyone had the opportunity to participate, even if they didn't own their own pair.

Sadly, the Ice Capades Chalet Skating Rink at the Brea Mall closed its doors in the late 1980s.

Ice Chalet
2701 Harbor Boulevard
Costa Mesa

The Ice Chalet skating rink in Costa Mesa served as a training ground for numerous world-class and professional skaters from the 1970s until its closure in 2001. Members of the community were heartbroken when the owners announced that the rink would be shutting down permanently on January 28 of that year.

The announcement left parents, coaches, and skaters stunned. The owners cited the declining number of skaters as the primary reason for the closure. Over time, the Ice Chalet, which had once been the oldest and only rink in Orange County, struggled to maintain the same level of popularity that it had enjoyed in its earlier years.

Klondike Skating Rink
Paularino Avenue
Costa Mesa

The Klondike Skating Rink was a popular attraction for ice skating enthusiasts during its time. It featured a spacious 95 x 212-foot rink, providing ample space for skaters to glide and twirl on the ice. The rink was built by George Baney, and its location near major highways and shopping centers made it easily accessible to residents and visitors alike.

Despite its initial popularity, the Klondike Skating Rink closed its doors in the 1970s. Unfortunately, it remained unused for an extended period, possibly due to various factors such as changing trends or economic considerations.

While the rink's closure marked the end of an era for ice skating enthusiasts in Costa Mesa, the memories of the Klondike Skating Rink and its contribution to the local community remained. The rink served as a place of joy and recreation for many, offering a fun-filled experience for skaters of all ages and skill levels.

Polar Palace
Beach Boulevard and Whittier
La Habra

The Polar Palace holds fond memories for many who grew up in the area during the 1970s. It served as a beloved ice skating rink and a popular destination for families seeking refuge from the scorching Orange County heat. The facility provided a unique opportunity for children to learn how to skate while enjoying a fun-filled day of activity.

The Polar Palace was more than just an ice-skating rink; it was a community hub that brought people together. During the 1970s, Saturdays at the Polar Palace were a tradition for many families. Children would spend hours on the ice, honing their skating skills, while parents watched proudly from the sidelines or joined in on the fun. The rink provided a safe and exciting environment for people of all ages to escape the heat and enjoy the thrill of gliding on ice.

Not only was the Polar Palace a recreational facility, but it also played a role in fostering local talent in ice hockey. The Whittier Polar Kings, a team that called the Polar Palace home, competed in the Southern California Amateur Hockey Association (SCAHA). The rink served as a training ground for aspiring hockey players, some of whom would go on to achieve success at the collegiate and professional levels. The Polar Kings' presence added to the rink's popularity, drawing in both players and fans eager to witness the exciting sport.

As the 1980s rolled in, the Polar Palace underwent a transformation. It evolved into a wedding venue, providing a picturesque setting for couples to exchange their vows. While this change brought new life to the building, many who had grown up skating there felt a sense of loss as the rink's original purpose faded away. Nevertheless, the memories of countless Saturdays spent at the Polar Palace remained etched in the minds of those who had experienced the joy of gliding across the ice.

MINIATURE GOLF

Holo Wai Miniature Golf Course
Glassell Street, across from Hart Park
Orange

This miniature golf course was an absolute gem. As you stepped onto the course, you were immediately transported to a tropical paradise. The center of the course boasted a sunken area adorned with mesmerizing waterfalls. Oh, the sound of cascading water was

HOLO WAI

"RUNNING WATER"

MINIATURE GOLF COURSE
576 SOUTH GLASSELL STREET
ORANGE, CALIFORNIA
Phone 532-2020

music to your ears! Everywhere you looked, there were Tikis, grass shacks, and fountains, creating an enchanting atmosphere.

The course was a sight to behold, with fishing nets and floats adding an authentic touch. The landscaping was simply marvelous, meticulously crafted to transport you to a faraway island. It truly felt like a miniature golf oasis.

Even professional golfers graced this course with their presence. The legendary Arnold Palmer himself was among those who played here, securing a spot on the top ten list of best scores.

As life often goes, change swept over the landscape. In the early '80s, progress took its toll. The miniature golf course had to make way for a freeway interchange. It's a bittersweet ending, as the only remnant of this beloved oasis is the restaurant that stood adjacent to it. Today, the restaurant has transformed into a Chinese eatery, while apartments now occupy the space where the course once thrived.

SKATEBOARDING

Sadlands
2271 West Crescent Street
Anaheim

Throughout the 1970s, Sadlands gained a reputation as a premier destination for skateboarders looking to push the boundaries of the sport. Its unconventional layout and innovative obstacles attracted riders of all skill levels, sparking creativity and fostering progression within the skating community.

During the early 1980s, Sadlands gained even more recognition in the skating world and became a haven for renowned skateboarders. One of the most notable skateboarders who frequented Sadlands was Tony Hawk, who considered it one of his favorite places to skate. With its distinctive terrain and reputation for fostering creativity, Sadlands played a role in shaping the careers of many influential skateboarders.

In 1989, modifications were made to the park in an effort to discourage skateboarding. This decision was met with disappointment from the skating community, as it altered the beloved features that had made Sadlands so iconic. Despite the changes, the park continued to hold a special place in the hearts of skateboarders who had experienced its unique challenges and thrills.

While Sadlands may no longer exist in its original form, its impact on the skateboarding community remains significant. It served as a catalyst for innovation and expression within the sport during its heyday, leaving a lasting impression on those who had the opportunity to skate its unique terrain. The memories and experiences shared by skateboarders at Sadlands continue to contribute to the rich history and culture of skateboarding.

SKATE CULTURE

The influence of skate culture can be seen in the numerous skateboarding communities that have formed throughout Orange County. These communities provide a supportive and inclusive environment for skaters of all ages and skill levels. Skateboarding is not just a sport or hobby; it is a way of life for many individuals who find solace and camaraderie within this tight-knit community.

Skate culture has also had a positive impact on the local economy. Skateboarding events, competitions, and demonstrations draw visitors from far and wide, boosting tourism and bringing revenue to the area. Local skate shops, too, benefit from the dedicated customer base and continue to be integral parts of the skateboarding ecosystem.

In addition to its economic and cultural contributions, skate culture has also played a role in shaping the identity of Orange County. The rebellious spirit and individuality associated with skateboarding have become intrinsic parts of the region's ethos. Orange County has become synonymous with a laid-back, free-spirited lifestyle that embraces creativity, self-expression, and a passion for adventure.

The influence of skateboarding in Orange County can be seen in various aspects of popular culture as well. Skateboarding has been featured in movies, television shows, and music videos, further cementing its place in the collective consciousness. The distinctive aesthetics of skateboarding, from the colorful graphics on skateboards to the edgy fashion choices of skaters, have permeated fashion, art, and design trends.

Additionally, skate culture has had a lasting impact on the broader skateboarding industry. Orange County-based companies continue to be at the forefront of skateboarding innovation, producing cutting-edge skateboarding equipment and apparel. The region's skateboarding heritage has created a legacy of excellence that continues to influence the global skateboarding community.

Skatopia
7100 Knott Avenue
Buena Park

Skatopia, a renowned skate park, was a hub of intense skateboarding action in the past. One of the main attractions at Skatopia was the iconic "Pipeline," a 175-foot half pipe. The Pipeline was one of the first half pipes built at the skate park and consistently remained a favorite among skaters. It measured 15 feet across and featured a spectator area on one side. The Pipeline began with a small snake run that gradually turned into a sloping track. Above the lip of the pipe, there was a pure vertical section that extended to the boundary wall, which ran flush to the run. This unique design element facilitated some of the most radical moments in skateboarding history.

In addition to the famous Pipeline, Skatopia boasted seven other bowls and runs within its two-acre park. These varied in difficulty, catering to everyone from beginners to advanced skaters. The park's large freestyle area received high praise from skateboarders, offering ample space for creative maneuvers. Another notable feature was the "Whirlpool," a four-bowl cloverleaf configuration. It consisted of two 20-foot bowls and two 10-foot bowls, with depths ranging from six to 12 feet.

Among the park's other attractions was the impressive 230-foot long "big snake." It featured an initial two percent grade that gradually increased to an eight percent grade, providing skaters with an exhilarating and challenging experience. The "big snake" also combined a slope with radical, sharp, high-banked turns. Skaters reveled in the intense action this run provided. Additionally, there was a smaller snake designed specifically for beginners, allowing novice skaters to hone their skills in a more manageable environment.

The park included other notable attractions such as the "Riptide." Resembling a regular swimming pool, the Riptide measured 18 feet by 30 feet and had depths ranging from four to eight feet, featuring up to three feet of vertical transition. Skaters embraced the challenges and opportunities for creative expression presented by this unique pool-like structure.

Another distinct feature was the "Escondido Bowl." This four-sided bowl boasted flat, 40-degree walls, offering skaters a varied area to explore different forms and styles of skateboarding. To add to the excitement, Skatopia featured a banked slalom run, providing an exhilarating and fast-paced experience for skateboarders.

For skaters who did not have their own safety gear, Skatopia provided the option to rent equipment at the pro shop. Safety gear items such as helmets, knee pads, and elbow pads could be rented for a nominal fee of 25 cents per item. This ensured that skaters could ride safely even if they didn't have their own gear. Skatopia aimed to make the skateboarding experience accessible and enjoyable for all enthusiasts. Skatopia was an extraordinary skate park, continually pushing the boundaries and providing skateboarders with an outrageous and dynamic environment to pursue their passion. The park closed in the late 1970s.

CHAPTER SEVEN

MUSIC

ORANGE COUNTY HAS PLAYED a significant role in the music scene, encompassing a wide range of genres from folk to punk. The first real band in the region, the Rhythm Rockers, was a group comprised of members of the Rillera family from Santa Ana. The Rilleras, a Mexican American family, brought their unique blend of rhythm and rock to the local music scene, contributing to the cultural diversity and musical heritage of Orange County starting in the late 1940s.

Orange County has been a breeding ground for talented musicians across various genres. The region has produced a diverse array of artists who have made significant contributions to the music industry. Some of the notable musicians who hail from Orange County include the Righteous Brothers, Jackson Browne, Avenged Sevenfold, and many more. These artists have achieved widespread success and have left an indelible mark on the music world.

Orange County's music scene also attracted numerous international acts. Led Zeppelin played at UC Irvine during their first American tour, leaving an unforgettable impression on local music fans. Throughout the 1970s, Orange County became a regular stop for a multitude of legendary artists, including David Bowie, Elvis Presley, KISS, Elton John, The Who, The Rolling Stones, and many others. The region's vibrant music community and enthusiastic audience made Orange County a sought-after destination for touring musicians.

Orange County is also home to Rickenbacker, a renowned guitar manufacturing company. Rickenbacker was founded in 1931 by Adolph Rickenbacker and George Beauchamp, and their guitars have since become iconic instruments used by countless musicians worldwide. The company's headquarters and manufacturing facilities remain in Orange County to this day, symbolizing the region's ongoing influence on the music industry.

In the late 1970s, Orange County was often associated with conservatism and suburban conformity. A group of young musicians and fans sought an alternative expression through punk rock. Bands like The Germs, Agent Orange, and Social Distortion emerged, infusing the county with a raw and aggressive sound that resonated with disenchanted youth.

What made the Orange County punk scene unique was its DIY ethos. Many bands and their fans created their own spaces to perform and connect. While some notable clubs like Cuckoo's Nest and Safari Sam's provided a platform for punk bands, many shows took place in unconventional venues like backyards, garages, and warehouses. These spaces allowed for an intimate and inclusive atmosphere, fostering a sense of community and shared rebellion.

The Orange County punk rock scene developed its distinct sound, known as the "Orange County sound" or "OC punk." Combining elements of punk, surf rock, and garage rock, this sound was characterized by fast-paced guitar riffs, aggressive drumming, and raw energy. Bands such as T.S.O.L. and Adolescents contributed significantly to shaping this unique sonic landscape.

While some iconic venues from Orange County's punk rock era are still remembered, such as Cuckoo's Nest, many of the places where the music thrived have faded into the anonymity of history. Backyards, garages, and warehouses that once hosted raucous shows have been repurposed or forgotten. However, the spirit of those times lives on through the memories and stories shared by those who experienced it firsthand.

ANAHEIM PUNK SCENE

Radio City, with its gritty atmosphere and DIY spirit, became a focal point for local and touring punk bands. The club provided a platform for underground acts to showcase their music and connect with like-minded individuals. The venue's intimate setting allowed for an up-close and personal experience, creating a unique bond between the performers and the audience.

Adjacent to Radio City in the same strip mall were two other notable clubs: Woodstock and Cartoons and Capers. These establishments further enriched the local punk rock scene, offering additional spaces for bands to perform and fans to gather. Each club had its own distinct character and contributed to the vibrant music culture of the area.

In addition to these dedicated punk rock venues, Anaheim boasted a range of other hardscrabble locations that became ad hoc performance spaces. Old VFW halls, warehouses, and various makeshift venues were transformed into stages for punk bands. These unconventional spaces allowed for a raw and unfiltered expression of the punk ethos, fostering an

environment where creativity thrived.

Anaheim's vibrant punk rock scene was characterized by its grassroots nature and do-it-yourself philosophy. Bands would book their own shows, create their own flyers, and distribute them throughout the community. The scene was fueled by a tight-knit network of musicians, fans, and promoters who supported one another and fostered the growth of the local punk rock community.

Spangler's Café, located at 3009 Ball Road in Anaheim, deserves a mention as well. While not exclusively a punk rock venue, it played a role in the broader music scene of the area. Spangler's Café hosted a diverse range of musical acts, including punk bands. Although it was only open for about six months, the club actively pursued booking bands straight from their living rooms and garages to try to give lesser-known bands exposure and help them build a platform.

Anaheim's status as a hotbed of punk rock venues can be attributed to several factors. The city's proximity to Los Angeles, which was a pivotal hub for the punk rock movement, made it an attractive destination for touring bands. Additionally, Anaheim's relatively affordable rent and ample supply of old buildings and warehouses made it an ideal location for establishing alternative music venues.

The legacy of Radio City and the other punk rock venues in Anaheim lives on in the memories of those who experienced the vibrant scene firsthand. While the physical spaces may have changed over time, the spirit of the DIY punk rock community continues to inspire musicians and fans alike.

Billy Barty's Roller Fantasy
464 W. Commonwealth Avenue
Fullerton

Back in the 1980s, Billy Barty's Roller Fantasy was a unique roller rink/concert venue. Barty, a beloved three-foot-nine actor known for his roles in movies and TV shows dating back to the 1930s, had made a wise investment with his earnings. He decided to create a roller rink that would not only cater to skating enthusiasts but also host concerts on Saturday nights.

Over the years, Roller Fantasy had gained a reputation for bringing in exciting acts such as The Plimsouls and Rick Derringer. It was on the fateful evening of October 23, 1982 that something truly extraordinary happened. A relatively unknown band called Metallica was scheduled to open for the popular band Ratt at the roller rink.

As fans eagerly gathered at the venue, little did they know that they were about to witness the birth of a legendary heavy metal band. Metallica brought an intense energy and raw talent to the stage that captivated the audience. The crowd, a mix of roller skaters and music enthusiasts, couldn't believe their luck as they skated around the rink while head banging to Metallica's electrifying performance.

Billy Barty's Roller Fantasy became a hub for rock, punk, and metal bands throughout the 1980s. The roller rink magically transformed into a stage where renowned acts would come to play, entertaining the crowd with their music and creating an unforgettable atmosphere. The unique combination of live music and roller skating created an experience unlike any other, drawing fans from far and wide. The venue closed down in 1983.

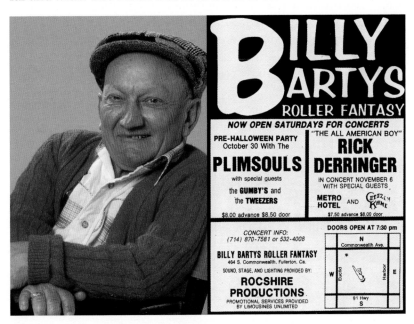

The Boogie
1721 S. Manchester Avenue
Anaheim

The Boogie was a legendary night club located in Anaheim. It had a rich history spanning over two decades and was renowned as one of the most popular clubs in the region. Over the years, it underwent several name changes, starting with The Warehouse, The Crescendo, then The Cowboy, The Bandstand, The Cowboy Boogie, and finally just The Boogie.

Originally established in the early 1970s as a popular live music venue (where everyone from Styx to Chuck Berry to Captain Beefheart performed), The Boogie took a dramatic turn in 1980 when entrepreneur Jack Wade seized the opportunity presented by the popularity of the film *Urban Cowboy*. He transformed the club into a country music Mecca, and it instantly became a sensation. Jack Wade spared no expense in creating an exceptional entertainment experience for club-goers.

The Boogie featured a bustling café, vibrant dance floors, a grand stage for live performances, lively bars, and a massive state-of-the-art sound and lighting system. It wasn't merely a nightclub; it had evolved into a cultural phenomenon, drawing music lovers and country music enthusiasts from all around. The club's ambiance and energetic atmosphere made it a sought-after destination for locals and visitors alike.

The Boogie even gained recognition in the film industry, serving as a filming location for the 1989 movie *Roadhouse*, further solidifying its place in history. As time went on, the club acquired a reputation for rowdiness and unruly behavior. The excessive activity played a part in its closure in 2007.

Although The Boogie is no longer operational, its legacy lives on in the memories of those who experienced its vibrant atmosphere and unforgettable performances. It remains a significant part of the nightlife history of Anaheim and Southern California.

Cattlemen's Wharf
1160 W. Ball Road
Anaheim

FOR RESERVATIONS (714) 535-1622

Cattlemen's Wharf was a highly popular nightclub located in Anaheim. Operating throughout the 1980s and 1990s, it offered a unique and diverse experience for its patrons. The club was known for its themed rooms, each providing a distinct ambiance and entertainment.

One of the notable areas within Cattlemen's Wharf was the Disco Fantasy Level. This floor catered to the disco scene, featuring vibrant lights, a pulsating dance floor, and energetic music that kept the crowd grooving all night long. It was a haven for those seeking the excitement and glamour of the disco era.

Another themed room was the Arabian Knights room, which transported guests into an exotic and enchanting atmosphere. Decorated with Middle Eastern-inspired elements, such as ornate tapestries, colorful cushions, and intricate patterns, it offered a unique escape for visitors looking for a different experience.

The Ben Franklin room provided a distinct setting, invoking a historical ambiance with elements reminiscent of the era when Benjamin Franklin lived. The room featured decor inspired by colonial America, including antique furniture, portraits, and other period-specific items.

The Garden Room offered a more relaxed and natural atmosphere, designed to resemble an outdoor garden setting. It boasted lush greenery, floral arrangements, and a serene ambiance, providing a refreshing break from the energetic dance floors and themed rooms.

Lastly, the Baron's Lounge was situated on the top level of Cattlemen's Wharf and catered to an older crowd who preferred live entertainment over the disco scene downstairs. This sophisticated lounge featured a bar and provided a more refined and relaxed setting for patrons to enjoy drinks and live performances.

Cattlemen's Wharf was a popular destination for club-goers in Anaheim during the 1980s and 1990s, offering a variety of themed rooms and entertainment options to suit different tastes and preferences. While it may no longer be in operation, it holds a place in the memories of those who experienced its unique and vibrant atmosphere.

The Clubhouse
2800 N. Main Street
Santa Ana

Located in what is now the bustling Main Place Mall in Santa Ana, there once existed a hidden gem of the 1970s music scene known as The Clubhouse. This intimate rock club holds a special place in the hearts of those who frequented it, despite its relative obscurity in the annals of music history. Hosting an impressive roster of artists, including the likes of Tina Turner and Peter Gabriel, The Clubhouse offered a unique opportunity to experience renowned performers in an up-close and personal setting.

Located at the heart of the vibrant Santa Ana music scene, The Clubhouse quickly gained a reputation for its exceptional sound quality and intimate atmosphere. The club's modest size created an immediate connection between the audience and the performers, allowing fans to experience the raw energy of live music in a way that larger venues couldn't replicate.

As word spread about the club's exceptional sound system and dedication to showcasing top-tier talent, The Clubhouse became a coveted destination for both emerging and established artists. Drawing in a diverse array of musicians from various genres, the venue offered an eclectic mix of rock, blues, funk, and soul performances. The Clubhouse prided itself on its ability to provide an intimate setting for fans to witness these iconic acts, far removed from the larger stadiums and arenas where they typically performed.

A legendary artist who left an indelible mark on The Clubhouse was Peter Gabriel. Known for his pioneering work as the lead vocalist of Genesis before embarking on a successful solo career, Gabriel mesmerized audiences with his theatrical stage presence and innovative musical style. Fans who were lucky enough to witness Gabriel's 1977 performance at The Clubhouse often recount it as an unforgettable experience that showcased his artistic genius up close.

Despite The Clubhouse's relative obscurity outside of those who were fortunate enough to attend its shows, it holds a special place in the hearts of music enthusiasts.

Celebrity Theater
201 E. Broadway
Anaheim

The Celebrity Theater in Anaheim holds a significant place in the history of entertainment in Southern California. Over the years, it played host to legendary performers such as The Beach Boys, George Carlin, and Howie Mandel, among others.

In its heyday, the Celebrity Theater was a popular venue for live performances and concerts. Its intimate setting and state-of-the-art facilities made it a favorite among both artists and audiences.

The theater's stage witnessed memorable performances by iconic musicians, captivating comedians, and talented actors, leaving a lasting impression on those who experienced the shows firsthand.

Unfortunately, despite its initial triumphs, the theater struggled to maintain its popularity and financial stability. The competitive landscape, with nearby performing arts centers and concert venues, posed a significant challenge. As other entertainment venues sprouted up in the area, drawing audiences and performers alike, the Celebrity Theater faced increased competition for bookings and ticket sales.

As a result, the theater's owners made the difficult decision to close its doors in 1994. The closure marked the end of an era, leaving behind a legacy of memorable performances and cherished memories.

The story of the Celebrity Theater did not end there. In 1997, the theater underwent a significant transformation and reopened under a new name: the Freedman Forum. The rebranding aimed to reinvigorate the venue and attract a fresh audience. Despite the efforts to revive the theater, the challenges it faced earlier persisted. The competition from neighboring performing arts centers and concert venues remained fierce, making it difficult for the Freedman Forum to regain its former glory.

Ultimately, the theater never truly found its footing again and struggled to establish a sustainable presence in the ever-evolving entertainment landscape. The combination of increased competition, changing audience preferences, and financial constraints proved too formidable to overcome. As a result, the Freedman Forum eventually faced its own closure, marking the end of the theater's legacy in Anaheim.

The Crazy Horse Saloon
Newport Freeway at Dyer Road
Santa Ana

The Crazy Horse was a renowned music venue located in Santa Ana. It played a significant role in the local music scene and became an iconic destination for both aspiring and established musicians and fans. From its humble beginnings in the 1960s to its closure in the early 2000s, the Crazy Horse left an indelible mark on the local music community.

The Crazy Horse started as a small club primarily featuring folk and acoustic music. In its early years, it provided a platform for emerging artists, nurturing their talent and helping them gain exposure. As the venue gained popularity, it expanded its musical offerings to include a wide range of genres such as rock, blues, jazz, and country.

During the 1970s and 1980s, the Crazy Horse became a hotspot for both local and national acts. Its intimate atmosphere and excellent acoustics made it a preferred venue for musicians to connect with their audience on a personal level. Many now-famous bands and artists performed on its stage, including Merle Haggard, Jerry Lee Lewis, Johnny Cash and Dolly Parton. These performances helped elevate the Crazy Horse's reputation and solidify its status as a premier music venue.

Apart from hosting live music, the Crazy Horse also served as a gathering place for music enthusiasts. It became a hub where musicians, industry professionals, and fans could come together to celebrate their shared love for music. The venue's welcoming and inclusive atmosphere fostered a sense of community, making it a beloved institution among locals. Over the years, the Crazy Horse faced various challenges, including changes in musical tastes, competition from other venues, and economic pressures. Despite these obstacles, it managed to adapt and evolve, consistently delivering memorable performances and maintaining its status as a cultural landmark.

Unfortunately, the Crazy Horse closed its doors in the early 2000s, marking the end of an era for Orange County's music scene. Its closure was met with sadness by many who had formed cherished memories within its walls. The venue's legacy, however, lives on through the countless musicians who launched their careers there and the fans who experienced unforgettable performances.

The Cuckoo's Nest
1714 Placentia Avenue
Costa Mesa

During the late 1970s and early 1980s, the Southern California punk rock scene flourished, giving rise to a slew of iconic venues that defined the era. Among them, the Cuckoo's Nest in Costa Mesa stood out as a legendary punk nightclub that hosted some of the most influential bands of its time. From its gritty atmosphere to its raw and rebellious energy, the Cuckoo's Nest became a beloved institution that left an indelible mark on the punk rock landscape.

The Cuckoo's Nest opened its doors in 1976 under the ownership of a man named Jerry Roach. Originally a country and western bar, Roach saw an opportunity to tap into the burgeoning punk rock movement and transformed the venue into a haven for punk music and culture.

What set the Cuckoo's Nest apart was its unpretentious and raucous atmosphere. The club's interior was grimy and dimly lit, with walls adorned by band posters, graffiti, and other punk-inspired artwork. The stage was small, putting the performers in close proximity to the crowd, fostering an intense and intimate experience.

The Cuckoo's Nest quickly gained a reputation for hosting groundbreaking punk rock acts. Some of the most influential bands of the time, both local and international, graced its stage. The list includes Black Flag, Dead Kennedys, Social Distortion, Circle Jerks, The Germs, X, and many more. These performances were often high-energy, chaotic, and occasionally controversial, reflecting the rebellious spirit of the punk movement.

The Cuckoo's Nest played a pivotal role in shaping the punk

JERRY ROACH PRESENTS
IGGY POP
THE HUMANS
NEOPHONICS
SAT. DEC. 1
CUCKOO'S NEST

rock scene in Southern California. It provided a platform for emerging punk bands to showcase their talent and gain exposure. The club's intimate setting allowed fans to connect with the music on a personal level, fostering a sense of community and unity among punk enthusiasts.

The Cuckoo's Nest's influence extended beyond its physical space. Its reputation as a punk hotspot attracted fans and musicians from across the country, further solidifying Southern California's reputation as a punk mecca. The club's legacy lives on in the memories of those who experienced its raw energy and in the ongoing influence of the bands that emerged from its stage.

Unfortunately, like many iconic venues, the Cuckoo's Nest met its demise in 1981 due to financial difficulties and legal challenges. Nonetheless, its impact on the punk rock movement had already been firmly established. The Cuckoo's Nest remains an enduring symbol of the rebellious and vibrant spirit of the punk rock era.

THE EAGLES
Tomorrowland Stage

The Tomorrowland Stage at Disneyland in Anaheim, California played a significant role in showcasing music history, particularly during the 1960s and 1970s. Located in Disneyland's Tomorrowland, it provided a platform for various musical performances that entertained park visitors.

During the early 1970s, one notable event occurred at the Tomorrowland Stage that would have a profound impact on the music industry. It was the birth of the band known as the Eagles, who initially served as a backing band for the talented singer Linda Ronstadt.

Ronstadt, a renowned artist in her own right, was performing at the Tomorrowland Stage in the early 1970s. She had become acquainted with the Eagles after hanging out with them at the famed Troubadour nightclub in Los Angeles, and, recognizing their exceptional musical abilities, invited them to join her on stage as her backing band for the evening. At that time, the Eagles consisted of Glenn Frey, Don Henley, Bernie Leadon, and Randy Meisner.

The collaboration between Linda Ronstadt and the Eagles was a significant turning point for both parties. It showcased the band's extraordinary talent and harmonies, ultimately leading to their own rise to stardom. The experience gained from performing with Ronstadt helped solidify the Eagles' sound and musical direction.

Following their time as Ronstadt's backing band, the Eagles went on to achieve incredible success in their own right. They became one of the most successful and influential bands of the 1970s, known for their timeless hits such as "Hotel California," "Take It Easy," and "Desperado." Their unique blend of rock, folk, and country music resonated with audiences worldwide.

While the Tomorrowland Stage at Disneyland may be primarily associated with the birth of the Eagles in the early 1970s, it also hosted numerous other musical performances throughout the 1960s and 1970s. Many popular artists of the era, including The Beach Boys, The Supremes, and The Temptations graced the stage and entertained visitors with their iconic music.

The Tomorrowland Stage provided a vibrant and memorable venue for both established and emerging artists, leaving a lasting impact on the music industry. Although the stage has undergone changes over the years and is now known as the Tomorrowland Terrace, its legacy as a platform for significant musical moments continues to be celebrated. It was replaced in 1977 by part of the Space Mountain rollercoaster ride.

FENDER TOUR
Leo Fender

Leo Fender, born as Clarence Leonidas Fender on August 10, 1909 in Anaheim, California, was an American inventor, engineer, and entrepreneur who revolutionized the music industry with his innovations in electric guitars and amplifiers. He is widely regarded as one of the most influential figures in the development of the modern electric guitar.

Growing up in a musical family, Fender showed an early interest in electronics and tinkering. After completing high school, he worked for a short time as an accountant but soon realized his true passion lay in electronics and music.

In the late 1930s, Fender opened a radio repair shop in Fullerton, California. This venture provided him with valuable experience and knowledge of electronics, which would later prove crucial in his guitar designs. In the early 1940s, he joined forces with Clayton Orr "Doc" Kauffman to form the K&F Manufacturing Corporation, producing lap steel guitars and amplifiers.

It was in 1946 that Leo Fender truly made his mark on the music industry when he founded the Fender Electric Instrument Manufacturing Company. His first breakthrough came with the introduction of the Fender Esquire, a solid-bodied electric guitar that offered improved sound and playability compared to traditional hollow-body guitars.

Fender's most significant contribution came in 1950 with the introduction of the iconic Fender Telecaster, the world's first commercially successful solid-body electric guitar. The

Telecaster's simple yet versatile design, durable construction, and distinctive twangy sound quickly made it a favorite among professional musicians.

Continuing his innovative streak, Fender went on to develop the Fender Precision Bass in 1951, the first mass-produced electric bass guitar. This invention revolutionized the way bass players performed and recorded music, providing a more reliable and portable alternative to the bulky and temperamental upright bass.

In 1954, Fender introduced another groundbreaking guitar model—the Stratocaster. With its sleek double-cutaway design, comfortable contours, and three-pickup configuration, the Stratocaster became an instant classic and has since become one of the most iconic and widely played guitars in the world.

Fender's contributions extended beyond guitar designs. He also developed revolutionary amplifier technologies, including the Fender Bassman and later the Fender Twin Reverb, which played a crucial role in shaping the sound of modern music.

In 1965, Fender sold his company to CBS Corporation due to health issues and a desire to focus on other interests. He remained active in the industry, starting a new company called Music Man in the late 1970s and later launching the G&L Musical Instruments brand.

Fender's impact on popular music cannot be overstated. His designs and innovations transformed the way musicians played, recorded, and experienced music. His guitars and amplifiers became the preferred choice of countless legendary musicians across different genres, shaping the sound of rock 'n' roll, blues, country, and many other styles.

Leo Fender passed away on March 21, 1991, but his legacy lives on. His instruments continue to be highly sought after, and the Fender brand remains one of the most revered and influential names in the music industry. Leo Fender's technical brilliance, entrepreneurial spirit, and dedication to innovation have left an indelible mark on the world of music and have cemented his place as a true pioneer and visionary.

Let's take a tour of some Fender-related lost landmarks in Fullerton. Our tour of Fullerton locations related to Leo Fender begins at 107 S. Harbor Boulevard, where Fender's Radio Service was located. This turn-of-the-century building became a city of Fullerton local landmark in 2010, in recognition of its historical significance. In the early 1940s, Fender's Radio Service offered various services, including radio and appliance repair, car stereo installation, musical instrument sales, and servicing early amplifiers.

If you visit the location today, you will notice a large mosaic on the rear of the structure created by artist Katherine England. The mosaic features an image of a guitar, paying homage to Leo Fender's contributions to the music industry. It adds a touch of artistic flair to the building.

It's worth noting that the business operating at this location has since changed its focus. Presently, it manufactures parts for the aerospace industry. While the nature of the business has evolved, the historical significance of the building and its association with Leo Fender remain noteworthy.

Next is the site of the original Fender factory, located at the Fullerton train station at 120 E. Santa Fe Avenue. The building that served as the factory from 1945–1952 is gone and has been replaced by a parking structure. To honor the legacy of Leo Fender and the impact of Fender guitars, a mural and plaque has been installed at the location. The mural serves as a tribute to the historic significance of Fender's presence in Fullerton and the contributions made by Leo Fender to the music industry.

Our final stop on the tour takes us to the primary Fender factory at 500 South Raymond Avenue in Fullerton. As Fender guitars gained worldwide recognition, this larger facility provided the necessary space to meet the growing demand for Fender guitars and amplifiers.

Despite its unremarkable appearance, this concrete-block building played a crucial role in Fender's early years and holds a significant place in the company's history.

Currently housing Jimmi's Nascar Bar & Grill and several auto repair shops, the building's exterior may not reflect its historical significance, but one can easily imagine the vibrant atmosphere that once filled the space. In its heyday before Disneyland opened, the building buzzed with activity as Fender employees, with cigarettes dangling from their lips, worked diligently.

It was within these walls that the first mass production of the iconic Stratocaster guitars took place. The Stratocaster, a groundbreaking model that became synonymous with rock 'n' roll, was crafted just a short distance away from where Jimmi's Budweiser tap now stands. Notably, the guitar Buddy Holly famously played during his 1958 appearance on the *Ed Sullivan Show* was likely handmade in this very location.

From 1953 to 1985, this building served as Fender's primary base of operations. It was a hub of creativity and innovation, where countless guitars and amplifiers were

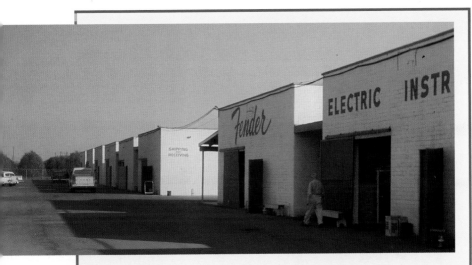

crafted, shaping the sound of popular music.

Although the building's current occupants may differ from its historic purpose, the Fender complex on South Raymond Avenue and Valencia Drive remains a testament to the legacy of Leo Fender and the impact of his instruments on the music industry. It stands as a reminder of the remarkable craftsmanship and entrepreneurial spirit that once thrived within its walls.

The Golden Bear
306 Pacific Coast Highway
Huntington Beach

The Golden Bear has a rich history as a restaurant and music club in Huntington Beach. It first opened its doors in the 1920s as a restaurant at 306 Pacific Coast Highway, across from the pier. By the early 1960s, it had become one of the most popular music clubs in the area.

During its time as a music club, the Golden Bear hosted

numerous renowned artists and bands including Dizzy Gillespie, the Byrds, Janis Joplin, and many others. Junior Wells, a blues musician, even recorded a live album at the Golden Bear.

In the 1970s, the Golden Bear underwent a change in ownership

but continued to thrive as a significant performance space. Esteemed acts such as Linda Ronstadt, Steve Martin, Blondie, and the Ramones graced its stage. Guitarist Robin Trower had the honor of playing the final show at the Golden Bear on January 26, 1986.

Unfortunately, a few months later, the original club was demolished. Parts of the structure were preserved and incorporated into the facade of a new Golden Bear that opened a few years later. Regrettably, this reincarnation of the club did not succeed, and it quickly disappeared amidst the ongoing redevelopment of downtown Huntington Beach. But the stories live on, such as these:

It was the early 1970s, and the Golden Bear in Huntington Beach was abuzz with excitement. Steve Martin, fresh on the stand-up comedy scene, was set to perform. The owner, eager to witness Martin's rising talent, was both thrilled and nervous about the night's events. As Martin took the stage, his zany energy filled the room. The audience was captivated by his unique brand of humor. But little did they know, Martin had something mischievous up his sleeve. Midway through his performance, Martin interrupted his routine and addressed the crowd. With a mischievous grin, he commanded all 300 patrons to stand up and follow him outside the club. Curiosity and anticipation filled the air as they obediently complied.

They marched single file across Pacific Coast Highway, drawing puzzled looks from onlookers. Their destination? A row of bushes that lined the front of Maxwell's restaurant. Martin's plan was about to unfold. He ordered everyone to kneel down quietly behind the bushes, waiting for the next unsuspecting person to walk out of the restaurant. Time seemed to stretch as they held their breath in anticipation. And then, as if on cue, Martin signaled for everyone to stand up and unleash their collective screams onto the unsuspecting passerby. Shrieks and laughter filled the air as the bewildered individual hurriedly passed by, wondering what on earth had just happened. Martin's impromptu prank brought a surge of adrenaline and joy to the participants.

With the prank successfully executed, Martin led the group back to the Golden Bear, the excitement and laughter lingering in the air. The owner, initially nervous about losing paying customers, was relieved when Martin returned with the entire entourage, unpaid checks in hand. The night continued with Martin's uproarious performance, leaving everyone in stitches. That night at the Golden Bear became a memorable tale, a testament to Steve Martin's comedic genius and his ability to create unforgettable experiences for his audience.

The night Peter Gabriel graced the stage at the Golden Bear in 1977 would forever be etched in the memories of those fortunate enough to witness it. The British singer-songwriter, on tour in support of his debut solo album, brought his unique style and infectious energy to the intimate venue.

As the concert neared its conclusion, Gabriel's performance had left the audience in awe. Little did they know that an unexpected twist awaited them. Unbeknownst to the crowd, earlier that day, Gabriel had purchased a boogie board at Jack's Surfboards, an iconic surf shop just a block away from the club. Seizing the opportunity for a spontaneous adventure, Gabriel slipped out of the back door of the Golden Bear, clutching his boogie board. With a mischievous smile, he crossed the Pacific Coast Highway, shedding his clothes along the way. Fully naked and with the board in hand, he made his way into the dark ocean for a midnight swim. The sight of Gabriel, illuminated by the moonlight, riding the waves on his boogie board, had to be nothing short of surreal. The ocean became his playground as he reveled in the freedom and tranquility of the late-night swim. Meanwhile, inside the Golden Bear, whispers spread among the astonished spectators as they realized what was happening. The unique combination of Gabriel's musical talent and spontaneous nature had created a moment that would be forever etched in their minds.

Clearly, the Golden Bear was no stranger to other incredible stories. One of the most remarkable involved a former dishwasher in the 1960s. This struggling singer-songwriter, known as Peter Tork, had found himself living in a modest basement apartment beneath the club. Financial constraints had made it difficult for him to afford a place of his own. Tork's dreams extended beyond washing dishes. He pursued his passion for music and eventually started doing auditions in Los Angeles. To his surprise and delight, he landed the role of Peter in the popular band The Monkees, propelling him to stardom and leaving the Golden Bear with a tale of its own.

When new owners took the reins of the Golden Bear in 1974, they faced a steep learning curve in booking concerts and managing the business. As a result, the club's success started to wane. A stroke of luck came their way when they managed to secure a week's worth of solo shows with Jerry Garcia, a legendary musician on a break from his band, the Grateful Dead. Garcia, known for his love of intimate venues and connection with his audience, thoroughly enjoyed his time at the Golden Bear. He quickly formed a bond with the staff, even taking the time to teach them a few guitar tricks. The experience was so positive for Garcia that, upon returning to the Bay Area, he began spreading the word among his musical friends about this hidden gem of a club in Huntington Beach. His endorsement helped the new owners overcome their initial struggles and put the Golden Bear back on the map.

Another captivating story from the Golden Bear involves the renowned muralist Wyland. In the late 1970s, Wyland, a local surfer, frequented the club and soaked up the vibrant atmosphere. It was during this time that Wyland created one of his first public works—an awe-inspiring mural that adorned the walls of the Golden Bear. This mural, a testament to Wyland's talent and love for the ocean, captured the spirit of the club and became an iconic piece of artwork within its walls. It served as a visual representation of the Golden Bear's connection to the local community, surfing culture, and the arts.

The Golden Bear was not only a venue for extraordinary musical performances but also a place where artists from various disciplines converged. It fostered an environment that nurtured creativity and inspired collaborations between musicians, painters, and other creative minds. These stories, from Jerry Garcia's endorsement to Wyland's mural, are just a glimpse into the rich tapestry of experiences that made the Golden Bear a cherished and legendary venue. It was a place where music, art, and community intertwined, leaving an indelible mark on the history of Huntington Beach and the memories of all who had the privilege of being part of its vibrant scene.

The Harmony Park Ballroom
1514 W. Broadway
Anaheim

The Harmony Park Ballroom, previously known as the Concordia Club Hall, has a rich history in Anaheim. It officially opened on July 4, 1922 and was initially constructed to serve as a venue for the Concordia Club's songfests, German plays, and social

gatherings. Notably, Diedrich Blankmeyer, a member of the building committee who was actively involved in various organizations like the Sons of Herman and men's chorus, composed "Greetings to Thee, My Anaheim," a poem set to music by Oscar Rasbach, which premiered during the opening day celebrations.

In the early 1960s, the Harmony Park Ballroom gained popularity as a nightclub, with Dick Dale and his band the Del-Tones serving as the house band during that period. Dick Dale, often referred

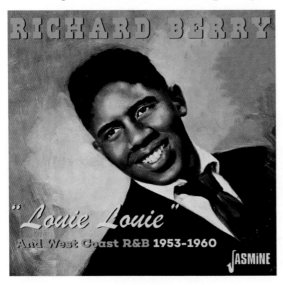

to as the "King of the Surf Guitar," was known for his energetic and influential performances, particularly in the surf rock genre.

Additionally, the Harmony Park Ballroom holds significance in the history of the song "Louie Louie," which was composed at the venue in 1955 by musician and songwriter Richard Berry. Within two years, the song was released on the FLIP record label and later recorded and popularized by The Kingsmen. "Louie Louie" went on to become an iconic rock and roll anthem.

In later years, the Harmony Park Ballroom underwent various transformations. It became the Pepper Tree Faire antique mall and later the Whole Earth Marketplace in the 1970s. Unfortunately, the venue was demolished in 1991, marking the end of its physical presence.

The Hop
18774 Brookhurst Street
Fountain Valley

In 1983, The Righteous Brothers, Bill Medley and Bobby Hatfield, opened a restaurant and dance club called "The Hop" in Fountain Valley. The establishment featured piped hits from the 1950s and 1960s, as well as live performances from renowned artists such as Chuck Berry, Chubby Checker, and The Righteous Brothers themselves. The Hop remained operational for several years before eventually closing down in 1993.

Hungry Joe's
1506 Pacific Coast Highway
Huntington Beach

Hungry Joe's, a cozy roadhouse, stood as a testament to the "old" Huntington Beach, where memories were forged and the spirit of

community thrived. Its unassuming facade painted with an honest slogan beckoned locals and travelers alike to step inside and experience a slice of authentic coastal charm.

Hungry Joe's was more than just a restaurant; it was a sanctuary where time seemed to slow, where laughter and camaraderie filled the air. As patrons crossed the threshold, they were transported to an era when life was simpler, when the sound of jazz permeated the walls and the scent of good food tantalized the senses.

This humble establishment not only satisfied hunger but also nourished the soul with its vibrant jazz scene. It became a revered music venue, attracting notable musicians and jazz aficionados from near and far. The likes of Kenny Burrell and Joe Pass graced its stage, their melodic notes intertwining with the clinking of glasses and the murmurs of conversation, creating an atmosphere of pure magic. Bonnie Raitt also loved playing here. Hungry Joe's became a haven for music lovers, a place where the spirit of jazz could be embraced and celebrated.

In 1977, tragedy struck as fire consumed Hungry Joe's, reducing it to ashes and taking with it a piece of Huntington Beach's soul. The loss was profound, leaving an unfillable void in the hearts of those who had shared countless memorable evenings within its walls.

Irvine Meadows Amphitheatre
8808 Irvine Center Drive
Irvine

The Irvine Meadows Amphitheatre holds a rich history as one of Southern California's premier outdoor music venues. Since its opening in the early 1980s, it hosted countless iconic performances and music festivals, becoming a beloved destination for music lovers of all genres. The amphitheater's inaugural rock concert took place on September 18, 1981, featuring Tom Petty and the Heartbreakers as the headlining act. This historic performance was made even more memorable when surprise guest Stevie Nicks joined the band on stage to perform their hit duet, "Stop Draggin' My Heart Around." This momentous occasion set the stage for the many legendary performances that would follow at Irvine Meadows.

In 1987, the Pacific Symphony Orchestra made Irvine Meadows its summer home, bringing a touch of classical music to the venue. This collaboration allowed music enthusiasts to enjoy a diverse range of genres, from rock and pop to symphonic compositions, all within the unique open-air setting.

One of the most significant annual events held at Irvine Meadows was the KROQ Weenie Roast, organized by the popular radio station KROQ. This festival brought together a lineup of alternative and rock acts, attracting a dedicated fan base year after year.

The amphitheater gained a reputation as a prime location for hosting major music festivals. Some of the most notable festivals held at Irvine Meadows included the Area2 Festival, Fishfest, Gigantour, Lilith Fair, Lollapalooza, Projekt Revolution, and the Uproar Festival. These events drew large crowds and showcased a diverse range of musical talent, making Irvine Meadows a must-visit destination for festival goers.

In June 1982, heavy metal legend Ozzy Osbourne recorded a live performance at Irvine Meadows titled *Speak of the Devil*. Originally released as a home video in Japan, it later became available on DVD in the United States in 2012. This recording captured the raw energy and electrifying atmosphere of a live concert at the amphitheater.

Throughout its existence, Irvine Meadows Amphitheatre provided a platform for both established and emerging artists to showcase their talents. The venue's picturesque outdoor setting, with sweeping views of the surrounding hills, created a unique and immersive concert experience.

Some other notable shows at the Irvine Meadows Amphitheatre:

1. **Bon Jovi:** As part of their highly successful Slippery When Wet Tour, Bon Jovi performed three consecutive nights at Irvine Meadows Amphitheatre from June 20 to June 22, 1987. These concerts allowed fans to witness the band at the height of their fame and showcased their infectious rock anthems.
2. **The Eagles:** The Eagles held a series of six consecutive shows at the amphitheater from May 27 to June 1, 1994, as part of their reunion tour titled "Hell Freezes Over."
3. **Grateful Dead:** The iconic band performed at the Irvine Meadows amphitheater a total of 15 times between 1983 and 1989.
4. **Iron Maiden, Motörhead, and Dio:** On August 24, 2003, Iron

Maiden, Motörhead, and Dio performed at the Irvine Verizon Amphitheater, which was the new name given to the Irvine Meadows amphitheater at that time.

5. **Michael Jackson:** The pop superstar Michael Jackson graced the stage of Irvine Meadows for three concerts from November 7 to November 9, 1988 during his "Bad" tour. These performances were highly anticipated, drawing massive crowds and further solidifying Jackson's status as a global music icon.

6. **Oingo Boingo:** Oingo Boingo, the iconic new wave and alternative rock band led by Danny Elfman, held their annual Halloween concerts at Irvine Meadows from 1986 through 1991. These shows became legendary for their energetic performances, theatrical stage presence, and the festive atmosphere they created. The band returned for one final Halloween concert in 1993 before moving subsequent shows to the Universal Amphitheatre in Los Angeles.

7. **Phish:** The renowned jam band Phish made their mark on Irvine Meadows with two single-night engagements. They performed at the venue in 1999 and 2000, delivering their signature improvisational style and captivating audiences with their eclectic blend of musical genres.

8. **Prince and The New Power Generation:** Prince and The New
   Power Generation performed at the Irvine Meadows amphitheater during the Jam of the Year Tour on October 12, 1997.
9. **Rush:** On June 29, 1990, the Canadian rock trio Rush brought
   their Presto tour to Irvine Meadows. Known for their intricate
   instrumentation and thought-provoking lyrics, Rush delivered a
   captivating performance that showcased their technical prowess and enduring appeal.
10. **The Smiths:** The Smiths played at the amphitheater on August
    28, 1986, as part of their "The Queen is Dead" tour.
11. **Tangerine Dream:** Tangerine Dream performed at the Irvine
    Meadows amphitheater on June 6, 1986. This performance was
    recorded and later released as a bootleg called *Sonambulistic
    Imagery.*

In April 2000, the amphitheater was renamed the Verizon
Wireless Amphitheatre as part of a sponsorship deal between Verizon Wireless and SFX Entertainment, the then-owner of the venue. The sponsorship deal lasted for seven years and was renewed
for another seven years until 2014. After the expiration of the second sponsorship deal with Verizon Wireless, the venue's name
reverted to its original name, Irvine Meadows Amphitheatre, in
2015. Gwen Stefani performed the final shows at the venue on October 29 and 30, 2016. Her performances marked the end of the Irvine Meadows Amphitheatre. The Irvine Company, the owner of
the land, informed the operators of the amphitheater that the land
lease would not be renewed after 2016. Consequently, the amphitheater was closed, and demolition began in November 2016, shortly after Gwen Stefani's final concert. The Irvine Company decided
to develop the land as a housing development. The entire space of
the original Irvine-based Lion Country Safari Park, including the
former amphitheater site, was transformed into a 3,700-unit housing development.

Joshua's Parlor Site
7000 Garden Grove Boulevard
Westminster

Joshua's Parlor was a prominent hard rock concert club in Orange

County during the mid-1980s. It played a significant role in shaping the local alternative rock and metal scene of that era. The club garnered attention by hosting a variety of bands, including the influential group Jane's Addiction. As one of Orange County's alt rock and metal hotspots in the 1980s, Joshua's Parlor attracted a dedicated following of music enthusiasts.

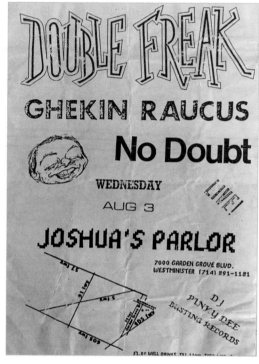

The venue provided a stage for both established and emerging bands, allowing them to showcase their talent and connect with a passionate audience. Jane's Addiction performed at Joshua's Parlor during their early years, leaving a lasting impact on the local music scene. The club's energetic atmosphere and commitment to live music made it a popular destination for fans seeking an authentic and immersive concert experience. Joshua's Parlor became known for its passionate crowds, intimate setting, and the raw energy that emanated from the stage.

Unfortunately, Joshua's Parlor closed its doors in the early 1990s, marking the end of an era for Orange County's alternative rock and metal scene. Today, the location where Joshua's Parlor once stood is occupied by a strip club, signaling a significant shift in the character and purpose of the venue.

Melodyland
400 Disney Way
Anaheim

Melodyland was Southern California's first theater in the round. It served as a venue for various pop concerts and later hosted a church in the round. Situated across Harbor Boulevard from Disneyland,

Melodyland had a seating capacity of 3,200 and opened on July 2, 1963.

In 1969, Reverend Ralph Wilkerson purchased Melodyland and repurposed it as a church. The church retained both the name and the original Melodyland sign. Unfortunately, Melodyland was demolished in 2003, and the property it occupied is now part of Anaheim Garden Walk, a lifestyle shopping center.

Throughout its existence, Melodyland hosted numerous notable concerts featuring renowned artists such as Bobby Darin, Ray Charles, The Beach Boys, Sly and the Family Stone, Jefferson Airplane, Grateful Dead, Simon and Garfunkel, Sonny and Cher, and many others.

NEWPORT POP FESTIVAL

The Newport Pop Festival was a music festival held in Costa Mesa over the weekend of August 3–4, 1968. It was one of the largest music festivals of its time, drawing a significant crowd and featuring prominent rock, folk, and psychedelic acts.

The festival took place at the Orange County Fairgrounds and was organized by promoter David Freeman, who had previously worked with the Monterey Pop Festival. Freeman aimed to create a similar atmosphere of music and cultural expression at the Newport Pop Festival. The lineup included a mix of well-known artists and emerging acts, representing a range of musical genres. Some of the notable performers included:

1. **The Byrds:** A influential folk-rock band known for songs like "Mr. Tambourine Man" and "Turn! Turn! Turn!"
2. **Grateful Dead:** An iconic rock band associated with the counterculture movement and known for their improvisational style.
3. **Iron Butterfly:** A psychedelic rock band famous for their epic song "In-A-Gadda-Da-Vida."
4. **Jefferson Airplane:** A popular psychedelic rock band known for hits like "Somebody to Love" and "White Rabbit."
5. **Sonny & Cher:** A popular duo known for their pop hits and variety show.
6. **Steppenwolf:** A rock band best known for their hit song "Born to Be Wild."
7. **Tiny Tim:** An eccentric performer known for his ukulele playing and falsetto singing.

In addition to the above artists, many other prominent artists performed at the Newport Pop Festival. Some of them included The Animals, Creedence Clearwater Revival, Canned Heat, Blue Cheer, Eric Burdon & the New Animals, and many more. The performances covered a mix of rock, blues, folk, and psychedelic music, reflecting the varied musical landscape of the late 1960s. The festival featured lengthy sets from many of the artists, allowing them to showcase their music and experiment with extended improvisations. Some performances lasted up to two hours, giving the audience an immersive and engaging experience.

The Newport Pop Festival embraced the countercultural spirit of the era. Attendees dressed in colorful and unconventional clothing, and the festival grounds were adorned with art installations and psychedelic decorations. This created an immersive environment that mirrored the cultural and artistic expressions of the time. The festival incorporated elaborate light shows and visuals to enhance the overall experience. Psychedelic projections, colorful lighting effects, and multimedia displays added a visually stimulating dimension to the performances, contributing to the sensory nature of the event.

Unlike many contemporary festivals, there is limited audio or video documentation of the Newport Pop Festival. Official recordings of the performances are scarce, making it challenging to fully capture the essence of the event. There are some bootleg recordings and photographs available that provide a glimpse into the festival's atmosphere.

The Newport Pop Festival attracted an estimated crowd of around 100,000 people over the two days. The diverse crowd of festival-goers included young people from various backgrounds and music enthusiasts. Tickets were reasonably priced compared to other contemporary events. Advance tickets for both days cost $5, and tickets at the gate were priced at $7.50. This affordability contributed to the large turnout.

The festival faced logistical challenges due to the unexpectedly large crowd. Insufficient facilities and resources strained the organizers' ability to manage the event effectively. Additionally, the festival faced some controversy and criticism from local authorities and residents who were concerned about the impact of such a large-scale event on the community.

Despite its general success, the Newport Pop Festival did not receive as much attention or recognition as other famous festivals of the era, such as Woodstock and the Monterey Pop Festival. The Newport Pop Festival did not continue in subsequent years, making the 1968 event a unique moment in Orange County's musical history.

The Newport Pop Festival holds historical significance as one of the early large-scale music festivals in the United States. It took place during a time of countercultural movements, social change, and the peak of the 1960s music scene. The festival provided a platform for artists and musicians to connect with their audience and express their music and ideas.

While the Newport Pop Festival did not become as iconic as Woodstock or Monterey Pop Festival, it played a part in the evolution of music festivals and paved the way for future large-scale events. It showcased the growing popularity of rock and psychedelic music, and its influence can be seen in the development of subsequent festivals that defined the 1970s and beyond.

Night Moves
5902 Warner Avenue
Huntington Beach

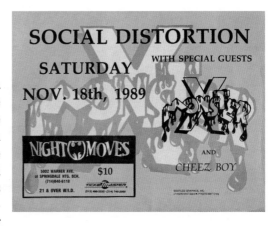

Night Moves was a significant club in the punk and alternative music scene from the mid-1980s to the early 1990s. It gained a reputation for its dark and smoky atmsphere, resembling a cavern. The club had a capacity of 295 people and became a hotspot for bands in the punk and alternative genres.

Many notable bands played at Night Moves during its five-year run. Sonic Youth, Hole, the Lords of the New Church, Soul Asylum, Bad Religion, and Circle Jerks were among the acts that performed there. The club's distinctive bat logo became an iconic symbol, and its memory is still cherished by fans today.

The club's existence came to an end, and the location underwent changes. Today, the space that used to be Night Moves is occupied by a gym. Despite the transformation, the legacy of Night Moves lives on through the memories of those who experienced its cramped yet classic atmosphere.

The Pav-a-Lon Ballroom
317 Pacific Coast Highway
Huntington Beach

The Pav-a-Lon Ballroom opened in 1938 and hosted numerous concerts featuring prominent bands of the time. Its spacious dance floor and lively atmosphere made it a sought-after venue for both established and up-and-coming musicians, drawing crowds from near and far. The ballroom's popularity continued to soar well into the 1950s and early 1960s, when iconic artists such as the Beach Boys, Ike, and Tina Turner graced its stage, captivating audiences with their electrifying performances.

As time went on, the ballroom underwent changes to adapt

to evolving tastes and demands. Eventually, it transformed into a restaurant called Maxwell's, offering patrons a unique dining experience with stunning views of the ocean. Maxwell's became a notable establishment in its own right, attracting diners seeking delicious cuisine served in a captivating setting.

Regrettably, by the late 1990s, the original Pav-a-Lon Ballroom structure was dismantled, making way for the construction of a popular beachside restaurant called Duke's. While the physical structure of the ballroom is no longer present, its legacy and the memories it created remain cherished by those who experienced its vibrant atmosphere and witnessed the performances of legendary musicians within its walls.

Today, Duke's stands as a testament to the ongoing evolution of Huntington Beach's coastal landscape. It offers patrons a chance to enjoy delicious cuisine while taking in the breathtaking vistas that have long made this area a sought-after destination. The Pav-a-Lon Ballroom's history is a testament to the rich cultural heritage of

Huntington Beach and its significance in the local entertainment scene. It served as a focal point for music and dance, providing a platform for renowned performers and offering the community an outlet for celebration and enjoyment.

The Prison of Socrates
106 Main Street
Newport Beach

The Prison of Socrates, a coffee house located on Balboa Island in the mid-1950s, was known for its subculture vibe and unconventional name. It quickly became a gathering place for singers, musicians, comedians, and poets who would come together to drink coffee and perform. The coffee house gained popularity as a hub for folk music during that era.

The establishment was adorned with Greek writings and scenes on the brick wall along the alley and in front of the building, creating a unique atmosphere. Many well-known artists of the time frequented the Prison of Socrates, including Steve Martin, Jose Feliciano, Hoyt Axton, Steve Gillette, and others. Their performances added to the coffee house's reputation and drew larger crowds.

Unfortunately, the Prison of Socrates closed its doors in the late 1960s. Its impact on the local cultural scene and the folk music community in Orange County was significant. The coffee house

provided a platform for emerging artists and fostered a sense of community among like-minded individuals. Its legacy lives on, reminding people of a vibrant era in the region's artistic history.

Today, the building that once housed the Prison of Socrates has been repurposed as a restaurant. While its function has changed, the memory of the coffee house and its contribution to the cultural landscape of Orange County remains an important part of the area's history.

The Rendezvous Ballroom
Intersection of Washington and Palm Streets
Newport Beach

The Rendezvous Ballroom, located on the beach of Balboa Peninsula in Orange County, holds a significant place in the history of public dancing and entertainment during the 1920s.

RENDEZVOUS BALLROOM

Built near this site in 1928, the Rendezvous became a showcase for Big Bands, especially during "Bal Week." For 38 years, the sounds of dance music echoed from this block-long ballroom, which was destroyed by fire in 1966. The music and dancing have ended, but the memories linger on.

Historical Site No. 35
Orange County Board of Supervisors
Orange County Historical Commission
City of Newport Beach
Placed 1986

The RENDEZVOUS BALLROOM
by the SEA at BALBOA Cal.

Constructed in 1928, the ballroom quickly became a popular destination for locals and visitors alike, drawn to the vibrant atmosphere and live music provided by popular bands and orchestras.

The ballroom was an impressive structure, boasting meticulous construction and luxurious features. Spanning an entire city block in length and half a block in width, it was a spacious venue that accommodated large crowds. The building's walls were made of reinforced concrete, ensuring stability and safety for its occupants. Inside, patrons were greeted with a meticulously crafted "floating" hardwood floor, providing the ideal surface for dancing enthusiasts to glide and twirl to the music. The ballroom was crowned with a tile roof, completing its elegant and stylish appearance.

Tragedy struck the Rendezvous Ballroom in 1935 when a fire engulfed the venue, severely damaging the building. The ballroom was not lost forever, though. Determined to resurrect this beloved establishment, it was rebuilt with a unique architectural feature inspired by the nearby Marine Corps' blimp hangars. The new design incorporated an arched roof supported by sectional girders of wood arranged in a cross pattern. This innovative construction method allowed for a spacious and open interior, reminiscent of the original ballroom's grandeur.

In addition to its role as a popular dance venue, the Rendezvous Ballroom attracted a lineup of notable musicians and bands that contributed to its rich musical history. One such notable figure was Stan Kenton, a renowned jazz band leader. Kenton not only performed at the Rendezvous but also originated a television show from the venue in 1957–1958. During his time at the ballroom, Kenton recorded two albums there: *Rendezvous with Kenton* in 1957 and *Back to Balboa* in 1958, capturing the energy and spirit of the venue.

Following a period of closure, the Rendezvous Ballroom experienced a resurgence when surf rock guitarist Dick Dale began performing there in 1960. Dale's energetic and exhilarating performances attracted crowds, and attendance grew rapidly from just a few hundred to a capacity crowd of 4,000 on Saturday nights. His unique blend of surf guitar and Middle Eastern influences left a lasting impact on the venue and helped solidify its place in the annals of rock and roll history. When Dick Dale left the Rendezvous in

1962 to perform at the Pasadena Civic Auditorium, the ballroom's popularity did not wane. It continued to draw large audiences with performances by legendary bands such as The Beach Boys, The Challengers, The Righteous Brothers, and many others. These influential acts further cemented the Rendezvous Ballroom's reputation as a hub for live music and entertainment during the heyday of the Southern California music scene.

Safari Sam's
411 Olive Avenue
Huntington Beach

Safari Sam's was a notable music venue in Huntington Beach that left a lasting impact despite its relatively short existence. It operated from September 1, 1984, until November 23, 1986. The venue hosted a range of influential bands and artists during its time.

Acts such as Black Flag, Social Distortion, 10,000 Maniacs, Jonathan Richman, and The Minutemen performed at Safari Sam's, among many others. One of the most legendary shows at the venue was the first-ever performance by Jane's Addiction on

October 13, 1985. They opened for Love & Terror using the misnomer "James Addiction." This performance holds significant historical importance for Jane's Addiction and their subsequent impact on the alternative rock scene.

The historic building that housed Safari Sam's is still standing today at 411 Olive Avenue in Huntington Beach. It currently serves as the home of the International Surfing Museum, preserving the cultural heritage of the area. Although Safari Sam's had a relatively short existence, its legacy lives on through the memories of those who attended its shows and the impact it had on the local music scene.

Spatz
16903 Algonquin Street
Huntington Beach

Spatz, which opened in 1985, was located in the Huntington Harbour Mall in the same space previously occupied by the Duke of Huntington, a new wave dance club. (It was also once occupied by a jazz club called the Ritz.) Under the ownership of entrepreneur Jack Richards, Spatz was initially intended to be a jazz dinner club. The venue quickly shifted its focus to local rock, new wave, and punk bands.

Soon after its transformation, Spatz began booking popular bands from Orange County and Los Angeles, including the Vandals, T.S.O.L., M.I.A., and many others. As the club gained popularity, it attracted emerging acts such as Stone Temple Pilots, Red Hot Chili Peppers, Black Flag, Fear, and the Dickies. These bands, among others, performed at the tucked-away corner club in the small Huntington Harbour neighborhood.

Unfortunately, in 1986, Spatz closed its doors for good due to rent disputes and ownership changes. Nonetheless, it left behind a rich and storied musical legacy, despite its relatively short existence. Today, the original site of Spatz is occupied by the Harbour Rack House, marking a different era for the location.

CHAPTER EIGHT

DAIRIES

DAIRIES PLAYED A SIGNIFICANT role in Orange County, starting back around the 1930s. During this time, the region was primarily rural, with vast stretches of farmland and open spaces. The establishment of dairies brought about numerous benefits, including a readily available supply of fresh dairy products, particularly through the innovative concept of drive-through dairies. The 1930s marked a period of growth and development for Orange County, as it transformed from an agricultural area into a thriving suburban community. Dairy farming became one of the key industries in the region, with numerous farms dotting the landscape. The moderate climate and fertile soil of Orange County provided ideal conditions for raising cows and producing high-quality milk and dairy products.

Drive-through dairies emerged as a convenient and popular way for families to access fresh dairy products. These establishments were designed to allow customers to remain in their vehicles while purchasing items such as butter, cream, milk, eggs, and more. Drive-through dairies provided a quick and efficient way to obtain these essential products without the need to leave the car or spend time inside a traditional store.

The concept of drive-through dairies was particularly advantageous for families, as it saved them time and effort. Parents with

young children could easily drive up to the dairy, purchase their required dairy products, and continue on with their day. This convenience proved to be a significant factor in the popularity of drive-through dairies, especially for busy households. In addition to their convenience, drive-through dairies also played a role in fostering a sense of community. They became gathering places where neighbors would often meet and socialize while waiting in line to purchase their dairy products. These dairies served as hubs for exchanging local news, sharing stories, and building relationships among residents of Orange County.

Over time, as Orange County experienced rapid urbanization and suburban development, the number of dairies declined. The once open farmlands were gradually replaced by housing tracts, shopping centers, and other developments. The rise of larger supermarkets and grocery chains also contributed to the decline of drive-through dairies, as consumers began to favor one-stop shopping. The memory of the importance of dairies in Orange County's history remains. Drive-through dairies symbolize a bygone era when the region was characterized by agriculture and a close-knit community. They represent a time when accessing fresh, locally sourced dairy products was not only easy but also a part of daily life.

Ed's Dairy
16561 Bolsa Chica Street
Huntington Beach

Located at the corner of Heil and Bolsa Chica in Huntington Beach, a rich dairy history spanning over a century unfolds. The story begins around 1910 when Justine Duc's family took ownership of the property. For several decades, they diligently operated a dairy on the property, fostering a legacy deeply rooted in the community.

In 1960, the property changed hands when it was acquired by Ed and Esther Gonsalves. Under their stewardship, the dairy evolved into Ed's Dairy, becoming a beloved local establishment. For 16 years, from 1960 until 1976, the Gonsalves family continued the tradition of providing the community with fresh eggs, milk, cream, butter, and more.

During its operation, Ed's Dairy not only served as a vital source of dairy products but also became a popular destination for school

field trips. Students would visit the dairy, gaining firsthand insight into the processes of milk production and dairy farming. These educational excursions allowed children to deepen their understanding of agriculture and the importance of dairy in their daily lives.

As time went on, the dairy faced challenges. Rising taxes and pressures from neighbors and developers prompted the Gonsalves family to make a difficult decision. In 1976, they relocated the dairy operation to Riverside County, seeking a more favorable environment for their business. Ultimately, in 1991, the family sold the dairy, marking the end of an era for Ed's Dairy in Huntington Beach.

The legacy of Ed's Dairy and its contribution to the community remains a cherished memory for many residents. The farm's longstanding presence and commitment to providing fresh dairy products left an indelible mark on the local area. It stood as a testament to the importance of agriculture and the bond between the community and its local farmers.

Although the physical dairy is no longer present at the Heil and Bolsa Chica intersection, the memories and stories of Ed's Dairy continue to resonate, reminding us of the enduring heritage of farming and the vital role it played in the development of Huntington Beach.

LA PALMA, AKA "DAIRYLAND"

La Palma is actually quite unique among the cities in Orange County. Unlike its neighbors, it didn't go through a gradual process of development from farmland to a bustling city. Instead, it made a leap from being farmland straight to becoming an incorporated city. If we take a step back in time to before 1955, you wouldn't find a town or any signs of urbanization in La Palma. There was no commercial center, no schools, and no post office. It was simply a region occupied by a group of determined and resilient farmers who were committed to preserving their rural way of life.

During the 1940s, dairy farmers started migrating into the area situated between Buena Park and Cypress. These farmers were forced to leave their previous locations in Los Angeles County due to the encroachment of new housing tracts. People from Torrance, Bellflower, Norwalk, Paramount, and other areas found themselves in search of new farmland. The majority of these farmers were of Dutch descent, although there were also a few Portuguese and Belgian families among them. By the early 1950s, approximately 30 dairy farms had taken root in the region. In addition to the dairy farms, there were a handful of chicken ranches and some row farmers. You would also come across a few scattered houses occupied by individuals who simply desired to live amidst the tranquility of the countryside.

This agricultural landscape of La Palma underwent a remarkable transformation in a relatively short period. The determined farmers, who initially settled there to continue their agricultural practices, were soon faced with the prospect of urbanization. The demand for housing and the growth of neighboring cities brought about significant changes to the area. And so, La Palma went from being a rural farming community to a fully incorporated city, making it a distinct anomaly in Orange County's development.

By the early 1950s, Orange County was experiencing a significant shift as urbanization, or more accurately, suburbanization, began to take hold. New communities were incorporating, and both old and new cities were expanding their boundaries through annexations. In 1953, Buena Park itself became an incorporated city and, within a span of just two years, tripled its city limits through further annexations. The trend of expansion continued when plans were announced to annex a substantial piece of territory to the south in early 1955. The dairy farmers in La Palma understood that once they became part of the city, the inevitable next step would be the development of subdivisions. They had already experienced being pushed out of their farmland before, and they were determined not to let it happen again. So, they put their heads together and came up with a unique solution—why not create their own city? A city that would maintain its rural character and exclude any subdivisions.

This idea of establishing their own rural city was born out of their desire to preserve their way of life and protect their agricultural land from being swallowed up by the expanding urban areas. They knew that if they didn't take action, they would likely face the same fate as before. So, with a strong sense of community and a determination to maintain their rural roots, they embarked on the journey of creating a city that would be distinct and free from the encroachment of subdivisions.

It's truly remarkable to think about the foresight and tenacity of these dairy farmers in La Palma. Their decision to chart their own course and establish a rural city demonstrates their commitment to preserving their agricultural heritage and ensuring that their land would not be lost in the wave of urban development sweeping across Orange County. In a nod to both the spirit of the times and the essence of their community, the dairy farmers of La Palma decided to name their newly created city "Dairyland." The year was 1955, the same year that Disneyland opened its magical gates. The name "Dairyland" had a certain ring to it, partly due to the influence of Disneyland's success. It was also a fitting and descriptive choice. Jack De Vries, the inaugural mayor of Dairyland, later explained that the name was chosen because the land belonged to them, and they had their dairies on it—thus, it was Dairyland.

The proposed City of Dairyland covered an area of just one mile and three-quarters square, and its population numbered a little over 500 residents. The important incorporation election took place on October 11, 1955. Despite having just one polling place, which happened to be in the garage of one of the homes, there was a respectable turnout. Out of the 92 registered voters, 74 individuals cast their ballots. The results of the incorporation vote were decisive, with 55 people in favor and only 19 against.

This overwhelming support for incorporation demonstrated the unity and shared vision of the community. The dairy farmers of Dairyland were determined to shape their own destiny and preserve their rural way of life amidst the rapidly changing landscape of Orange County. The successful incorporation vote marked the beginning of a new chapter for Dairyland as an independent and distinctive city within

the region.

The city council election wasn't as straightforward as you might think. There were six candidates vying for five seats, but things got interesting when they had to count the five absentee ballots to determine who would claim the fifth seat. In the end, Peter D. Bouma (not to be confused with his cousin, Councilman Peter G. Bouma) ended up losing. The new council decided to compensate by appointing him as the City Clerk and Treasurer. Interestingly, after all the dust settled, the council consisted of four dairymen and one chicken farmer. It's quite a unique mix, don't you think?

Their first official order of business was to establish zoning restrictions aimed at keeping subdivisions out and preserving the local agricultural landscape. It's worth noting that

this was perhaps the first time in California's history that a city was incorporated specifically to maintain its agricultural character. Surprisingly enough, this idea gained popularity. In 1956, the City of Dairy Valley was incorporated just across the border in Los Angeles County, and the following year, Dairy City incorporated in Orange County. Dairy City changed its name to Cypress after a short while.

Dairyland, despite attracting a few more dairies, remained the smallest city in Orange County in terms of both size and population. Throughout the first half of 1962, the population only grew by a mere six people. Even by the middle of 1963, there were still only 649 residents in Dairyland, along with thousands of cows.

During that period, rumors started circulating that subdivisions were on the horizon. This caused some concern among the locals.

The real issue, though, was the impending arrival of schools. Despite its small size, Dairyland was divided among five different school districts: Centralia, Buena Park, and Cypress elementary school districts, as well as Anaheim and Fullerton union high school districts. These districts had realized that agricultural land in Dairyland was more affordable than land in residential areas, so they began purchasing it.

Back in 1963, public schools in Dairyland had only around 50 kids attending, but surprisingly, there were already three schools within the city limits, with more in the pipeline. Most of these school sites were acquired through eminent domain. Eventually, the schools occupied a significant portion of the city, taking up about one-tenth of its total area.

Under such circumstances, Dairyland was left with no choice but to surrender to the inevitable changes. In 1964, a new master plan was drafted, outlining the future development of the city for residential and commercial purposes. The plan envisioned a population of 18,000 people. In February 1965, local voters gave their approval to the plan. Simultaneously, residents also voted to change the city's name from Dairyland to La Palma. This renaming decision was primarily driven by pragmatism, as the city fathers believed that La

Palma Avenue would inevitably become the city's main business street. By the autumn of 1965, the first residential subdivisions began opening up, and one by one, the dairies that had once defined the landscape started to depart. Nowadays, the city of La Palma has fully embraced suburbanization, transforming into a typical suburban community.

Lily Creamery Site

6586 Beach Boulevard
Buena Park

The site of Lily Creamery holds historical significance as the location of the first evaporated milk cannery in California. Originally established in 1889 by J.M. Pitblado, it was known as the Pacific Condensed Milk, Coffee, and Canning Co.

The creamery played a pioneering role in the state's dairy industry by introducing the production of evaporated milk, a condensed form of milk with a longer shelf life. This innovation allowed for milk to be preserved and transported more efficiently, providing increased accessibility to dairy products. Ownership of the creamery transferred to the influential Bixby family in 1896, who would operate the factory until its closure in 1907. During their ownership, the Bixbys contributed to the growth and development of the creamery, further solidifying its position as a significant industrial establishment in Buena Park.

After the closure of the Lily Creamery, the site's purpose shifted, and it was subsequently utilized as a tomato cannery. This transition reflects the adaptability and versatility of the location, as it continued to contribute to the local economy and agricultural industry.

Today, while the original creamery no longer stands, the site serves as a historical marker commemorating the early beginnings of the dairy and canning industry in Buena Park. It stands as a reminder of the entrepreneurial spirit and innovation that shaped the region's economic landscape during the late 19th and early 20th centuries.

Todd's Ranch
Northeast corner of Bushard Street and Ellis Avenue
Fountain Valley

Todd's Ranch, later known as Fountain Valley Dairy Farm, was a beloved dairy farm located in Talbert, which is now part of Fountain Valley. Established in the late 1930s, Todd's Ranch gained popularity in the 1940s and 1950s. The ranch became a symbol of innovation and community involvement.

One of the most notable features of Todd's Ranch was its commitment to transparency and education. They designed a unique space called the hostess room, where visitors could observe the milk processing procedures. This room provided an opportunity for people to ask questions and witness the precise methods employed in the production of milk and ice cream. The hostess room was open to school classes, clubs, and any other interested groups, offering them a chance to learn about the dairy farming process. It also served as a venue for lunch or dinner meetings, fostering a sense of community engagement.

Todd's Ranch was dedicated to delivering the highest quality products and became renowned as one of the finest and most modern creameries on the West Coast. Their commitment to efficiency and meticulous planning set them apart from other dairy farms of the time. The ranch prioritized the well-being of their cows and the cleanliness of their facilities, ensuring that customers received only the best dairy products.

Throughout its existence, Todd's Ranch remained deeply rooted in the local community. It was a gathering place for families and friends, creating lasting memories for those who visited. The farm's friendly atmosphere and dedication to quality made it a cherished landmark in the area. Its legacy as a community-friendly and innovative dairy farm continues to be remembered fondly by those who experienced it. The contributions of Todd's Ranch to the dairy industry and the local community remain an important part of Fountain Valley's history.

CHAPTER NINE

AGRICULTURE

THE CONFUSION SURROUNDING HOW Orange County got its name arises from the common misconception that it was named after the abundance of orange groves in the area at the time of its establishment. Historical records indicate that this is not entirely accurate. When Orange County officially separated from Los Angeles County in 1889, it was primarily an agricultural region, but oranges were not the predominant crop.

During the late 19th century, California's major agricultural products were grain and raisin grapes, rather than citrus fruits. While there were a few scattered orange trees in the area, they were not significant in terms of commercial production. The decision to name the county "Orange" was not directly tied to the presence of orange groves, but rather for aesthetic and evocative reasons.

The name "Orange County" was chosen because it sounded pleasant and conjured up images of a tropical paradise, reflecting the attractive and idyllic nature of Southern California. The region's year-round warm climate and natural beauty were reminiscent of exotic locales, and the name aimed to capture that essence.

It wasn't until after 1900 that the citrus industry began to flourish and dominate the local economy. A blight devastated many of the local vineyards, leading to a shift toward citrus cultivation. The newly constructed railroads played a crucial role in the growth of the citrus industry by facilitating the efficient transportation of fresh fruit across the country.

By the 1920s, the citrus industry in Orange County employed approximately one-third of the local workforce, highlighting its significance and economic impact. As the population continued to grow and urban development expanded, the cultivation of oranges gradually declined. The demand for land for residential, commercial, and industrial purposes led to the conversion of orange groves into urban areas.

Prior to World War I, Orange County had a diverse agricultural landscape that went beyond citrus cultivation. The region was known as the walnut producing capital of the world, with extensive walnut orchards dotting the landscape. New insect threats in the 1910s and 1920s, such as the walnut husk fly, posed significant challenges to walnut production, making it less profitable for farmers.

In the late 19th century and early 20th century, Orange County was also a leading source of celery in the nation. The marshy soil around Westminster and Huntington Beach provided ideal conditions for celery cultivation. However, around 1905, a blight struck the celery crops in the region, causing significant damage and reducing its profitability as a major cash crop.

Another significant agricultural venture in Orange County during the late 19th century was the cultivation of sugar beets. Vast fields of sugar beets were grown, and the first of five sugar factories was established in the 1890s. This industry thrived for a time, contributing to the local economy and providing employment opportunities.

Chili peppers were also a major cash crop in Orange County from the early 1890s until the 1920s. The region's climate and soil conditions were favorable for chili pepper cultivation, leading to successful harvests and economic prosperity for many farmers.

In the 1910s, the commercial growing of berries began to gain traction in Orange County. One notable figure in this industry was Walter Knott, located near Buena Park. Knott's success became renowned when he introduced the boysenberry to the world in 1934. The boysenberry, a hybrid berry developed by Rudy Boysen, who later became Anaheim's park superintendent, became synonymous with Knott's Berry Farm, a popular tourist destination in Orange County.

By 1915, Orange County boasted over 20,000 acres of orange groves, signaling the rapid growth and success of the citrus industry in the area. By 1936, Orange County had become a major player in the national citrus market, producing one-sixth of the nation's Valencia orange crop. The citrus industry became a major source of income for the county, generating around two-thirds of its agricultural revenue. Along with Valencia oranges, lemons, limes, grapefruits, and other varieties of citrus fruits were also grown in Orange County, contributing to the diversity of the local citrus industry.

In addition to the previously mentioned crops, Orange County also had successful cultivation of bean varieties such as Lima beans and black-eyed peas. These legumes thrived in the region's favorable climate and played a significant role in the local agricultural economy.

All that said, it was the commercial Valencia orange groves that

ultimately became the backbone of Orange County's agriculture for over half a century. The citrus industry, particularly the cultivation of Valencia oranges, dominated the landscape and economy of the region. The citrus growers' association and cooperatives wielded considerable influence in civic life, shaping policies and supporting the interests of citrus farmers.

For many years, the scenic vistas of Orange County were adorned with expansive orange groves, creating an iconic image that defined the region. The citrus industry provided employment opportunities, generated revenue, and contributed to the local identity and culture.

Originally, individual citrus growers were responsible for picking, packing, shipping, and marketing their own crops. As the industry grew and the need for more efficient distribution and marketing emerged, growers began to form cooperative packing and marketing associations. These associations allowed growers to have more control over the processing, packaging, and marketing of their citrus fruits.

By the 1930s, there were more than 40 local packing houses scattered across Orange County, stretching from one end of the county to the other. These packing houses served as central hubs for processing and preparing citrus fruits for shipment. The cooperative nature of these associations enabled growers to collectively negotiate better prices and access broader markets, enhancing their profitability and competitiveness.

The establishment of cooperative packing and marketing

associations played a crucial role in the success of the citrus industry in Orange County. It provided growers with a unified voice, improved efficiency in handling and distributing the fruit, and facilitated the growth and development of the industry as a whole. The cooperative spirit and infrastructure established during this period laid the foundation for the continued growth and expansion of the citrus industry in Orange County, solidifying its position as a leading citrus-producing region in the United States.

Most of the local packing houses in Orange County during that time period were members of the Southern California Fruit Exchange, better known by their trademark, Sunkist. The Southern California Fruit Exchange, including its Sunkist brand, was a prominent cooperative organization that represented a significant portion of the citrus industry in the region. Other packing houses belonged to the Mutual Orange Distributors or other smaller organizations. These cooperative organizations, led by the Southern California Fruit Exchange, played a vital role in the marketing and promotion of Orange County's citrus fruits by sponsoring many major advertising campaigns across the country in the early 20th century.

As part of these promotional efforts, brightly colored citrus labels were utilized. Each packing house used several different labels to indicate the various grades of fruit. These labels featured distinctive designs, bold colors, and large lettering, making them easily recognizable and eye-catching. They became an integral part of the marketing strategy, particularly during auction sales where wholesale buyers could readily spot the labeled crates of fruit. The citrus labels served as visual representations of the quality and brand identity associated with the fruit. They helped establish a sense of trust and familiarity among consumers, as well as provided a means for distinguishing the different grades of citrus fruits available. The striking and vibrant designs of these labels not only attracted attention but also conveyed the freshness, flavor, and appeal of Orange County's citrus produce.

The advertising campaigns and the use of citrus labels by organizations like Sunkist and other regional cooperatives greatly contributed to the success and widespread consumption of oranges and orange juice across the nation. They played a significant role in making oranges an everyday household item rather than a seasonal indulgence, ultimately shaping consumer habits and preferences.

The decades following World War II brought significant changes to Orange County. Rapid urban development and population growth resulted in the conversion of agricultural land into residential, commercial, and industrial areas. As cities expanded and housing demand increased, many orchards and groves were replaced by suburban neighborhoods and shopping centers.

Additionally, the citrus industry in Orange County faced challenges from the citrus virus, which affected the health of citrus trees and reduced the productivity of groves. These factors, coupled with the increasing costs of production and competition from other citrus-growing regions, led to a decline in the citrus industry's prominence and profitability in Orange County.

Today, Orange County is a bustling metropolitan region that encompasses a wide range of industries, including technology, tourism, finance, healthcare, and more. While the legacy of the citrus industry can still be seen in some pockets of the county, it no longer holds the same level of prominence it once did. Orange County's name serves as a reminder of its historical ties to agriculture and the allure of Southern California's tropical ambiance.

Remnants of Orange County's rich citrus history can still be experienced at the Irvine Ranch Historic Park. This 16½-acre park, located in the heart of Orange County, was once the epicenter of citrus cultivation and hailed as the world's greatest producer of Valencia oranges. The Irvine Ranch, established by James Irvine and his son James Irvine II in the late 1800s, encompassed vast stretches of land that were devoted to agriculture, including extensive orange groves. The fertile soil and favorable climate of the region made it an ideal location for citrus farming.

At its peak, the Irvine Ranch boasted over 60,000 acres of orange groves, earning it a reputation as a major player in the citrus industry. Valencia oranges, known for their sweet and juicy flavor, were the primary variety grown on the ranch. The abundance and quality of the oranges produced on the Irvine Ranch helped solidify Orange County's association with citrus farming.

Today, the Irvine Ranch Historic Park serves as a reminder of this citrus heritage. The park features preserved orange groves that harken back to the ranch's agricultural past. Visitors can stroll through the groves, taking in the fragrant aroma of citrus blossoms and marveling at the beauty of the mature orange trees. The park also offers educational programs and interpretive exhibits that provide insights into the history of the Irvine Ranch and its pivotal role in Orange County's citrus industry. Visitors can learn about the cultivation techniques, the harvesting process, and the significance of the citrus industry in shaping the region's identity.

The Anaheim Packing District
440 S. Anaheim Boulevard
Anaheim

The Anaheim Packing District gained popularity due to its fusion of historical charm and modern amenities. The 1919 citrus packing house, with its industrial architecture and vintage aesthetics, provided a distinctive backdrop for the various food vendors and bars housed within.

The food court featured a diverse selection of culinary options, ranging from international cuisines to local specialties. Visitors could enjoy a wide array of gourmet dishes, creative fusion foods, and artisanal treats. The presence of local vendors gave the district a community-oriented feel, offering visitors the opportunity to support small businesses and experience the flavors of Anaheim and its surroundings.

In addition to the food court, the Anaheim Packing District boasted several bars that catered to different tastes. These bars offered craft cocktails, locally brewed beers, and a welcoming ambiance for socializing and relaxing. The combination of food, drinks, and the overall atmosphere made the district a popular spot for both locals and tourists alike.

Frances Packing House
14407–14493 Culver Drive
Irvine

At the site of the old Frances Packing House in Irvine, there is a marker that commemorates the historical significance of the building and its operations. The marker provides details about the scale and processes involved in the packing house's activities.

The packing house featured two fumigation rooms. These rooms were used to fumigate beans and grains in order to eliminate pests and preserve the quality of the produce. Each fumigation room could hold 500 sacks, with each sack weighing 100 pounds. The fumigation process involved the use of canisters filled with methyl bromide, a chemical used for pest control. Fumigating 500 sacks took approximately 24 hours, indicating the thoroughness of the process. The marker at the site of the old Frances Packing House in Irvine provides a glimpse into the scale, operations, and specific facilities within the building. It showcases the significant role the packing house played in processing and preparing beans and grains for distribution.

Hass Avocados
426 West Road
La Habra

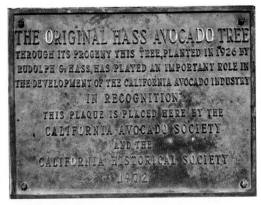

The Hass avocado, which constitutes about 80 percent of all avocados in the United States, technically has its roots in Orange County since La Habra Heights is on the border of Orange and Los Angeles counties.

Rudolph Hass, a mailman in the 1920s, developed an interest in avocados after seeing a magazine ad depicting dollar bills growing on an avocado tree. Intrigued by the potential of avocados as a business venture, he started purchasing seeds and grafting the initial sprouts to expand his crop.

During the grafting process, Hass encountered a stubborn baby tree that refused to accept a graft. Instead of discarding it, he decided to keep it as an experiment. This tree, which grew from a Guatemalan seed of unknown parentage, eventually bore fruit that surpassed the creamy and flavorful qualities of the prevalent Fuerte variety at the time.

Hass was delighted with the quality of these avocados. In August 1935, Hass patented his avocado tree and entered into an agreement with Harold Brokaw, a nurseryman from Whittier, California, to grow and sell Hass avocados. Under the agreement, Hass was entitled to receive 25 percent of the proceeds. The terms of the

agreement were widely violated by other
growers. These growers would purchase
a single tree from Mr. Brokaw, who had
the exclusive rights to produce nursery
trees, and then propagate their entire
groves using the bud wood from that one
tree. This practice undermined Hass'
ability to collect royalties from the widespread cultivation of Hass avocados. As a
result, Hass received less than $5,000 in
royalties over the life of the patent, which
at the time had a term of 17 years. Despite

the limited financial gains, Rudolph Hass can be credited as the
first person to have a producing grove of Hass avocados.

The success of the Hass avocado variety led to its widespread
cultivation in Orange County and throughout California. Its popularity soared due to its rich, creamy texture and exceptional flavor.
Today, the Hass avocado remains one of the most widely consumed
and commercially important avocado varieties in the United States
and beyond. It owes its success taste and texture, but also the vast
efforts of Rudolph Hass, who played a significant role in its early
cultivation and commercialization.

In 2002, the 65-foot tree standing beside Hass' home succumbed to root rot and had to be removed. Today, the wood from
the original Hass avocado tree is preserved at the Brokaw Nursery
in Ventura. A plaque, erected in 1973 by the California Avocado Society at the tree's original site, recognizes Rudolph Hass's contribution and the tree's impact through its progeny. The inscription
on the plaque highlights the tree's pivotal role in the development
and growth of the avocado industry in California. It serves as a reminder of the pioneering efforts of Rudolph Hass and the enduring
legacy of the Hass avocado variety.

Macadamia Trees
608 Macadamia Lane
Placentia

The Macadamia trees found here are Macadamia tetraphylla,
known for producing Australian nuts. They hold the distinction

of being the oldest Macadamia tetraphylla trees in California. These trees were planted before 1890 by the Societas Fraternia, a local spiritualist health colony. The members of the Societas Fraternia were dedicated to

exploring and experimenting with various fruits and nuts to supplement their strict vegetarian diet. The Macadamia trees were among many plant varieties they cultivated.

The colony thrived and remained active until the 1920s, with its members continuing their pursuit of a healthy and holistic lifestyle. The Macadamia trees planted by the colony have stood the test of time, serving as a living testament to the colony's dedication to natural and sustainable living.

Sandi Simon Center for Dance
(Former Villa Park Orchards Association packing house site)
350 N. Cypress Street
Orange

In 1967, the Villa Park Orchards Association acquired a packing house from the Santiago Orange Growers Association. Then, in 2004, Chapman University purchased the packing house from the Villa Park Orchards Association. Since then, the building has been repurposed to house the Sandi Simon Center for Dance, showcasing how historic structures can be adaptively reused for different purposes while retaining their historical significance.

The Villa Park Orchards Association packing house's inclusion on the National Register of Historic Places demonstrates the recognition of its importance in preserving the heritage and history of the Orange community. Its continued existence serves as a reminder of the region's agricultural past and the significant role played by the orange industry in the area's development.

SUGAR BEETS

Sugar beets played a significant role in the development of Orange County, particularly in the late 19th and early 20th centuries. The region's marshy and wet areas provided ideal conditions for cultivating sugar beets, leading to the establishment of sugar beet processing plants.

The first sugar beet processing plant in Orange County was constructed in Los Alamitos in 1897 by the Los Alamitos Sugar Company, who had the land donated to them by Bixby Land Company. The plant was located at 3651 Sausalito Street. This marked the beginning of the local sugar beet industry, which saw substantial growth in subsequent years. The fertile lands of Orange County allowed for extensive sugar beet cultivation, with over 30,000 acres dedicated to sugar beet farming at its peak.

The introduction of the sugar beet processing plant brought about significant economic opportunities and development to the area. The industry created jobs and stimulated growth, leading to the emergence of the new town of Los Alamitos. The processing plant provided employment for local residents and attracted workers from surrounding areas, further fueling the town's growth.

In 1911, the Holly Sugar Plant was established in Huntington Beach, becoming a prominent industry in the area. The plant processed locally grown sugar beets, contributing to the economic prosperity of the region. For several years, the Holly

Sugar Plant served as Huntington Beach's primary industry, providing employment opportunities and fueling local economic growth.

Another Holly Sugar Plant, located in South Santa Ana near the 55 freeway, holds nostalgic memories for many who grew up in Orange County. The iconic plant was built in 1912 by the Santa Ana Co-Operative Sugar Co., which was formed by James Irvine in 1911. The purpose of establishing the cooperative was to secure better prices for sugar beets grown in the area. Holly Sugar Co. acquired the Santa Ana Co-Operative Sugar Co. in 1918, thus taking ownership of the sugar plant. During World War I, Orange County had four sugar factories, and it was a significant supplier of refined sugar, accounting for about one-fifth of the nation's sugar production.

The dominance of the sugar beet industry in Orange County would eventually diminish with the discovery of oil in 1920. The newfound oil industry brought significant economic changes to the region, transforming the landscape and redirecting the focus of development.

In 1926, the Los Alamitos Sugar Company's processing plant closed due to various challenges, including nematode infestations and changes in the economy and market conditions. Despite the closure of the plant, the town of Los Alamitos continued to thrive and grow. The foundation laid by the sugar beet industry and the town's initial development provided a solid basis for further expansion and diversification of the local economy.

By 1930, the Santa Ana plant was the only one still in operation. It continued to be owned by Holly Sugar Co. until its closure in 1982. The plant was subsequently demolished in 1983, marking the end of an era for the sugar industry in Santa Ana.

Dyer Road, located in the vicinity of the former Holly Sugar Plant in Santa Ana, is named after the Dyer Company of Cincinnati, Ohio. The Dyer Company was responsible for designing and constructing the sugar factory. The road serves as a reminder of the historical significance of the plant and its impact on the local community.

CHAPTER TEN

⊙IL

BEGINNING IN THE 1890S, the oil industry played a pivotal role in boosting Orange County's economy. Oil drilling had already been taking place since the 1860s in Brea Canyon, and occasional discoveries were made by the 1880s. The significant boom, though, occurred in 1897 when the first successful well was drilled in Olinda, located in Carbon Canyon. As a result, a small town began to develop around the oil field, and in 1899, the Santa Fe railroad constructed a spur line to connect the wells.

The discovery of oil in Olinda sparked interest and investment, leading to further exploration across the region. As oil explorations expanded throughout the hills of Northern Orange County, Brea emerged as the focal point of the local oil industry by 1910. However, it was the noteworthy strike in 1919 by Union Oil in CC Chapman's lemon grove in Placentia that truly revolutionized the oil industry in the area. This discovery opened up an entirely new area for oil exploration along the north side of the Santa Ana Canyon, attracting numerous investors seeking rapid wealth.

With the growth of the oil industry, Orange County experienced significant economic benefits. The extraction of oil brought about job

Oil Scene, - near L.A. Habra Cal.,

opportunities, attracting workers to the region. The establishment of oil-related businesses and support services further stimulated the local economy. As oil exploration expanded, the population of Orange County grew, leading to increased demand for housing, transportation, and other services.

In 1920, the oil industry in Orange County experienced even greater progression when Standard Oil Number One struck oil at Huntington Beach. This discovery marked a significant shift in the oil boom toward the coastal region. Shortly after, Bolsa Chica Number One also struck oil at Huntington Beach, transforming the once quiet beach town into a bustling hub of oil production.

By the middle of 1921, there were approximately 700 producing wells in Orange County, reflecting the rapid expansion of the industry. The demand for oil exploration led to thousands of acres of farmland being optioned for drilling. Wildcat wells were drilled not only in Orange and Fountain Valley but also in El Toro and the Santa Ana Mountains.

During this time, gasoline emerged as the primary product of the oil industry. By 1924, the oil industry was generating around $50 million annually, surpassing the citrus industry, which produced just under $18 million per year. It is worth noting that the majority of the citrus revenue remained with local growers, while a significant portion of the oil revenue went to big oil companies and investors from outside the county.

Over time, many of the oil wells in Orange County have been decommissioned or removed, leading to a decline in the region's status as a petroleum powerhouse. The impact of the oil industry during its heyday in the 1920s played a crucial role in the county's economic development and transformation.

Discovery Well Park
6720 Summit Drive
Huntington Beach

On May 24, 1920, the first oil well that demonstrated Huntington Beach as a viable source of oil was drilled near the present-day intersection of Golden West and Clay. The *Orange County Register* reported at the time that the well produced 70 barrels of oil per day. This discovery marked the beginning of the oil boom in Huntington Beach.

Then, on November 6, 1920, the Bolsa Chica Number One well struck a gusher, producing a remarkable 1,742 barrels of oil. The oil

flowed from the Mesa into the low-lying areas, prompting a rapid response from 500 men equipped with mules and scrapers. Their task was to construct a dyke to contain the overflow of oil, preventing it from spreading uncontrollably. This event had a transformative effect on the city of Huntington Beach, with the oil industry rapidly developing and changing the landscape.

Today, Discovery Well Park in Huntington Beach stands as a commemoration of this significant event that altered the city virtually overnight. The park features a marker to honor the discovery well and its role in the oil boom that shaped the history and development of Huntington Beach.

The Olinda Oil Museum
4025 E. Santa Fe Road
Brea

The Olinda Oil Museum is a remarkable 12-acre historical park located in Brea. It holds great significance as the place where Edward Doheny discovered crude oil in 1897, which later became a crucial resource for the Santa Fe railroad. The museum offers visitors a unique opportunity to delve into the rich history of the oil industry in the region.

The centerpiece of the museum is the Olinda Oil Well No. 1, which holds great historical value as it is still actively producing oil. This functioning well serves as a testament to the longevity and importance of the oil industry in the area. Visitors can witness the well in action and gain insights into the extraction process that has been ongoing for over a century.

Another notable feature of the museum is the former field office building, constructed in 1912. This building was once the nerve center of the bustling Olinda oil operation, overseeing the daily activities of the workers involved in oil production. Today, it serves as a captivating exhibit space, filled with artifacts that provide a glimpse into the past. The original safe and warehouse, once used

for storing and organizing equipment and parts, are also preserved within the field office building.

As visitors explore the museum, they will encounter a variety of antique oil operation tools, each representing a different aspect of the oil extraction process. These tools showcase the ingenuity and craftsmanship of the early oil industry workers and allow visitors to envision the challenges they faced.

One of the unique aspects of the Olinda Oil Museum is its ability to transport visitors back in time by capturing the sights, sounds, and smells of the first commercial oil production in the Los Angeles basin. The museum's immersive experience aims to create an authentic atmosphere, enabling visitors to imagine themselves in the midst of the bustling oil operation of the past.

CHAPTER ELEVEN

SURFING

SURF CULTURE PLAYED A crucial role in shaping the history of Orange County. From its early beginnings to the present day, the region's coastal lifestyle, with its emphasis on surfing, beach culture, and a laid-back attitude, has become an integral part of Orange County's identity.

In the early 20th century, Orange County's pristine beaches and consistent waves attracted a small community of surfers who recognized the region's potential for riding waves. These early surfers, often referred to as "watermen," were drawn to the ocean's power and the exhilaration of riding waves on wooden boards. Surfing quickly gained popularity, and by the 1950s and 1960s, it had become a significant part of the local culture.

On June 20, 1914, an iconic moment in the history of surfing took place. At the time, Henry Huntington, a prominent railroad magnate, was promoting a recently constructed concrete pier in Huntington Beach and sought to promote the area as a recreational destination.

To achieve his goal, Huntington hired renowned Hawaiian surf pioneer George Freeth to demonstrate the art of surfing to the public. Freeth, armed with his wooden surfboard, boarded one of Huntington's Pacific Electric red cars in Los Angeles, embarking on a journey to Huntington Beach. As the train arrived at the new pier, Freeth stepped out and prepared to showcase his surfing skills to the onlookers.

With the waves as his canvas, Freeth rode the swells with finesse and grace, captivating spectators with his mastery of the sport. This exhibition marked the first public display of surfing on the shores of Huntington Beach and left an indelible mark on the city's identity.

The significance of this event cannot be overstated. Freeth's demonstration sparked an enduring fascination with surfing and laid the foundation for Huntington Beach's reputation as a premier surfing destination. The seeds of "Surf City" were planted that day, and the city would go on to embrace its association with the sport, becoming a hub for surf culture and hosting numerous surfing competitions and events.

One of the other key figures in the rise of surf culture in Orange

County was legendary surfer Duke Kahanamoku. He introduced the sport to the area in the early 1920s and helped popularize it through his Orange County demonstrations and exhibitions. Kahanamoku's influence, along with the growing accessibility of surfboards and the establishment of surf clubs and competitions, contributed to the rapid expansion of surf culture in the region.

Orange County's surf culture was further propelled by the advent of surf music and the popularity of beach movies in the 1960s. Bands such as The Beach Boys and Jan and Dean, with their catchy tunes and lyrics celebrating the beach lifestyle, helped to spread the California surf culture worldwide. Movies like *Gidget* and *The Endless Summer* showcased the thrill and freedom associated with surfing, attracting even more enthusiasts to the sport.

The influence of surf culture extended beyond the waves and into other aspects of Orange County's identity, too. Surf-inspired fashion, characterized by board shorts, Hawaiian shirts, and flip-flops, became a distinctive style associated with the coastal lifestyle. Surfboard manufacturing and related industries flourished, creating job opportunities and contributing to the local economy.

As time went on, Orange County's surf culture continued to evolve. It embraced innovations in surfboard design and witnessed the rise of professional surfing as a competitive sport. The region became home to numerous renowned surf spots, including Huntington Beach, Newport Beach, and San Clemente, attracting surfers from all over the world.

Today, surf culture remains deeply ingrained in the fabric of Orange County. The area hosts world-class surf competitions, such as the U.S. Open of Surfing in Huntington Beach, attracting top surfers and large crowds of spectators. Surfing schools and surf shops are prevalent throughout the county, catering to the ongoing passion for the sport. And not all surf landmarks are lost. Case in point, Harbour Surfboards at 329 Main Street in Seal Beach, established by Rich Harbour.

Rich Harbour is a prominent figure in the surfing world, known for his iconic surf shop in Seal Beach and his surfboard shaping expertise. His story began when he was a teenager living in Seal Beach and had his surfboard stolen from his yard. Determined to continue pursuing his passion for surfing, he took matters into his own hands and built himself another board.

This incident sparked Harbour's passion for surfboard shaping. Motivated by the need to replace his stolen board, he delved into the art of shaping and honed his skills over time. As he gained experience and refined his craftsmanship, he started to gain recognition for his high-quality surfboards.

In due course, Harbour opened his surf shop on Main Street in Seal Beach. It quickly became renowned as one of the most famous surf shops in Orange County. The shop's prime location allowed it to thrive and attract surfers from the local community and beyond. What sets Harbour's surf shop apart is its longstanding operation in its original location. Many surf shops have come and gone over the years, but Harbour's shop has endured, making it a significant part of the local surf culture in Seal Beach.

The success of Harbour's surf shop can be attributed to his dedication to producing exceptional surfboards and providing excellent customer service. His boards were highly regarded for their quality, performance, and attention to detail. The shop became a go-to destination for surfers seeking top-notch equipment and expertise.

Harbour's legacy as a surfboard shaper and the longevity of his surf shop in Seal Beach is a testament to his passion for the sport and his commitment to his craft. By turning a setback into an opportunity, he built a successful business that has left a lasting impact on the surf community in Orange County. Rich Harbour passed away in 2021, and his legacy will undoubtedly live on through his surf shop and the impact he made on the sport of surfing. His contributions to surfboard shaping and the surf culture in Orange County will continue to be remembered and celebrated by surfers and enthusiasts for years to come. As for the landmarks that no longer exist, let's explore those now.

Duane, Gordon
13th Street and Pacific Coast Highway
Huntington Beach

Gordon Duane, born in 1930, led a remarkable life and made significant contributions to the surfing community in Huntington Beach. His journey began as a star water polo player during his high school years, showcasing his athletic abilities. In 1950, at the age of 20, Duane joined the Navy and was stationed in Pearl Harbor, Hawaii.

It was during his time there that he discovered the thrill of surfing and became captivated by the sport. After completing his service in the Navy, he settled in Huntington Beach and began crafting balsa wood surfboards in his garage.

Duane's passion for surfboard shaping led him to make a groundbreaking deal. He rented four rooms under the Huntington Beach pier for a mere $10 per month, where he established his first surfboard shop. The setup was unique and efficient, with each room dedicated to a specific stage of the surfboard production process. This iconic shop quickly became a popular hangout spot for

surfers and a hub for the local surf community. It was known for its vibrant atmosphere and memorable late-night parties.

Unfortunately, in 1959, a mysterious fire destroyed Duane's shop under the pier. Undeterred by this setback, he soon took over an old oil field welding shop located on Pacific Coast Highway at 13th Street. This new location became one of the most renowned surfboard shops in Orange County, coinciding with the explosive growth of the sport. Duane's shop thrived during a time when surfing was gaining popularity, capturing the attention of surfers and enthusiasts. The shop became synonymous with quality surfboards and played a significant role in shaping the local surf culture.

Duane's involvement with The Hole in the Wall Gang, a well-known surf team from the '70s, further highlights his passion for the sport (he was called their "Spiritual leader"). The Hole in the Wall Gang were known for hitting the waves before surfing became as popular as it is today. It's fitting that the surf team received a star on the Surfing Walk of Fame just a week after Duane's passing, honoring their contributions to the surfing community.

In 1984, the property where the shop was located underwent redevelopment, leading to the closure of Duane's shop. Despite this, the brand and legacy associated with Duane's surfboards continued to resonate within the surfing community. Gordon Duane's contributions to surfboard shaping and his role in fostering the surf culture in Huntington Beach are widely recognized. His entrepreneurial spirit and dedication to his craft left an indelible mark on the local surf scene.

The Endless Summer
Salt Creek Beach
Dana Point

The Endless Summer, a documentary filmed in the early 1960s, captivated audiences as it followed two Californian surfers on their global journey to ride the waves. Filmmaker Bruce Brown chose the title to represent a surfer's ultimate dream—a perpetual summer that could be achieved by traveling around the world at the right speed. The film not only introduced the sport of surfing to new audiences, but also uncovered one of the world's most renowned surf spots: Cap St. Francis in South Africa.

One of the most iconic aspects of *The Endless Summer* is its movie poster, which has become widely recognized worldwide. The poster was created by John Van Hamersveld, a surfer who was studying graphic design at the time. Van Hamersveld crafted the poster at his kitchen table in Dana Point, and his artistic contribution earned him a stipend. Little did he know that his work would propel him into a successful career in graphic design.

Interestingly, more people recognize the movie poster than have actually seen the film itself, highlighting the immense popularity and impact of the poster's imagery. The photograph used as the basis for the poster was taken at Salt Creek Beach in Dana Point, featuring Bruce Brown, Robert August, and Mike Hynson as models. This photograph, along with Van Hamersveld's creative vision, resulted in the creation of one of the most iconic pieces of surf imagery in the world.

Hobie Surfboards
34195 Pacific Coast Highway
Dana Point

Hobie Alter, with his passion for woodworking and a deep connection to the sea, began crafting surfboards out of balsa wood in his father's garage during the summer of 1950. Four years later, in 1954, his father purchased a vacant lot for $1,500, and Alter built his own

surf shop there. This surf shop, located on Pacific Coast High-way in Dana Point, is believed

to be the first surf shop in Southern California. Hobie's Surf Shop was more than just a retail store. It became a gathering place for surfers, a spot where they could share stories, exchange ideas, and immerse themselves in the surf culture. The shop's friendly and welcoming atmosphere contributed to the growth of the surfing community and the development of the action sports lifestyle.

The introduction of Hobie surfboards brought about a revolution in surfboard manufacturing and played a significant role in shaping the ocean sports lifestyle we know today. These new boards were lighter, faster, and easier to ride than anything else in the water at that time. Their superior performance quickly caught the attention of surfers, and the demand for Hobie surfboards soared.

Hobie surfboards not only changed the surfing experience but also sparked a surge in interest in the sport. Suddenly, everyone wanted to be a surfer, and having a Hobie surfboard became a coveted possession among surfers. The impact of Hobie surfboards on the surfing world cannot be understated, as they set a new standard for surfboard design and performance.

Today, Hobie surfboards continue to be recognized and cherished by surfers worldwide. The legacy of Alter and his innovative approach to surfboard manufacturing lives on, and his contributions have left an indelible mark on the history of surfing.

As for Hobie's Surf Shop, although it has since been transformed into a taco surf restaurant, the original structure still stands just two blocks south.

Holden Surfboards
17443 Beach Boulevard
Huntington Beach

Holden Surfboards was a renowned surfboard shop that made significant contributions to shaping the sport of surfing. Bill Holden, the master surfboard shaper behind the brand, played a pivotal role in molding the surfboard industry into what it is today.

With a passion for surfing and a keen eye for design, Holden became a well-known figure within the surfing community. He honed his skills as a surfboard shaper, crafting boards that were highly regarded for their quality and performance. Through his expertise and innovation, Holden helped push the boundaries of surfboard design and enhance the surfing experience.

Holden Surfboards, under Bill Holden's guidance, became a hub for surfers seeking high-quality boards tailored to their specific needs. The shop attracted surfers from near and far, drawn by the reputation for exceptional craftsmanship and attention to detail. Holden Surfboards quickly established itself as a go-to destination for surfers in Huntington Beach and beyond. Holden's dedication to his craft helped elevate the art of surfboard shaping. His creations not only provided surfers with the tools to ride the waves but also contributed to the development of the sport itself. His commitment to innovation and continuous improvement left a lasting impact on the surfing community.

Jack Haley Surf Shop
501 Marina Drive
Seal Beach

Jack Haley was a notable figure in the surfing community and had a significant impact on surf culture in Southern California. Haley was born on August 15, 1933 and grew up in Seal Beach, California. He perfected his surfing skills riding the waves of Huntington Beach.

In 1959, Jack Haley became the first-ever winner of the West Coast surfing championships held at Huntington Beach. The following year, his brother Mike Haley also won the event, showcasing the family's talent in the sport. Jack Haley went on to open Jack Haley Surf Shop in Seal Beach in 1961. His surf shop became quite popular among surfers in the area, contributing to the local surf scene.

In addition to his involvement in the surfing industry, Jack Haley expanded his ventures and opened Captain Jack's restaurant in Sunset Beach four years later. Captain Jack's has remained popular over the years and is still operating today. Tragically, Jack Haley passed away in 2000 after battling cancer. Despite his untimely death, his contributions to the surfing community and the local area are still remembered and appreciated.

It is worth noting that while Jack Haley had a successful career in surfing and entrepreneurship, his son, Jack Haley Jr., pursued a different path in professional basketball. Jack Haley Jr. played two seasons with the Los Angeles Lakers from 1988 to 1990.

Olson's
223 Seal Beach Boulevard
Seal Beach

Bob "Ole" Olson, a notable figure in the surfing world, made significant contributions to the sport as a surfboard shaper. He began his journey by opening his first surfboard shop in a Quonset hut in Sunset Beach. He soon relocated to Bay Boulevard, which has since been renamed Seal Beach Boulevard.

Olson's fascination with surfing began in 1937 when he witnessed early surfers riding the waves at Palos Verdes. Inspired by their skill and the allure of the ocean, he embarked on his own surfing journey. In 1948, he paddled out and caught his first wave off the Huntington Beach pier, marking the beginning of his lifelong love for the sport.

To further develop his skills as a surfboard shaper, Bob Olson sought mentorship from renowned figures in the industry. He learned the art of shaping from influential shapers

O L E CUSTOM SURFBOARDS

We will custom build a board to your exact requirements that will give you utmost performance.

Prices start at $95 for 8' to 8'6" size.

223 BAY BLVD. • SEAL BEACH
Across from Naval Ammo. Depot
Phone GEneva 0-2008

Hobie Alter and Harold Walker. Drawing knowledge and inspiration from their expertise, Olson honed his craft and eventually established his own surfboard shop in 1958.

Over the years, Bob "Ole" Olson gained recognition for his exceptional craftsmanship and innovative designs. His surfboards became highly sought after by surfers seeking quality and performance. In 1971, Olson made a significant move and relocated to Hawaii, where he continues to shape boards to this day.

Hawaii's rich surf culture and challenging waves presented Olson with new opportunities to refine his shaping skills. His presence in Hawaii has contributed to the local surf community and allowed him to connect with surfers from around the world.

Olson's dedication and passion for shaping surfboards have left an enduring impact on the sport. His commitment to craftsmanship and his willingness to seek knowledge from industry pioneers have solidified his place in surfing history. Today, his legacy lives on as he continues to shape boards in Hawaii, leaving his mark on the ever-evolving world of surfing.

Velzy Surf Shop
9 W. Avenida San Gabriel
San Clemente

Dale Velzy, born in 1927, was a prominent figure in the early days of surfing and played an influential role in shaping surf culture in Southern California. He began his surfing journey in 1936 when he was just nine years old. By the time he turned ten, he started shaping balsa/redwood laminate surfboards for himself and his friends under the Hermosa Beach pier.

Velzy is widely recognized as one of the pioneers of modern longboarding and is credited as being the first surfer to hang ten, a maneuver where a surfer walks to the front of the board and hangs all ten toes over the nose of the surfboard. This iconic move became synonymous with longboarding and helped shape the evolution of the sport. After serving in World War II, Velzy returned to Manhattan Beach and began commercial surfboard shaping. In 1950, he ventured to Hawaii, where he continued to shape and sell surfboards. His experience in Hawaii further expanded his knowledge and skills in board shaping.

In a significant partnership, Velzy teamed up with Hap Jacobs to establish Velzy-Jacobs Surfboards in Venice Beach. Together, they brought innovation to surfboard design and played a crucial role in the growth of the surf industry. In 1958, they opened a second surf shop in San Clemente, which became immensely popular and remains an important part of Orange County's surfing history.

Velzy's contributions to surfboard shaping and surf culture were significant. He was known for his craftsmanship, attention to detail, and passion for the sport. Through his surfboards and surf shops, he helped popularize surfing and played a pivotal role in its development as a global phenomenon.

Dale Velzy passed away on July 26, 2005, leaving behind a lasting legacy in the surfing world. His innovative designs, entrepreneurial spirit, and love for the ocean continue to inspire surfers and shape the future of the sport.

CHAPTER TWELVE

MILITARY

ORANGE COUNTY BECAME AN important military area during World War II. The U.S. Navy established several facilities in the county, including the Naval Weapons Station Seal Beach, Naval Air Station Santa Ana, and Naval Training Center San Diego (Camp Noyes), which all had an impact on the county's development.

Orange County's coastal location made it strategically significant for military operations and defense. Its proximity to the Pacific Ocean and major ports like Long Beach and Los Angeles made it an ideal location for naval bases and defense installations. The military presence led to the establishment of training centers and bases in the region. These facilities provided training for thousands of military personnel, boosting the local economy and contributing to the growth of surrounding communities.

The establishment of military bases and defense-related industries created numerous job opportunities in Orange County. The influx of military personnel and defense workers stimulated economic growth and provided employment during a time of economic uncertainty. The war effort necessitated the expansion of industries such as aerospace, shipbuilding, and manufacturing in Orange County. Companies like Douglas Aircraft Company (now Boeing) and North American Aviation (now part of Boeing) played significant roles in producing military aircraft and equipment, contributing to the county's industrial development.

The military presence and associated industries also led to a population boom in Orange County. Military personnel, defense workers, and their families relocated to the area, resulting in increased urbanization and the development of new communities. The need to accommodate the growing population and military activities also drove infrastructure development. Highways, airports, and housing projects were constructed to support the military and civilian needs, shaping the county's physical landscape.

As well, the military presence brought diverse groups of people to Orange County, contributing to the region's cultural diversity. The interaction between the military personnel and local residents led to the exchange of ideas, traditions, and cultural influences. The war effort fostered a sense of unity and camaraderie among residents as they supported the troops and contributed to war-related initiatives. Community organizations, volunteer efforts, and support networks emerged during this time.

The military history, particularly the beginning of World War II, had a profound impact on Orange County. It led to the establishment of military installations, stimulated economic growth, drove population growth and urbanization, and brought cultural and social changes. The legacy of this military history can still be seen in the county's infrastructure, industries, and diverse community, so let's look at some of the important lost landmarks.

El Toro Marine Corps Air Station
Valencia Avenue and Armstrong Road
Tustin

El Toro Marine Corps Air Station, also known as Marine Corps Air Station (MCAS) El Toro, was a United States Marine Corps airbase located in Southern California. It was situated near the city of Irvine in Orange County. The base served as a crucial military installation for a significant part of the 20th century.

The history of El Toro dates back to 1942 during World War II, when the United States Navy acquired a portion of the land for the construction of an airfield. The site was chosen due to its strategic location and proximity to the Pacific coastline. Construction began rapidly, and the airfield was commissioned on December 17, 1942, as Naval Air Station (NAS) Santa Ana.

During the war, NAS Santa Ana primarily served as a training base for Marine Corps and Navy pilots. It provided instruction in various aspects of aviation, including flight training, gunnery, and carrier operations. The base played a vital role in preparing pilots for combat duty in the Pacific Theater. After the end of World War II, the base was renamed Marine Corps Air Station El Toro in 1948. El Toro became a significant center for Marine Corps aviation operations during the Cold War era. It served as a key base for fighter squadrons, supporting the defense of the West Coast and

participating in various military exercises and deployments.

El Toro underwent several expansions and upgrades over the years to accommodate the changing needs of the Marine Corps. New facilities, including hangars, barracks, and administrative buildings, were constructed. The airbase also played a role in the testing and development of new aircraft and aviation technologies.

In addition to its military operations, El Toro played a crucial role in humanitarian efforts. The base served as a staging area for disaster relief missions, including the response to major earthquakes and wildfires in California. As the Cold War came to an end and the military's requirements shifted, the decision was made to close MCAS El Toro. In 1993, the Base Realignment and Closure (BRAC) Commission listed El Toro for closure along with other military installations across the country.

The closure process of El Toro took several years, and the airbase officially ceased operations in July 1999. The closure marked the end of a significant era for the military and the local community. The land once occupied by El Toro has since undergone extensive redevelopment, with the former base transformed into a mixed-use development known as the Orange County Great Park.

The transformation of El Toro into the Orange County Great

Park has been a gradual process that has spanned over two decades. The goal was to create a space that would serve the community and provide recreational opportunities while preserving the historical significance of the site.

The development of the Orange County Great Park has involved extensive planning, design, and construction efforts. The former military buildings and infrastructure were demolished to make way for new park amenities, including sports fields, playgrounds, picnic areas, and walking trails. The park also features a large man-made lake, gardens, and a wildlife corridor. One of the park's most notable features is the iconic Great Park Balloon, a helium balloon that offers visitors a panoramic view of the surrounding area. The balloon has become a symbol of the park and a popular attraction for both locals and tourists.

In addition to recreational facilities, the Orange County Great Park has embraced its military heritage by preserving and repurposing certain elements of the former base. The iconic "red horse" squadron barns, originally used for maintenance and storage, have been restored and transformed into a cultural center and event space. Another significant historical feature that has been preserved is Hangar 244, a massive aircraft hangar that once housed military aircraft. The hangar has been repurposed as the Great Park Gallery, a venue for art exhibitions and cultural events. The

development of the Orange County Great Park has not been without challenges. The scale of the project, along with funding limitations and various regulatory requirements, has resulted in a phased approach to construction. The park's transformation has taken place in stages, with different areas being developed and opened to the public over time.

Despite the ongoing development, the Orange County Great Park has already become a popular destination for outdoor activities, community events, and cultural experiences. The park continues to evolve and expand, with plans for additional amenities and features in the future.

The legacy of the El Toro Marine Corps Air Station lives on

through the Orange County Great Park, which has successfully repurposed the land to serve the needs of the local community. It pays tribute to the military history of the site while providing a space for recreation, relaxation, and community engagement. (Note: Tragically, as this book was going to press, the massive and historic north hangar in Tustin was all but destroyed by a fire.)

German POW Camp
Garden Grove Boulevard and Palm Street
Garden Grove

The story of the German prisoner of war (POW) camp in Garden Grove during World War II is a lesser-known chapter in the region's history. The camp housed more than 1,100 German soldiers near the end of the war. Today, there are no remnants of the camp, and the site has been transformed into a strip mall and tract homes, without even a plaque to mark its historical significance.

During World War II, approximately 10,000 German prisoners of war were sent to California to work on farms, although most of the 500 or so camps were located in rural areas of the South and Southwest. In the case of the Garden Grove camp, it was established in 1945 by Citrus Growers Inc., a citrus farming organization. Around 600 POWs arrived that year, with an additional 500 arriving in 1946.

The camp was set up on 15 acres of land, surrounded by citrus groves that covered approximately 75,000 producing acres. The rural setting and the vast expanse of citrus groves made escape attempts difficult for the prisoners. The camp itself consisted of five large tents and was considered a low-security facility. It was patrolled by military guards and dogs to ensure the prisoners' confinement.

The German POWs in California were assigned various roles within the camp and its surroundings. They worked as cooks, mechanics, and janitors, contributing to the day-to-day operations of the camp. Despite being prisoners, they were not subjected to harsh conditions and were generally treated fairly.

After the war, the German POWs were taken to the Santa Ana Army Base, where they continued working in various capacities until being repatriated to Germany in 1947. The Santa Ana

Army Base provided an opportunity for the former prisoners to contribute their skills in support roles, assisting with the base's operations.

While the German prisoner of war camp in Garden Grove no longer exists, its historical significance sheds light on the unique circumstances of World War II and the efforts to utilize POW labor in various industries across the United States. Although the site has been repurposed for modern development, it is important to remember and acknowledge the events that took place there as part of the region's history.

Although there is limited information available regarding the specific experiences and sentiments of the German prisoners of war at the Garden Grove camp, it is believed that some of them developed a fondness for California and returned to the state even after their repatriation to Germany. The pleasant weather, with its mild winters and abundant sunshine, may have played a role in their affinity for California. Compared to the harsh conditions many of them experienced during the war, the favorable climate of the region must have been a welcome change. The allure of the California lifestyle, with its opportunities for outdoor activities and the possibility of finding employment in various industries, also may have contributed to their desire to return.

While it is difficult to ascertain the exact number of former POWs who chose to come back to California, anecdotal evidence suggests that several individuals were drawn back to the state.

Nike Missile Site
Puente Hills
Brea

The former Nike missile site in Brea is a historical site that played a significant role in the nation's defense during the Cold War era. As the only Nike missile site in Orange County, it holds particular importance in the region's military history. Situated between the 57 Freeway and Harbor Boulevard, off Vantage Pointe Drive, the site's original structures and equipment are no longer present. What remains today are the foundations and stairs that once formed part of the missile installation. Accessing the site can be challenging as it is located on private property, and public access may be restricted.

It is advisable to seek permission or visit during times when the property is open to the public. The Nike missile site in Brea operated from 1958 to 1971. During this period, it served as a defense installation for the Nike missile system, which was developed by the United States Army to protect against potential aerial attacks. The Nike missile system was designed to intercept and destroy enemy aircraft or missiles.

These Nike missile sites were strategically located throughout the United States to provide a defense network against potential threats. They typically consisted of radar installations, launchers, and missile assembly and storage areas.

While the Brea site no longer retains its original structures, it represents an important piece of the region's military history and the nation's defense efforts during the Cold War. It serves as a reminder of the significant role these missile sites played in safeguarding the country during a tense period of international relations.

Santa Ana Army Air Base
88 Fair Drive
Costa Mesa

The Santa Ana Army Base, located in Orange County, California, holds a significant historical and cultural significance in the region. While it is now the site of the Orange County Fairgrounds, its past as a military base is a fascinating tale.

The origins of the Santa Ana Army Base can be traced back to the early 1940s during World War II. In response to escalating global conflict, the United States government sought to establish military installations across the country to support the war effort. The Santa Ana Army Base was one such facility, constructed in 1942.

Initially, the base served as a training ground for the 40th Infantry Division, a National Guard unit from California. The soldiers stationed at the Santa Ana Army Base received intensive training in various military tactics, including infantry maneuvers, combat training, and logistical operations. The base played a crucial role in preparing soldiers for deployment overseas.

Following the end of World War II, the base underwent several transformations. It was briefly utilized as a repatriation and demobilization center for returning soldiers. As the military's needs changed, the Santa Ana Army Base was repurposed for other purposes.

In the early 1950s, the base became home to the U.S. Army Reserve 63rd Regional Support Command. The facility served as a training center for reservists, providing them with the necessary skills and knowledge to support active-duty forces during times of conflict or emergencies. The Santa Ana Army Base continued to fulfill this role for several decades.

As the Cold War era drew to a close and the military's requirements shifted once again, the decision was made to close the Santa Ana Army Base. In 1994, the base was decommissioned, and plans were set in motion to repurpose the land for civilian use.

Given its central location in Orange County, the site was deemed suitable for a variety of community-oriented purposes. The Orange County Fairgrounds, known as the OC Fair & Event Center, emerged as the new occupant of the former Santa Ana Army Base. The fairgrounds became a hub for entertainment and cultural events.

Today, the Orange County Fairgrounds hosts a wide range of activities throughout the year. It features a multitude of recreational events, including concerts, trade shows, exhibitions, and, most notably, the Orange County Fair. The fair, which takes place annually, attracts visitors from all over Southern California, offering a mix of entertainment, food, carnival rides, and agricultural displays.

The transformation of the Santa Ana Army Base into the Orange County Fairgrounds represents the adaptive reuse of a historic military facility into a vibrant community space. It stands as a testament to the region's evolving needs and the importance of preserving and repurposing historical sites for the benefit of the local community.

WWII BUNKERS

The elaborate system of World War II bunkers developed as part of the Bolsa Chica Gun Club during World War II served as a significant defensive structure along the coast of Southern California. These bunkers were strategically positioned to protect the coastline from potential enemy attacks during the war.

The Bolsa Chica Gun Club was established as a coastal defense installation, equipped with artillery pieces and manned by military personnel. The gun club featured a network of interconnected bunkers that housed the weaponry and provided shelter for the soldiers. These bunkers were built to withstand enemy fire and bombings, ensuring the safety of the personnel within.

Over the years, the bunkers fell into disuse and were eventually sealed up due to various reasons. One of the primary factors leading to their closure was the occurrence of disruptive activities in the 1970s, '80s, and '90s. Teenagers and young adolescents would trespass into the sealed bunkers, using them as hangout spots. Unfortunately, these unauthorized visits often resulted in vandalism, graffiti, and other forms of

destructive behavior.

To prevent further damage and maintain public safety, authorities made the decision to seal off the bunkers completely. This involved closing entrances and reinforcing the structures to discourage access and ensure that they could no longer be used as gathering places.

Today, the sealed bunkers of the Bolsa Chica Gun Club serve as remnants of a significant historical period. While they are no longer accessible to the public, they stand as silent witnesses to the wartime efforts and the coastal defense measures undertaken during World War II. The sealing of the bunkers was necessary to protect their integrity and preserve them as historical landmarks, safeguarding their historical significance for future generations.

In addition to the World War II bunkers at the Bolsa Chica Gun Club, there is also a bunker located at Crystal Cove. While the structure still stands, it is only viewable if you know where to look. If you are on a boat close to shore, you can spot the viewing slit straight above Abalone Point, just below the power lines on the hill. At Crystal Cove State Park, there is also a trail that leads within 50 feet of the bunker.

Over time, measures have been taken to restrict access to the bunker. More recently, the top of the bunker has been covered in dirt and boulders to prevent people from going inside through the steel hatch on top.

These actions have been taken to protect the integrity of the bunker and ensure public safety. Although the bunker at Crystal Cove is not easily accessible, it serves as a hidden reminder of the area's history and the coastal defense efforts during World War II. Its presence adds to the historical significance of Crystal Cove State Park and preserves a piece of the region's military heritage.

CHAPTER THIRTEEN

PLANES AND TRAINS

EARLY AIRPORTS AND TRAIN travel played significant roles in the development of Orange County, contributing to its growth, connectivity, and economic progress. Here's an overview of their importance.

Early airports, such as Fullerton Municipal Airport, Eddie Martin/Orange County Airport, and Meadowlark Airport, provided essential air transportation infrastructure in the region. They facilitated travel, trade, and communication, connecting Orange County to other parts of California and beyond. These airports supported the growth of the aviation industry, attracting flight schools, aviation firms, and aircraft-related businesses. They served as bases for flight training, aircraft maintenance, and corporate aviation, contributing to job creation and economic development. The airports also fostered a sense of community and recreational aviation. Residents could witness flights, enjoy air shows, and experience the thrill of flying. These airports became beloved landmarks and gathering places for aviation enthusiasts.

Additionally, the advent of railroads in Orange County brought significant economic benefits to the county. Rail lines connected the county to major cities, such as Los Angeles and San Diego. In the early 20th century, the Pacific Electric train system played a vital role in the transportation infrastructure of Orange County. From the 1920s through the 1950s, the electric interurban railway connected various cities and towns, providing residents with a convenient and efficient way to travel. It also facilitated the transportation of goods, enabling trade and commerce to flourish.

Train travel also played a crucial role in promoting tourism and attracting visitors to Orange County. The accessibility provided by rail lines allowed tourists to explore the region's natural beauty, beaches, and attractions, contributing to the growth of the hospitality industry. Rail lines influenced the development of cities and towns, too. Stations served as transportation hubs and focal points for urban growth. The expansion of rail networks often led to the establishment

of new communities and the growth of existing ones. Train travel brought people together, fostering social connections and cultural exchange. It facilitated the movement of people, enabling commuting, leisure travel, and the exchange of ideas and experiences.

With the rise of automobiles and the construction of extensive freeway systems, the demand for public transportation declined. The Pacific Electric train system faced challenges in competing with the convenience and flexibility offered by cars. As a result, the railway gradually lost its prominence, and by the 1950s, most of the lines were discontinued and dismantled. Despite the disappearance of the Pacific Electric train system, there are several remnants that stand as reminders of its legacy, including a couple of repurposed train stations.

The preservation of these repurposed train stations serves as a tribute to the ingenuity and impact of the Pacific Electric train system. They provide visitors with a tangible link to the past, allowing them to imagine the bustling platforms, the hum of the electric trains, and the vibrant atmosphere that once characterized these stations. By repurposing these structures, Orange County has managed to retain a physical connection to its transportation history, ensuring that the legacy of the Pacific Electric train system is not forgotten.

AIRPORTS

Eddie Martin Airport
18601 Airport Way
Santa Ana

Eddie Martin Airport, which later became known as Orange County Airport, had its origins as a private landing strip built by aviation pioneer Eddie Martin in the 1920s on land owned by the Irvine Company. In 1923, Martin established Martin Aviation, which became one of the nation's oldest aviation firms.

In 1939, Orange County Airport became a publicly owned facility through a land swap between the Irvine Company and the County of Orange. During World War II, the airport served as a military base. After the war, it was returned to the county by the federal government.

In 1967, a new terminal building measuring 22,000 square feet was constructed at the airport. Initially, it was named the Eddie Martin Terminal to honor the airport's founder. In recognition of the late movie star John Wayne, who was a resident of Newport Beach and known for his love of aviation, the terminal was renamed John Wayne Airport.

The original Eddie Martin Terminal was eventually demolished in 1994, making way for modernization and expansion projects at the airport. Today, John Wayne Airport is a significant transportation hub in Orange County, serving both commercial and general aviation flights.

Meadowlark Airport
5241 Warner Avenue
Huntington Beach

Meadowlark Airport was a small general aviation airport located in Huntington Beach. It operated as a private airport in the 1940s and then as a public airport from the 1950s until its closure in 1989. The airport was purchased by the Nerio family, who were of Japanese-American descent, in 1947, and they remained the owners throughout its existence.

Initially, Meadowlark Airport featured a short strip primarily used by student pilots for practicing touch-and-go landings. Over the years, it grew in popularity and became a beloved community landmark. The runway was eventually extended to a length of 2,070 feet, providing space for approximately 150 aircraft. Several hangars, a well-liked restaurant called the Meadowlark Café, and fuel facilities were also added to the airport over time.

The airport attracted local residents who would bring their children to watch the small private planes take off and land each day. It served as a community hub for decades, fostering a sense of aviation enthusiasm and community spirit among the locals.

Meadowlark Airport ultimately closed down due to the increasing development in the surrounding area. As a result, a shopping center and a park were built on the site where the airport once stood. While the airport is no longer in operation, its memory lives on among the residents who cherished its presence and the sense of community it brought to Huntington Beach. A plaque can be found at the old runway terminus in Gibbs Park.

Seal Beach Airport
Near Seal Beach Boulevard and Pacific Coast Highway
Seal Beach

Originally known as Crawford Field and later renamed Seal Beach Airport, this small airport was developed in the 1920s. Like Meadowlark Airport, it primarily catered to private pilots and became quite popular within the community.

Adjacent to the airport, across Pacific Coast Highway, was a restaurant called the Glide'er Inn. It provided meals for the pilots and offered snacks in wicker baskets. The restaurant was a convenient gathering place for pilots and aviation enthusiasts who frequented the airport.

Today, the restaurant has been relocated further down Pacific Coast Highway and is now called Mahe. While the airport itself no longer exists, the restaurant's history and association with the aviation community in Seal Beach are still remembered and appreciated by locals.

TRAINS

Buena Park Train Marker
9700–9732 Holder Street
Buena Park

The Buena Park Marker commemorates the historic significance of the Pacific Electric Railway in Southern California. The railway system, established by Henry Huntington in 1895, played a vital role in connecting Los Angeles, Orange, Riverside, and San Bernardino counties. Stretching over 1,000 miles, the Pacific Electric Railway operated a vast network of trolleys, with up to 2,700 scheduled trips daily.

The trolleys of the Pacific Electric Railway were known for their distinctive colors, with the most famous and iconic being the "Big Red Cars." These electric trolleys became symbolic of the era and were a common sight, transporting commuters and sightseers throughout Southern California.

The extensive railway system provided transportation to various destinations, including cities, fruit groves, beach areas, ranchlands, and even the historic Spanish Missions. It played a significant role in shaping the growth and development of the region, facilitating movement between different communities and providing access to key locations.

The Buena Park Marker serves as a reminder of the rich history and impact of the Pacific Electric Railway in Southern California, reflecting the importance of this transportation system in connecting and shaping the region over more than half a century.

The Capistrano Depot
26701 Verdugo Street
San Juan Capistrano

The Capistrano Depot is a historic building that was originally constructed in 1894. It underwent renovations in 1974–1975 to transform it into a restaurant. The renovation project aimed to preserve the original Mission-style architecture, as this was one of the first train stations to feature this architectural style. The exterior of the depot was retained to maintain its historical appearance.

To accommodate the restaurant, modifications were made to the interior of the building. Given the limited space, freight and passenger cars were added to expand the available seating area. This creative solution allows for more patrons to be accommodated within the small interior of the depot.

Additionally, the platform area outside of the depot was enclosed in glass to create additional seating space for the restaurant. This enclosure provides a comfortable dining environment while still allowing visitors to enjoy the historic setting of the depot.

The Capistrano Depot,

with its unique combination of Mission-style architecture, creative interior modifications, and a glass-enclosed platform, stands as a testament to the adaptive reuse of historic structures and the preservation of architectural heritage.

The Children's Museum at La Habra

(Former La Habra Pacific Electric Train Depot)
301 S. Euclid Street
La Habra

The La Habra Pacific Electric Train Depot holds historical significance as a symbol of the transformative development that took place in the fertile La Habra Valley. The depot served as a vital hub for the La Habra Line, which played a prominent role in the progress of Southern California.

The establishment of the La Habra Line brought about a new era of connectivity and transportation in the region. The train line facilitated the rapid movement of early crops, supplies, and resources, including those needed for

the burgeoning oil fields. The popular "Big Red Cars" of the Pacific Electric Railway system provided efficient transportation options for both passengers and freight.

The train depot served as a central point for the loading and unloading of goods and passengers, enabling the smooth flow of commerce and contributing to the economic growth of the area. The arrival and departure of trains at the La Habra Pacific Electric Train Depot became a familiar sight, signifying the vitality and progress of the region. The La Habra Line and its depot played a significant role in shaping the development of La Habra Valley and its surrounding areas. They facilitated the transportation of goods and people, connecting communities and supporting economic activities crucial to the region's prosperity.

Today, it's The Children's Museum at La Habra, which opened in December 1977. This repurposing of the train depot to house a children's museum adds to its historical significance and provides a unique setting for engaging and interactive exhibits.

As an interactive enrichment center, The Children's Museum at La Habra offers a variety of hands-on exhibits spanning different areas of learning. Children, along with their parents and teachers, can explore 10,000 square feet of exhibits that cover topics such as arts, sciences, cultures, and everyday life. These exhibits are designed to stimulate the imagination and promote learning through play.

The Children's Museum at La Habra serves as a valuable resource for the community, offering a fun and educational environment where children can learn, explore, and grow. Its location within a repurposed historic train depot adds to its charm and creates a memorable experience for visitors of all ages.

Orange Street Cars

Marker located at intersection of West Chapman Avenue and Chapman Avenue

Orange

The history of the Orange Street Cars is fascinating and showcases the development of transportation in the city. The first motorized streetcar in Orange was affectionately known as the "Peanut Roaster" due to its distinctive high-pitched whistle. It marked the

beginning of a new era in transportation for the community.

The streetcar system in Orange began in 1888 with a horse-drawn car that traveled through the Plaza to Santa Ana. Over time, the system expanded and became part of the Pacific Electric network, connecting Orange with various points throughout Southern California by 1901. Due to declining ridership, the streetcar service ceased operations in 1930 and was replaced by bus service. Subsequently, the depot that once stood at this location was repurposed as a bus station by Pacific Electric, reflecting the evolving nature of transportation in Orange. Despite the end of streetcar operations, freight rail service continued from the site, serving the citrus packing houses located to the north.

In 2018, during the excavation for the Old Towne West Metrolink Parking Structure (which stands at the site today), original tracks from the streetcar era were discovered. A portion of these salvaged tracks has been installed in the landscaping surrounding the marker, providing a tangible connection to the city's transportation history.

Pacific Electric Red Car
Electric Avenue near Main Street
Seal Beach

The presence of an actual Pacific Electric Red Car in Seal Beach provides a tangible connection to the region's transportation history. Located on the old Pacific Electric right-of-way near Electric Avenue and Main Street, this rare Pacific Electric tower car was built in 1925 and has undergone restoration and painting.

The Pacific Electric Red Car served as a roving machine shop, dispatched to troubleshoot problems along the 40-mile Pacific Electric Los Angeles to Newport line. It played a crucial role in maintaining the electric train system and ensuring smooth operations along the route.

While the car is currently empty and no longer serving as the Red Car Museum headquarters, it remains visible from the street. Its presence, along with the original pieces of track it sits on, offers a glimpse into the past and helps visitors appreciate the significance of the electric train system in Orange County's history.

The Pacific Electric Red Car system was once an integral part of Southern California's transportation infrastructure, connecting various cities and communities. It provided a convenient and efficient mode of transportation for residents, workers, and tourists alike. The sight of the preserved Red Car in Seal Beach serves as a reminder of the region's reliance on electric trains and the impact they had on shaping Orange County's development.

Visiting the Pacific Electric Red Car and standing next to it allows individuals to immerse themselves in the history of the electric train system. It offers a unique opportunity to reflect on the past, appreciate the engineering marvels of the era, and understand

the importance of transportation networks in fostering growth and connectivity within a community.

Preservation efforts such as maintaining the Red Car and displaying it in a prominent location contribute to preserving the historical legacy of Orange County's transportation system. The Red Car provides residents and visitors with a chance to connect with the region's past and gain a deeper appreciation for its rich history.

CHAPTER FOURTEEN

SPORTS

ORANGE COUNTY HAS A rich sports history that dates back to the 1880s and has seen the growth and popularity of various sports throughout the years.

The presence of oil companies in the region during the 1880s led to the formation of company baseball teams, creating a foundation for sports culture in the area. In addition to company teams, there were Mexican leagues and merchant leagues featuring local business owners who competed in baseball. These grassroots and community-based leagues showcased the passion for sports among the residents of Orange County. And who can forget the Orange Lionettes, the celebrated women's softball team that dominated in the 1940s and '50s?

Of course, there are also the major league professional teams that have left a mark on the region's sports landscape. The California Angels (now Los Angeles Angels) arrived in Anaheim in 1966, bringing Major League Baseball to the area. The Los Angeles Rams football team also played in Orange County for many years before moving. The Anaheim Ducks, an NHL team, continue to be popular and represent the region in professional ice hockey.

Throughout Orange County's history, there have been numerous landmarks and venues that symbolize the popularity of sports in the area. While some of these landmarks may no longer exist, they hold a significant place in the memories and stories of sports enthusiasts in Orange County.

Amerige Park
300 W. Commonwealth Avenue
Fullerton

Amerige Park was built in the 1930s as part of a Works Progress Administration (WPA) project. It served as the spring training grounds for various Pacific Coast League teams, including the Hollywood Stars, San Diego Padres, Portland Beavers, Los Angeles

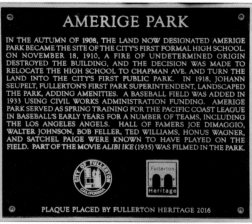

AMERIGE PARK

IN THE AUTUMN OF 1908, THE LAND NOW DESIGNATED AMERIGE PARK BECAME THE SITE OF THE CITY'S FIRST FORMAL HIGH SCHOOL. ON NOVEMBER 18, 1910, A FIRE OF UNDETERMINED ORIGIN DESTROYED THE BUILDING, AND THE DECISION WAS MADE TO RELOCATE THE HIGH SCHOOL TO CHAPMAN AVE. AND TURN THE LAND INTO THE CITY'S FIRST PUBLIC PARK. IN 1918, JOHANN SEUPELT, FULLERTON'S FIRST PARK SUPERINTENDENT, LANDSCAPED THE PARK, ADDING AMENITIES. A BASEBALL FIELD WAS ADDED IN 1933 USING CIVIL WORKS ADMINISTRATION FUNDING. AMERIGE PARK SERVED AS SPRING TRAINING FOR THE PACIFIC COAST LEAGUE IN BASEBALL'S EARLY YEARS FOR A NUMBER OF TEAMS, INCLUDING THE LOS ANGELES ANGELS. HALL OF FAMERS JOE DIMAGGIO, WALTER JOHNSON, BOB FELLER, TED WILLIAMS, HONUS WAGNER, AND SATCHEL PAIGE WERE KNOWN TO HAVE PLAYED ON THE FIELD. PART OF THE MOVIE *ALIBI IKE* (1935) WAS FILMED IN THE PARK.

PLAQUE PLACED BY FULLERTON HERITAGE 2016

Angels, and Hollywood Stars, among others. The park attracted notable players such as Joe DiMaggio, Satchel Paige, Ted Williams, Rogers Hornsby, Gary Carter, and Ernie Vaughn. Honus Wagner, who was coaching the Pittsburgh Pirates at the time, was also present at Amerige Park in the early 1930s when the team played an exhibition game. The Pirates had trained in San Bernardino and made their way to Amerige Park for the exhibition match.

While the field itself remains, most of the original grandstands have been replaced over time. However, the park still retains some of its historical elements, such as the flagstone columns that outline the original ballpark.

Athletic Park
Atchison Street and E. Broadway
Anaheim

In 1904, the city of Anaheim constructed a baseball park called Athletic Park near the Santa Fe railroad station. The *Los Angeles Times* reported that Anaheim had acquired a lease for the park, which was expected to become the finest baseball park in Orange County at the time. The park had a seating capacity of over 1,000 spectators, making it a popular venue for various teams. People from nearby areas such as Santa Ana, Olinda (now Brea), and Placentia would come to watch games at the park.

An interesting event took place here on Sunday, July 20, 1905, when the local team from Olinda (Brea) played two games at Athletic Park. One of the games was played during the day, and the other was held at night against a team of Sioux Indians from South Dakota. An advertisement for the event promoted the use of 50 arc lamps to illuminate the grounds for the evening game. This night game was one of the earliest instances of night baseball being played. Approximately 1,000 fans attended the night game, paying 25 cents per ticket. Athletic Park only existed at that location for a few years and there is no marker at the site today.

Brea Bowl
265 S. Crispen Avenue
Brea

The Brea Bowl holds a significant place in the history of the area, particularly in relation to a legendary baseball game that took place

on October 31, 1924. The Brea Bowl was an open area used by local oil companies for baseball games in the 1920s.

The game that made the Brea Bowl notable occurred when Walter Johnson, a local legend and one of the greatest pitchers in baseball history, returned to his hometown to participate in a charity game. Johnson assembled his own team of all-stars, while the other team was led by none other than iconic baseball figure Babe Ruth.

The game attracted immense attention and drew thousands of spectators from all over Southern California. It featured many notable players, including the future Hall of Famer Sam Crawford.

During the game, Babe Ruth hit two home runs off Walter Johnson, one of which was said to have traveled nearly 600 feet. According to local folklore, the ball disappeared into a nearby oil field, adding to the mystique and legend of the event. The match between Johnson's team and Ruth's team has become one of the most mythical games in baseball history.

Over time, the Brea Bowl site underwent development, and homes were built where the field once stood. Nevertheless, the memory of the historic baseball game and the presence of legendary players such as Walter Johnson, Babe Ruth, and Sam Crawford remains etched in the folklore of Brea, preserving the significance of the Brea Bowl in local history.

Hang Gliding (Birthplace of the Sport)
2200 San Miguel Drive
Newport Beach

During the mid to late 1800s and early 1900s, a group of pioneering individuals dedicated themselves to unraveling the mysteries of flight and finding ways to soar through the skies. In their pursuit, they constructed various simple gliders, which eventually became known as "hang gliders." These early aircraft often featured a pilot who would hang beneath the glider and launch and land on their feet, or make attempts to do so.

At this address, a marker stands to commemorate a significant moment in history. On May 23, 1971, this site became the birthplace of the worldwide sport of hang gliding, as enthusiasts for personal human flight gathered here for the world's first hang gliding meet. Word had spread rapidly about the event, even in the absence of the internet, attracting an unexpectedly large number of hang gliders and enthusiasts. The excitement was palpable as individuals arrived, eager to witness and participate in this groundbreaking endeavor. The presence of a National Geographic photographer further added to the significance of the occasion, as they captured the moments and prepared to feature the modern "birdmen" in an article.

Although some of the gliders present were not able to achieve airborne flight from the shallow hillside at this location, they persevered. To overcome the challenge, hand towing using ropes was employed to assist in launching the gliders.

Among the various designs showcased at the event, one notable biplane named the "Hang Loose" stood out. It was the brainchild of Jack Lambe, a school teacher, who had his students build one.

Lambe had also drawn up simple plans for the glider, which were made available for purchase at a cost of $3. This accessibility allowed others to construct their own versions of the "Hang Loose."

The hillside overlooking MacArthur Boulevard provided a prominent vantage point for onlookers during the hang gliding event. The sheer number of participants caused traffic to come to a standstill, drawing the attention of the Newport Beach police. In an effort to address the unpermitted gathering, the officers sought out the organizer, only to be met with repeated claims of individuals not knowing of any specific organizer. Frustrated, the police approached the owner of the cemetery adjacent to the hillside, requesting that the gathering be dispersed from his property. To their surprise, the owner expressed his lack of concern and allowed the hang gliders to continue their activities. This unexpected response led to humorous speculation that the cemetery owner saw potential for future business related to hang gliding, creating a lighthearted joke among the participants. With the owner's support of the event, the police eventually left the scene.

The events of that memorable day in May 1971 marked the beginning of a new era in aviation. The passion, innovation, and determination exhibited by those early hang gliding enthusiasts paved the way for the development of a global sport that continues to captivate individuals worldwide.

Hawley Park
North side of Ninth Street, just west of Bristol Street
Santa Ana

Hawley Park was built by Alfred E. Hawley, a sporting goods dealer who arrived in Santa Ana in 1887. In 1906, as part of an effort to boost sales of his sporting equipment, Hawley built the park and sponsored a team called the Santa Ana All Stars to play at his ball field. The park quickly became one of the most popular places to watch baseball in Orange County.

Hawley Park hosted notable players like Walter Johnson, who pitched there on several occasions. In 1910, the Santa Ana Yellow Socks also played at Hawley Park. They were part of the ill-fated Southern California Trolley League, which included teams such as the Redondo Beach Wharf Rats, Long Beach Sand Crabs, Los

Angeles McCormicks, and Pasadena Silk Socks. The league got its name because teams would travel from city to city by streetcar. Unfortunately, the league lasted only one year.

The ballpark had a relatively short lifespan, existing for about 10 years before being replaced by the neighborhood that now occupies the area. There is no sign or marker indicating the location of the former ballpark.

La Palma Park
1151 N. La Palm Parkway
Anaheim

La Palma Park Stadium began construction on December 16, 1937, and was completed in March 1939. La Palma Park Stadium was a

multi-use stadium that was designed for both football and baseball. Originally, it shared the same name as the park in which it is situated, La Palma Park. The funding for the stadium was provided by the Works Progress Administration, which was a New Deal agency established during the Great Depression.

The inaugural event at the stadium took place on March 12, 1939. It was a Pacific Coast League spring training baseball game between the Seattle Rainiers and Sacramento Senators. The Sacramento Senators used the stadium for their spring training and played 10 games there in 1939.

Additionally, Connie Mack, the legendary manager and owner of the Philadelphia Athletics (now the Oakland Athletics), brought his team to La Palma Park for spring training in 1940. In 1941, La Palma Park served as the home of the Anaheim Aces, a charter member of the Class C California League in professional baseball. The St. Louis Browns utilized it as their spring training home for the 1946 season. From 1947 to 1948, the stadium was home to the Anaheim Valencias of the Class C Sunset League.

The legendary baseball player Joe DiMaggio played at La Palma Park while he was stationed nearby during World War II. DiMaggio, known as "The Yankee Clipper," is one of the greatest players in baseball history. In the early 1950s, Jackie Robinson, the iconic baseball player who broke the color barrier in Major League Baseball, appeared as himself in a movie about his life that was shot at La Palma Park. This film showcased Robinson's remarkable journey and impact on the sport.

In 1956, the stadium underwent renovations. Instead of constructing a new football stadium, the Anaheim City Council decided to add grandstands to La Palma Park, which would be more cost-effective. These grandstands were built across the outfield, spanning from left field to right-center. As a result, the size of the baseball field was reduced, and the football stadium was subsequently named La Palma Stadium.

In 1971, the football stadium was renamed Glover Stadium in honor of Richard Glover, who served as an assistant and head football coach at Anaheim High School from 1931 to 1957. This renaming was a tribute to Glover's significant contributions to the local football community. In 1987, the baseball field within the stadium was renamed Dee Fee Field. It was named after Dee Fee, who dedicated 50 years of service to the Anaheim Parks Department, starting from 1937 until his retirement in 1987.

Apart from hosting professional and minor league baseball games, the stadium has also been a venue for American Legion Baseball and California Interscholastic Federation (CIF) high school baseball games, providing a platform for local teams to compete in these events.

As for football, the first game held at the stadium took place on September 21, 1956, between Anaheim High School and Redlands High School. Since that time, the stadium has been regularly used as a venue for CIF high school football games in the area.

La Palma Park Stadium (Glover Stadium) has also been a venue for community college and NCAA Division I college football games. In 1983, the Cal State Fullerton Titans football team played two of their three home football games at the stadium. The first game took place on October 1, 1983, against the Pacific Tigers, and the second game was held on November 12, 1983, against the UNLV Rebels. These games were relocated to Glover Stadium due to inclement weather and field conditions at Cal State Fullerton's regular home football stadium, Anaheim Stadium.

In January 1976, Glover Stadium also hosted a rugby union match between the United States national team and Australia. Approximately 7,000 fans attended the game, which marked the first match played by the USA team after the formation of USA Rugby. Australia emerged as the victors, winning the game with a score of 24–12.

Additionally, Glover Stadium has been used to host soccer games, rodeos, circuses, and even high school graduations from the surrounding area. It is still in use today.

Rams Football Practice Site
215 N. Ventura Street
Anaheim

This is where the Los Angeles Rams found an unexpected home in 1980–1994, at the former Juliet Lowe Elementary School in Anaheim. It quickly became a magical playground for both kids and football enthusiasts alike.

Picture this: a vibrant campus, once filled with the laughter and chatter of eager students, now transformed into a hub of excitement and anticipation. As news of the Rams' temporary residence spread like wildfire, kids from all corners of the city flocked to this enchanted spot, their hearts pounding with the hopes of catching a glimpse of their beloved football heroes.

The air crackled with anticipation as young fans lined the sidewalks, brandishing pens and footballs, ready to embark on their autograph-collecting quests. Wide-eyed and full of wonder, they exchanged whispered rumors about the players they longed to meet. Oh, the stories they would tell their friends once they had secured their prized signatures!

As the school doors swung open, little football enthusiasts scurried through the corridors, their tiny feet echoing with excitement. They discovered hidden nooks and crannies where they would eagerly wait, hoping for a chance encounter with their idols.

Every day at the former Juliet Lowe Elementary School was an adventure, with surprises lurking around every corner. Kids would giggle as they stumbled upon impromptu football matches in the playground, where they could witness the Rams' skill and finesse up close. The echoes of cheers and laughter reverberated throughout the campus, creating an atmosphere of pure joy and camaraderie.

The former Juliet Lowe Elementary School became a place where dreams came true, where the world of football collided with the innocent wonder of childhood. It was a treasure trove of memories, etched forever in the hearts of those fortunate enough to experience its magic.

The Women's Individual Road Race
22128 Antigua
Mission Viejo

The 1984 Summer Olympics marked the first inclusion of women's cycling events in the Olympic program. The race took place here on Sunday, July 29, 1984, starting at 9:00 A.M. Jeannie Longo-Ciprelli from France was considered the favorite for the event, with strong competition expected from Connie Carpenter-Phinney and Rebecca Twigg, both representing the United States.

A decisive breakaway occurred midway through the race, involving Longo-Ciprelli, Carpenter-Phinney, and Twigg. With less than a kilometer remaining, Longo-Ciprelli and another participant collided, causing Longo-Ciprelli's bike chains to come off. This incident eliminated her from the race, leaving only Twigg and Carpenter-Phinney to contend for the victory.

Twigg was anticipated to have the advantage in the final sprint. However, in a thrilling finish, Twigg initially led the sprint, but Carpenter-Phinney employed a "bike pumping" technique she had learned from her husband, who was participating in the Men's Olympic Individual Road Race. This technique involved standing on the pedals and vigorously pumping them to gain extra speed.

Carpenter-Phinney managed to catch Twigg and won the race by a narrow margin, crossing the finish line just inches ahead.

Connie Carpenter-Phinney's victory in the Women's Individual Road Race at the 1984 Olympics marked a historic moment in women's cycling and was a memorable achievement for her and the United States. A marker here honors the spot.

World Cup Soccer Training Facility
27200 La Paz Road
Mission Viejo

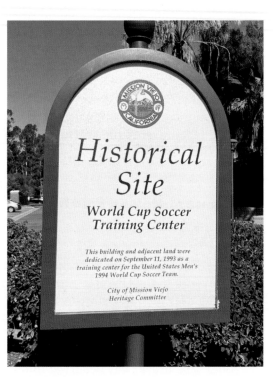

This site was dedicated on September 11, 1993 as a training center for the United States Men's 1994 World Cup Soccer Team. The facility was used by the team to prepare for the 1994 FIFA World Cup, which was held in the United States. Mission Viejo, located in Orange County, was chosen as the site for the training center. The facility and the adjacent land were specifically designated for the purpose of providing a training venue for the national team in preparation for the World Cup tournament. The training center provided state-of-the-art facilities and resources to support the team's training sessions, tactical preparations, and physical conditioning. It played a vital role in shaping the team's performance and readiness for the prestigious international tournament. A plaque marks the history.

CHAPTER FIFTEEN

WEIRD, WONDERFUL, AND ONE-OF-A-KIND

WHILE ORANGE COUNTY IS renowned for its breathtaking beaches, thriving cities, and iconic landmarks, it is also a treasure trove of hidden gems that defy categorization. These peculiar places—many of which are no longer standing but are etched in the memories of those who experienced their eccentricity—continue to cast a spell on our collective imagination. From unique buildings and strange structures to oddly captivating attractions, this chapter unravels the enigmatic and elusive essence of these lost landmarks that sometimes defy description.

The Bolsa Chica Gun Club

Bolsa Chica wetlands
Huntington Beach

The Bolsa Chica Gun Club, which opened in 1899, holds a significant place in the history of Orange County. Nestled within the picturesque Bolsa Chica wetlands, it initially served as a retreat for wealthy industrialists from Los Angeles, Pasadena, and other areas during the early 1900s. This exclusive establishment provided an ideal sanctuary for influential individuals seeking privacy and solace.

As the 20th century progressed, the gun club underwent several transformations. During World War II, the site was repurposed as a military installation to safeguard against potential oceanic attacks. This strategic positioning exemplified the club's importance and its role in protecting the region's coastal areas.

Following the war, in the 1950s, the Bolsa Chica Gun Club transitioned into a social club. It continued to serve as a gathering place for socializing, networking, and fostering relationships among its members. The club became a hub for the local elite, offering

them opportunities to connect and engage in various recreational activities.

Unfortunately, the club's existence came to an end in the early 1960s when it was torn down. Despite its demolition, the gun club's legacy and historical significance endure. Today, remnants of the club can still be found atop the upper Mesa of the Bolsa Chica wetlands, serving as a tangible reminder of the area's rich past.

Boy Scout Jamboree
1103A Newport Center Drive
Newport Beach

The Third National Jamboree held in Orange County in July 1953 stands as a significant milestone in the history of Scouting in the United States. With an astonishing attendance of around 50,000 Scouts and Scouters from all corners of the country, the event left an indelible mark on the region and the hearts of those who participated.

Interestingly, the decision to host the Jamboree in Orange County was somewhat serendipitous. During a meeting of California Scout Executives in early 1952 in Los Angeles, the topic of potential Jamboree sites was being discussed. Various locations were being considered when "Skip" Fife, the Scout Executive of the Orange Empire Area Council, casually suggested that "the only place big enough around here to handle that many kids would be the Irvine Ranch."

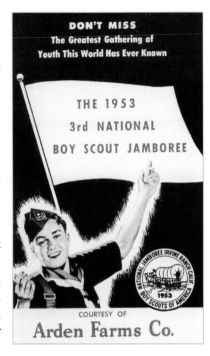

DON'T MISS
The Greatest Gathering of
Youth This World Has Ever Known

THE 1953
3rd NATIONAL
BOY SCOUT JAMBOREE

COURTESY OF
Arden Farms Co.

The mere mention of the Irvine Ranch as a possible venue sparked interest and ignited the imagination of those present. Located in Orange County, the Irvine Ranch was an expansive and picturesque area that spanned thousands of acres. Its vast and diverse landscape, which included rolling hills, open fields, and scenic vistas, made it an ideal backdrop for such a grand event.

Recognizing the potential of the Irvine Ranch, Scouting officials wasted no time in exploring the feasibility of hosting the Jamboree there. Subsequent discussions and negotiations took place between the Boy Scouts of America and the Irvine Company, which owned the ranch. Eventually, an agreement was reached,

paving the way for the Third National Jamboree to be held on this extraordinary site.

The Jamboree preparations were immense. The Irvine Ranch underwent extensive transformations to accommodate the influx of Scouts and Scouters. Temporary campsites, activity areas, and infrastructure were constructed to ensure a smooth and enjoyable experience for all participants. The event organizers left no stone unturned in their efforts to create an atmosphere of fellowship, adventure, and fun.

When the Jamboree finally commenced in July 1953, it exceeded all expectations. The Irvine Ranch buzzed with energy and excitement as tens of thousands of Scouts and Scouters arrived from across the United States. The seven-day event was packed with a plethora of activities, including educational workshops, group competitions, outdoor adventures, and cultural exchanges. Scouts had the opportunity to interact with fellow Scouts from different regions, fostering friendships and building lifelong memories.

With the departure of the Scouts and the closing of the event, the 1953 Jamboree became a part of history, leaving behind unforgettable memories and experiences for those who participated. The Jamboree also left a lasting impact on Orange County. The region experienced an economic boom during the event, as local businesses benefited from the influx of visitors. It also put Orange County on the map as a destination capable of hosting large-scale events, setting the stage for future endeavors.

CARNEGIE LIBRARIES

Carnegie libraries were public libraries built across the United States and several other countries through the philanthropic efforts of Andrew Carnegie, a Scottish-American industrialist and philanthropist. During the late 19th and early 20th centuries, Carnegie funded the construction of thousands of libraries worldwide, with the aim of providing free access to knowledge and education for all.

The Carnegie library movement began in 1881 when Carnegie offered a grant to his birthplace, the city of Dunfermline, Scotland,. Inspired by the impact of this initial library, Carnegie expanded his philanthropic endeavors, primarily in the United States. His grants were offered on the condition that the local community would provide the land and commit to maintaining and operating the library.

Carnegie libraries were designed to be functional and aesthetically pleasing structures, often featuring classical architectural styles. They became community hubs, offering not only books but also educational programs, lectures, and cultural events. Carnegie libraries played a vital role in democratizing access to education and fostering a love of learning in communities across America.

Over time, as communities grew and library needs changed, many Carnegie libraries faced challenges in meeting modern requirements. Some libraries were expanded, while others were eventually replaced by larger facilities. However, rather than demolishing these historic buildings, many communities recognized their architectural and historical value and opted for adaptive reuse.

Orange County had three Carnegie libraries: one in Huntington Beach that burnt down in the 1960s, one in Fullerton, and one in Anaheim. Thankfully, the building where the Carnegie library in Anaheim was located in still exists.

The original Carnegie library in Anaheim was constructed in 1908 and served as a public library for several decades. It

was a cherished institution in the community, providing access to books and knowledge. To preserve the historical significance of the building and provide a contemporary space for cultural exhibitions and events, the Carnegie library was transformed into a dynamic museum and cultural center called Muzeo Anaheim. The repurposed space now showcases art exhibitions, historical displays, and various community-driven programs.

Muzeo Anaheim maintains the architectural integrity of the original Carnegie library while incorporating contemporary design elements. Visitors can experience the unique blend of history and culture as they explore the exhibitions and engage in educational activities within the repurposed space.

By repurposing the former Carnegie library, Muzeo Anaheim pays homage to the community's intellectual heritage while continuing to foster cultural enrichment and engagement. It stands as a testament to the enduring legacy of Carnegie libraries, which have left an indelible mark on communities around the world.

Casa de Tortuga
10455 Circulo De Zapata
Fountain Valley

In the 1960s and 1970s, Casa de Tortuga, located in Fountain Valley, was a normal residence that housed a large number of rare turtles. It offered tours for those interested in seeing the collection or adopting a turtle. The property, which was collector Walter Allen's home, included the habitats of over 450 turtles and tortoises. Allen's private collection at Casa de Tortuga was the largest of its kind in Orange County, showcasing more than 100 different species. It was the only private collection in the area that was open to the public.

Apart from the live turtles, the house also boasted an impressive display of turtle memorabilia. With over 20,000 turtle-related items, including mobiles, plaques, fountains, drawings, planters, ashtrays, and statues, it was a paradise for turtle enthusiasts. Walter Allen started collecting turtles and tortoises as a hobby back in 1967 and over time, his collection grew exponentially, prompting his move to Fountain Valley when it reached 100 animals. Allen found great joy and purpose in engaging with people about turtles and embarking on global journeys to observe and contribute to the preservation of wild turtle populations.

China House
2889 Way Lane
Corona Del Mar

China House, a remarkable architectural gem in Orange County, was a testament to the beauty and allure of Eastern Asian-inspired design. Constructed in 1929, this enchanting residence stood as a testament to the artistic vision of its owner, Lindsay, and his wife, whose passion for Eastern aesthetics shaped the stunning features of the home. One of the most striking elements of China House was its distinctive tiled roof, which boasted a pagoda style. This unique architectural feature added an air of elegance and exoticism to the property. The ornate fixtures adorning the house further accentuated its Eastern influences, creating a captivating atmosphere for both the inhabitants and visitors.

At the entrance of China House, a magnificent carved dragon greeted all who stepped foot inside. This intricately crafted piece added a touch of grandeur and symbolism, signifying power, wisdom, and good fortune. It served as a remarkable testament to the attention to detail and craftsmanship that permeated every aspect of the dwelling.

For several decades, China House stood as a cherished landmark, capturing the imagination of those who encountered its splendor. Sadly, in 1987, the home was torn down, making way for the construction of two luxury houses. Although China House may no longer grace the landscape of Corona del Mar, the memory of its architectural grandeur lives on. Its unique blend of Eastern-inspired design elements and meticulous craftsmanship serves as a testament to the enduring appeal of cultural exchange and the power of architectural beauty to transcend time. While the loss of China House was undoubtedly a great disappointment to all who appreciated its beauty, remnants of its legacy remain.

One of the fortunate outcomes of the demolition of China House in 1987 was the foresight and dedication of John Hamilton, a long-time resident of China Cove. Recognizing the historical significance of the structure, Hamilton worked out a deal with the homeowners, Jim and Martha Beauchamp, as well as Ernie and Donna Schroeder, who were replacing China House with their own luxury homes.

Hamilton's agreement allowed him to salvage pieces of the historic structure before its demolition. He carefully stored these remnants in a warehouse, envisioning a future where they would resurface as poignant reminders of the house that once stood in all its glory. True to his word, Hamilton found a unique way to incorporate the salvaged pieces into his own property. The roof tiles, which had adorned China House's pagoda-style roof, were repurposed and used in the construction of a small building situated just above his garage on Way Lane. This location, approximately 50 yards from the original site of China House, provided a fitting tribute to the lost architectural treasure.

By reusing the salvaged roof tiles in such a close proximity to the original location, Hamilton ensured that the spirit and essence of China House would live on in the neighborhood. The little building, adorned with these historic pieces, served as a tangible reminder of the beauty and cultural significance that once graced China Cove.

Today, China Cove in Corona del Mar serves as a treasured hideaway, preserving the memory of China House and the allure of its original surroundings. The cove's picturesque beauty continues to captivate residents and visitors alike, offering a tranquil retreat from the bustling urban life of Orange County.

Dana Point Auditorium
24699 Del Prado Avenue
Dana Point

This marker in Dana Point highlights the historical significance of the original Dana Point Community Center, specifically focusing on the auditorium. The marker features a picture depicting the Woodruff Sales staff and potential buyers standing in front of the community center.

The auditorium was originally constructed for Sidney H. Woodruff, who used it as his headquarters. In addition to serving as Woodruff's base of operations, the auditorium was also utilized for community events and large sales promotions. It played a central role in showcasing the advantages of the planned community in the 1920s.

At that time, Dana Point's location was praised for several

reasons. It was known for its ample water supply, excellent views, and a coastline that ran east-west, providing a southern exposure. The area was free from dangerous riptides and undertow, making it an appealing destination for residents and potential buyers.

Throughout its history, the building that housed the auditorium has served various purposes. It has been utilized as a warehouse, a garage, an antique shop, a music school, and a restaurant. This highlights the adaptive reuse of the structure, with different businesses and organizations making use of the space in different ways over the years.

The marker in Dana Point serves to commemorate the original Dana Point Community Center and its auditorium, offering a glimpse into the history of the area and the development of the planned community.

The Dana Point Elevator
24443 Dana Point Drive
Dana Point

The Dana Point elevator was a historic structure that was constructed in 1930 with the purpose of providing access to a pocket beach for the Dana Point Inn. The elevator was intended to serve as a means for guests to reach the hotel lobby from the beach, as part of a larger development project that included the construction of the Dana Point Inn on the bluff's edge.

The structure consisted of a doorway that provided entry to a

tunnel measuring 165 feet in length. This tunnel led to an elevator that would transport guests 135 feet up to the hotel lobby.

But the development project faced unfortunate circumstances. The stock market crash of 1929, which marked the beginning of the Great Depression, had a significant impact on the economy and led to the abandonment of many construction projects, including the Dana Point Inn. Consequently, the hotel was never built, and the elevator remained unfinished.

Although the Dana Point Inn was never realized, remnants of the hotel arches can still be seen above the elevator structure. These remnants serve as a reminder of the ambitious development plans that were disrupted by the economic downturn of the 1929 stock market crash. Today, the Dana Point elevator stands as a historical landmark, representing the unrealized vision of the Dana Point Inn and the impact of the Great Depression on the local area. It provides a glimpse into the architectural plans and aspirations of the past, preserving a piece of Dana Point's history.

Disneyland Bandstand
2301 San Joaquin Hills Road
Newport Beach

The marker at Rogers Garden nursery in Newport Beach commemorates the historical significance of the Bandstand that was originally located in Disneyland's Town Square, Main Street, USA. It notes that on July 17, 1955, bandleader Mickey Mouse led his 16-piece band from this very Bandstand on the day Disneyland opened.

Originally, the Bandstand was situated in Town Square, but before Disneyland's Grand Opening, Walt Disney realized that its placement obstructed the view from the Disneyland Railroad Station to Sleeping Beauty's Castle. As a result, the Bandstand was moved to Carnation Plaza Gardens.

In 1956, the Bandstand was relocated once again, this time to what is now known as New Orleans Square. It served as an entertainment venue, and during Easter Week 1958, the Mouseketeers performed there daily. Additionally, from 1959 to 1961, the Kid's Amateur Dog Show took place in front of the Bandstand, with

judging and awards ceremonies held within its structure.

Eventually, in 1967, the Bandstand was retired to the "backstage" area just before the debut of New Orleans Square. The marker at Rogers Garden nursery serves as a reminder of the Bandstand's significant role in Disneyland's early years and its connection to iconic events and performances, including Mickey Mouse leading his band during the park's opening day.

Doll Museum
The White House Banquets & Event Center
1238 Beach Boulevard
Anaheim

The White House Banquets & Event Center is a one-half scale replica of the original White House in Washington D.C. It was constructed in 1978 by Jay and Bea DeArmond as part of Hobby City.

The venue once housed an iconic doll museum featuring over 4,000 toys and dolls, including a large Barbie and Ken collection. However, the doll museum closed in 2008. The White House Banquets & Event Center has since transformed into a premiere event facility, featuring the West Wing Grand Ballroom and the Rose Garden Courtyard.

Farmers Gun Club
5660 Orangewood Avenue
Los Alamitos

In the vibrant eras of the 1920s and '30s, when much of coastal and near-the-coast Orange County sat amidst marshes and wetlands, it was a hotbed for gun clubs. The Farmers Gun Club stood as a testament to the enthusiasm for shooting sports that permeated the region.

One particularly notable event in the club's chronicles occurred in October 1927 when two legends of America's favorite pastime, Babe Ruth and Lou Gehrig, made an extraordinary visit. Fresh off their triumphant World Series win with the illustrious New York Yankees' "Murderers' Row" team, the dynamic duo ventured westward to explore the charms of California. Accompanying them on their journey was Glenn Thomas, a local car dealer and club member who undoubtedly relished the opportunity to showcase the Farmers Gun Club to these baseball icons.

The occasion was a rare one, as it marked Gehrig's sole visit to the Golden State throughout his illustrious career. A treasured photograph, capturing the three legendary figures together, immortalizes this exceptional rendezvous. It stands as a testament to the Farmers Gun Club's allure and the magnetic appeal that drew people from all walks of life to its hallowed grounds.

Today, while the Navy Golf Course has transformed the landscape, a few of the original waterways that once intersected the Farmers Gun Club still weave through the grounds, offering a glimpse into the past. They serve as a poignant reminder of the club's heyday and the vibrant era of gun clubs that once thrived in Orange County.

Some trivia: At the very golf course that now occupies the site of the former Farmers Gun Club, a young prodigy by the name of Tiger Woods honed his game, setting the stage for a legendary career that would captivate the world.

FOUNTAIN VALLEY HISTORY

The historic marker in Fountain Valley commemorates three significant sites in the area. Here's a description of each site as outlined on the marker:

1. **Country Stores:** The marker mentions the presence of two country stores in the area. The first store was established between 1896 and 1898 by John Corbett. It then passed through the ownership of Tom Talbert, Joe Parsons, and finally Bob Harper. In 1916, another store was built across Bushard Street by Bob Harper. These country stores served as gathering places for the community and played a role in providing essential goods and services to the residents of Fountain Valley.

2. **First Post Office:** In 1899, a Post Office was established in Fountain Valley within the Country Store. Initially named Fountain Valley, it was later renamed Talbert due to duplication with another post office. In 1907, the Talbert Post Office was combined with the Santa Ana Post Office. The marker also notes that the post office was later re-designated as Fountain Valley in 1957. This site represents an important aspect of the community's history and its postal services.

3. Original Circus Site: This site was once the location where the Escalante Circus set up its annual performance tent. The marker highlights that the circus parade would begin at this site and proceed east to Ward, then north to Warner, west to Wintersburg (which is

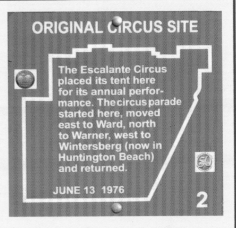

now in Huntington Beach), and finally return. The presence of the circus in this area was a notable event that brought entertainment and excitement to Fountain Valley.

The Grant Boys
1750 Newport Boulevard
Costa Mesa

After 66 years of selling outdoor goods, Levi's, and firearms, The Grant Boys, a beloved old business in Orange County, closed its doors in 2015. The Costa Mesa shop, originally named Grant's War Surplus, was established in 1949 by Edward "Buddy" Grant and his mother, Minnie Stone. Initially located near the future site of The Triangle shopping center, the hardware and surplus store quickly gained popularity among locals.

In 1953, Grant's War Surplus relocated a few blocks away to its current location, which became recognizable to many due to its charming Wild West storefront. Over the years, the store became a cherished part of the community, serving generations of customers with a wide range of outdoor merchandise, durable Levi's clothing, and firearms.

Following the passing of Edward "Buddy" Grant, the store's ownership was transferred to his daughter, Alexa, and her husband, Randy Garell. The couple diligently carried on the family business and continued to provide quality products to their loyal customer base. Alexa and Randy dedicated their lives to the store, having started working there as teenagers. Now in their mid-60s, they decided that it was time to retire and pursue their passion for fishing.

The closing of The Grant Boys marked the end of an era for Orange County residents who have relied on the store for their outdoor and Levi's needs for over six decades. It served as a testament to the enduring entrepreneurial spirit of the Grant family and their commitment to the local community. The store is fondly remembered for its warm customer service, vast selection of goods, and its iconic Wild West façade that captured the imagination of passers-by.

Randy acknowledged in a 2004 interview with the *Orange County Register* that while firearms were a significant part of their business, the store's focus extended beyond that. He emphasized that the gun industry was not highly profitable, requiring substantial labor and navigating through numerous regulatory requirements. He humorously remarked that anyone contemplating entering the gun business should consider seeking medical help, as it was not an easy industry to thrive in. Despite the challenges, The Grant Boys persevered and maintained a reputation as a reliable source for firearms and related products.

THE GREETER

In Laguna Beach, there lived a man named Eiler Larsen. Born on March 27, 1890, Larsen was a Danish vagabond who wandered across continents, embracing the adventures that unfolded before him. After a lifetime of exploration and discovery, he found his way to Laguna Beach at the age of 52, where he would leave an indelible mark on the community. Larsen was a man of simple pleasures and extraordinary warmth. Although he occasionally worked as a gardener, his true calling was something far more enchanting. Every day, without fail, Larsen would find himself standing on a street corner, ready to greet every passing car and pedestrian with his infectious smile and booming voice.

With his shaggy hair and heavily bearded face, Larsen became known as "The Greeter" of Laguna Beach. From the

1940s until the early 1970s, he became a beloved cultural icon for both locals and tourists alike. His signature greeting, a resounding "Halloo-oo-oo!" echoed through the streets, filling the air with joy and a sense of community. Larsen's genuine warmth and affection touched the hearts of all who encountered him. Visitors to Laguna Beach were instantly captivated by his charm and the genuine interest he showed in each person he greeted. He became a symbol of the town, a living landmark that welcomed people from near and far, enveloping them in the spirit of friendship and hospitality.

The people of Laguna Beach recognized the treasure they had in Eiler Larsen. Local patrons rallied around him, offering their support in various ways. Generous souls provided him with a rent-free room, ensuring he had a place to call home. Others offered free meals and essential services, understanding the significance of his presence in their community.

In 1964, the mayor of Laguna Beach bestowed a remarkable honor upon Larsen. He was officially proclaimed as Laguna's Official Greeter, a title that encapsulated the love and appreciation that the town held for him. Larsen's infectious personality and unwavering dedication to greeting everyone with open arms had become an integral part of the town's identity.

Throughout his life, Larsen found himself immortalized in various forms of art. Paintings, postcards, photographs, and sculptures captured his essence, ensuring that his spirit would endure beyond his years. The people of Laguna Beach recognized that Larsen was more than just a man; he was a living embodiment of their community's heart and soul. When Larsen passed away on March 19, 1975, the town mourned the loss of their beloved greeter. But his legacy lived on, forever etched in the memories of all who had been touched by his kindness. The story of Eiler Larsen, the vagabond turned greeter, continued to inspire generations with its message of embracing others with open hearts and spreading joy through simple acts of kindness.

To this day, the spirit of Larsen lives on in the hearts of Laguna Beach residents and visitors alike. There are two large statues of Larsen in Laguna Beach. The first statue, called "Hello-o-o-o-o-o- How Ar-r-re You?," is a painted cement casting that was created by sculptor Charles Beauvais in the 1960s. This statue can be found outside the Pottery Place along Pacific Coast Highway. There is a plaque dedicated to Larsen, describing him as a philosopher, gardener, and friend of man who spent his spare time spreading goodwill and cheer. The second statue, created in 1986 by Guy Angelo Wilson, is a life-sized redwood carving located at a downtown corner outside Greeter's Corner restaurant. This statue was named in Larsen's honor. These statues serve as tributes to Larsen's contributions and his impact on the community.

Hanging Tree
Accessed by taking a strenuous 10-mile hike led by an Irvine Ranch
Conservancy docent
Tustin

Deep within the serene confines of the Irvine Ranch Natural Landmarks, within a small canyon, lies a cluster of seven majestic sycamore trees. These towering beauties, with their distinctive deep green leaves and tall, straight trunks, hold within their ancient roots a tale of outlaw history that has become notorious in Orange County.

During the mid-19th century, a notorious band of outlaws known as the Flores Gang wreaked havoc throughout the region. Their audacious robberies spanned from Los Angeles to San Juan Capistrano, striking fear into the hearts of the local residents. It was their brazen ambush of Los Angeles County Sheriff James Barton that etched their name into the annals of infamy.

The tragic event, known as the "Barton Massacre," claimed the lives of Sheriff Barton and three others. The shocking incident sent shockwaves throughout the community and ignited a relentless pursuit to bring the perpetrators to justice. The hunt for the notorious Flores Gang and their leader, Joaquin Flores, became the stuff of legends.

After tireless efforts, Flores was eventually captured and met his fate at the hands of the law. In a dramatic spectacle witnessed by several thousand spectators, he was hanged in downtown Los Angeles, marking the end of his reign of terror. However, the pursuit of justice did not end there. Two of Flores' accomplices, Francisco Ardillero and Juan Catabo, were relentlessly pursued, their paths leading them to the grove of sycamore trees that still stand proudly within the Irvine Ranch Natural Landmarks today. In a climactic ending, Ardillero and Catabo were finally apprehended and met a similar fate as their leader. They were hanged at the very spot where the sycamore trees now bear witness to their dark legacy.

Over the years, the grove of sycamore trees has become a haunting reminder of the turbulent times that once gripped Orange County. It stands as a silent witness to the pursuit of justice and the triumph of law and order over lawlessness. The stories of the Flores Gang, the Barton Massacre, and the subsequent hangings have become deeply ingrained in the folklore of the region, a testament to the enduring power of history.

As visitors wander through the Irvine Ranch Natural Landmarks and come across the grove of sycamore trees, they are transported back to a time when outlaws roamed the land. The trees, swaying gently in the breeze, serve as a poignant reminder of the past, a reminder of the pursuit of justice and the ultimate price paid by those who sought to challenge the law.

Throughout the years, there has been a persistent misidentification of the location of the hanging tree associated with the notorious killings. Many believed it to be situated along Santiago

UNDER THIS TREE GENERAL
ANDRES PICO HUNG TWO
BANDITOS OF THE FLORES
GANG IN 1857.
DEDICATED
EL VIAJE DE PORTOLA RIDE
APRIL   1967

Canyon Road, near the turnoff to Modjeska Canyon. But the true site of these dark events was unknown to the public for a significant period of time.

In 1967, an equestrian group erected a monument to mark the authentic location of the hangings. As the years went by, the monument became obscured by the overgrowth of mustard plants and weeds, fading from sight and memory. It seemed as though the site and its historical significance would remain hidden indefinitely.

Then, in 2007, the devastating Santiago Fire swept across Loma Ridge, leaving destruction in its wake. As the flames raged through the area, the intense heat consumed the obstructing vegetation, revealing the long-forgotten monument to the public eye once again. The site, not far from the 241 Toll Road, bore witness to the chilling words engraved upon a plaque: "Under this tree, General Andres Pico hung two banditos of the Flores Gang in 1875."

This revelation sparked renewed interest in the dark history associated with the Flores Gang and their ultimate demise. General Andres Pico, a prominent figure at the time, had taken it upon himself to deliver swift justice by carrying out the hangings. The plaque serves as a somber reminder of the events that unfolded under the very branches of the tree it stands beneath.

The unearthing of the monument and its subsequent exposure to the public has allowed for a deeper understanding of the region's past. It has become a place of pilgrimage for those who seek to connect with the tales of the Flores Gang, the Barton Massacre, and the pursuit of justice that followed. The plaque beneath the tree stands as a testament to the enduring power of history and the need to remember even the darkest chapters of our collective past.

Huntington Inn
Eighth Street and Pacific Coast Highway
Huntington Beach

Back in 1905, the beautiful Huntington Inn hotel opened its doors in Huntington Beach, right at the intersection of Eighth Street and the Pacific Coast Highway. It was a grand building, constructed in the popular craftsman style that was all the rage at the time. The hotel was designed to cater to both tourists and local officials who often held meetings there. As the years went by, the hotel saw its fair share of changes. In 1917, a flamboyant boxer named Tommy Burns purchased the property and transformed it into a health spa. It was an unexpected twist for the hotel, but it seemed to strike a chord with the changing times and the desires of visitors. The most significant transformation came in 1920 when the oil boom hit Huntington Beach. The Standard Oil Company saw the potential in the hotel's location and acquired it to house many of its new employees. The hotel became a bustling hub for oil workers, providing them with a place to live and rest after long days in the oil fields.

For several decades, the hotel thrived as an important part of the community. But in 1969, its fate took a sad turn. The iconic Huntington Inn hotel was torn down, marking the end of an era. It was a heartbreaking moment for many locals who had grown up with the hotel as a prominent landmark in their lives.

Despite its demolition, the memories and significance of the Huntington Inn hotel remain deeply ingrained in the fabric of Huntington Beach's history. The hotel's early days as a tourist hotspot, its transformation into a health spa, and its role in housing oil workers during the boom years have left an indelible mark on the community.

La Vida Mineral Hot Springs, Calif.

La Vida Mineral Springs Resort
Carbon Canyon Road, east of Brea
Brea

La Vida Mineral Springs was a popular resort that operated from 1910 to the 1980s in Carbon Canyon, located on the Brea side of the canyon just east of Olinda Village. The resort was known for its mineral springs, which were believed to have therapeutic properties and attracted visitors seeking relaxation and wellness.

The mineral waters of La Vida Springs were first discovered and tapped during oil drilling operations in 1893. At that time, the primary objective of the drilling was to extract oil from the region. During the drilling process, the workers encountered underground mineral springs instead. The discovery of the mineral springs during oil drilling was unexpected but intriguing. Recognizing the potential value of the mineral waters, the owners of the land decided to capitalize on this newfound resource by establishing La Vida Mineral Springs as a resort.

Guests at La Vida Mineral Springs could enjoy a range of amenities and activities. The resort offered mineral baths, which were thought to have healing benefits for various ailments. People would soak in the mineral-rich waters to promote relaxation and improve their overall well-being. In addition to the baths, La Vida Mineral Springs featured a hotel, cabins, and camping facilities, allowing

Cottages at LaVida Mineral Springs, Calif.

guests to stay overnight or for extended periods.

The natural surroundings of Carbon Canyon provided a beautiful backdrop for outdoor activities. Visitors could go hiking, horseback riding, or picnicking in the scenic canyon area. The resort also had recreational facilities such as swimming pools, tennis courts, and even a dance pavilion, offering a variety of entertainment options for guests.

Unfortunately, as the 1980s arrived, La Vida Mineral Springs faced challenges that led to its closure. Factors such as changing tourism trends, the decline in mineral springs' popularity, and the impact of urban development in the area contributed to the resort's demise.

Magic Lamp Motel
1013 W. Katella Avenue
Anaheim

Hotels and motels have played a crucial role in the development of Orange County, particularly due to its transformation into a popular tourist destination. The emergence of theme parks like Disneyland and Knott's Berry Farm significantly contributed to the growth of tourism in the region. Themed tourist motels, adorned with the magic of imagination, once thrived around such iconic attractions as these. These distinctive accommodations were more than mere places to rest one's weary head; they were immersive experiences that transported guests into the realms of fantasy, adventure, and wonder. Each hotel embodied a unique theme, enchanting visitors with its own brand of magic.

One example was the Magic Lamp Motel, once located in Anaheim. The Magic Lamp Motel was known for its distinctive Arabian Nights theme, which added a touch of enchantment to the motel experience. The exterior of the motel featured ornate architectural details reminiscent of Middle Eastern palaces, complete with domes, arches, and intricate patterns. This thematic design created an immersive atmosphere, transporting guests to a world of fantasy and adventure as soon as they stepped foot on the property.

One of the most memorable elements of the Magic Lamp Motel was its neon sign. Standing tall and proud, the sign featured a shining lamp with billowing smoke, evoking the imagery of the mystical genie's lamp from the tales of Arabian Nights. The neon lights of the sign illuminated the night, guiding weary travelers to the motel's welcoming embrace.

Inside the Magic Lamp Motel, guests were treated to comfortable accommodations that blended modern amenities with the motel's whimsical theme. Each room was thoughtfully designed to reflect the Arabian Nights concept, featuring colorful textiles, ornate furnishings, and decorative accents that transported guests to a magical oasis. The motel provided a respite for weary travelers, offering a unique and memorable stay in the heart of Anaheim.

Sadly, like other motels of its time, the Magic Lamp Motel eventually succumbed to the changing tides of progress and development. As the demand for larger and more modern hotels grew, these charming roadside motels gradually lost their popularity. The Magic Lamp Motel, with its distinctive theme and nostalgic ambiance, was eventually torn down, making way for new developments in the area.

While the physical presence of the Magic Lamp Motel may no longer grace the streets of Anaheim, its memory lives on as a part of the city's motel history. The Arabian Nights-inspired motif, the enchanting neon sign, and the whimsical experiences it offered to its guests remain a cherished part of Orange County's past.

The Main Street Arch
Main Street and Pacific Coast Highway
Huntington Beach

The famous arch that once graced the intersection of Pacific Coast Highway and Main Street in Huntington Beach holds a special place in the city's history. Constructed around 1930, it stood as a towering symbol that welcomed visitors and residents alike to this small coastal city.

The grand arch, adorned with a large Huntington Beach sign at its pinnacle, became an iconic landmark, representing the spirit and identity of the community. It served as a beacon, guiding people towards the heart of the city and invoking a sense of excitement and anticipation as they entered its boundaries.

For a decade, the arch stood as a testament to the pride and character of Huntington Beach. By the late 1930s, the city faced a significant challenge in maintaining the arch's integrity. The

corrosive effects of the salty ocean air took a toll on the metal structure, posing ongoing maintenance and financial concerns.

Ultimately, recognizing the impracticality and expense of preserving the arch in the face of relentless exposure to the coastal elements, the decision was made to dismantle it. Although the arch was dismantled and never replaced, its legacy and significance endure in the collective memory of the community.

Moon Park
3337 California Street
Costa Mesa

Orange County has a rich history in aerospace and space exploration, with companies like McDonnell Douglas and Boeing playing significant roles in shaping this industry. Huntington Beach in particular has been a hub for aerospace activities and has contributed to some notable achievements in space history.

Moon Park is a unique recreational space that serves as a tribute to the monumental achievement of the Apollo 11 Moon landing on July 20, 1969. Much of the original has been lost, but parts of this interesting park still remain and the essence of its lunar theme remains intact.

One notable feature of Moon Park is the 30-foot cratered gray concrete dome that replicates the texture and appearance of the lunar surface. This dome serves as a focal point and reminder of the historic Moon landing. Visitors can explore the dome and experience a simulated lunar environment, allowing them to imagine what it might have been like for the astronauts who walked on the moon.

Previously, Moon Park had outer-space themed playground equipment that added to the immersive experience for children. However, these have since been replaced by more traditional slides and jungle gyms, likely due to maintenance or safety concerns. While the original playground equipment is no longer present, the park still offers a unique atmosphere that sparks the imagination and sense of wonder associated with space exploration.

Within the park, there is a plaque dedicated to Neil Armstrong, the first person to set foot on the moon. The plaque features his famous quote, "That's one small step for man, one giant leap for

mankind," which encapsulates the significance of the Moon landing and its impact on human history. The plaque serves as a reminder of the courage, ingenuity, and determination that led to this momentous achievement.

Ocean View Mushroom Growers
18100 Goldenwest Street
Huntington Beach

Ocean View Mushroom Growers was a mushroom farm located in Huntington Beach. The farm was owned by Victor DiStefano, who had a background in the mushroom business and decided to settle in Southern California after serving in World War II. The farm was situated on a parcel of land on Golden West Street, north of Ellis Avenue. Ocean View Mushroom Growers had 36 dark, air-conditioned grow houses filled with compost and mushrooms. The compost used at the farm was made from a blend of racetrack bedding, winemaking residue, rendered cow belly, and chicken manure. To work in the near darkness, pickers at the farm wore miner helmets.

During its operation, the farm had 220,000 square feet of growing space, and a successful crop yielded approximately five pounds of mushrooms per square foot. The farm eventually shut down in the 1980s. Following the closure of Ocean View Mushroom Growers, the city of Huntington Beach engaged in a lengthy battle to acquire the property, and won.

The Post Brothers' Plow
15261 Brookhurst Street
Westminster

The Post Brothers' Plow is a significant piece of agricultural machinery that was built by Charles R. Post in 1937. Its purpose was to reclaim farmlands that had been devastated by floods. This plow holds the distinction of being recognized as the world's largest plow.

In terms of its dimensions, the Post Brothers' Plow is an impressive piece of equipment. It measures 37 feet in length, 12 feet in height, and 11 feet in width. The blade of the plow itself is 86 inches long, highlighting its substantial size and capacity for soil displacement. To power and operate this massive plow, five 100 drawbar horsepower D-8 Caterpillar tractors were employed.

These tractors were harnessed together to provide the necessary pulling force to move the plow through the soil. The construction and use of the Post Brothers' Plow exemplify the innovative

and ambitious efforts made by Charles R. Post to reclaim and cultivate flood-damaged farmlands. Its large size and the power required to operate it reflect the magnitude of the task at hand. The Post Brothers' Plow holds a place of significance in the history of agricultural machinery, particularly due to its size and the purpose it served in reclaiming flood-ravaged farmland.

San Juan Hot Springs
33401 Ortega Highway
San Juan Capistrano

In the 1960s and early 1970s, San Juan Hot Springs flourished as a popular gathering place for hippies. It served as a haven for those seeking an escape from the constraints of society. The allure of the natural hot springs, combined with the countercultural spirit of the time, made it an ideal spot for communal gatherings, music, and free-spirited expression. It was here that locals and visitors alike flocked to immerse themselves in the healing waters and embrace a lifestyle of peace and harmony.

Before its hippie heyday, San Juan Hot Springs had a predecessor known as San Juan Capistrano Hot Springs. Established in the 1800s, the San Juan Capistrano Hot Springs was a testament to the therapeutic properties of the natural springs. It served as a retreat for people seeking respite and rejuvenation long before the 1960s. This earlier incarnation also adds another layer of history to the site, showcasing its enduring appeal. Unfortunately, the original resort met its demise and was abandoned in the 1940s, leaving behind echoes of a bygone era.

During the vibrant 1960s and 1970s, the new San Juan Hot Springs became a haven for both locals and notable figures. The legendary comedian Red Skelton was said to be a regular visitor, finding solace and inspiration amidst the serene surroundings. The site became synonymous with the counterculture movement, attracting a diverse array of individuals seeking freedom, self-discovery, and a break from societal norms.

Although the springs experienced a revival from 1980 to 1992, they eventually succumbed to neglect and fell into disrepair. Today, access to the hot springs requires a wilderness permit, adding an air of exclusivity to the experience. Adventurers and nostalgia-seekers can embark on a short hike beyond the hot springs to discover the remnants of the old entrance and sign, providing a tangible connection to the past. These relics serve as a testament to the enduring allure of this once-thriving retreat.

The Sea Breeze Auto Court and Trailer Park
21010 Pacific Coast Highway
Huntington Beach

The Sea Breeze Auto Court and Trailer Park in Huntington Beach was a popular destination from the 1930s to the 1950s. Located

on Ocean Avenue, which is now Pacific Coast Highway near First Street, the campground was initially leased by the city from the Huntington Beach Company. It was later purchased by William Ebert, who opened a gas station at the corner of First and Ocean and transformed the area into the Sea Breeze Auto Court and Trailer Park.

The Sea Breeze Auto Court and Trailer Park boasted the title of the "Largest Auto Court and Trailer Park in California." It featured 65 cottages and could accommodate up to 600 trailers. The facilities included a market, café, and dance hall, among other amenities. Its convenient location and range of offerings attracted visitors from all over the country, and it is estimated that over one million people stayed at Sea Breeze throughout its existence.

During its heyday in the 1930s, the Sea Breeze Auto Court and Trailer Park offered affordable accommodations. Cottages were available at a daily rate ranging from $1 to $5, while trailers and camping cost 35 to 50 cents per day. This pricing structure made it an accessible choice for travelers.

The campground had the capacity to accommodate several thousand people per day and night. During the peak season, it often reached its maximum capacity, attracting a significant number of visitors. The popularity of the Sea Breeze Auto Court and Trailer Park made it a bustling destination, with people from all over the country enjoying their stay.

The slogan "A Fine Place for the REST of Your Life" reflects the idyllic and relaxing atmosphere that the Sea Breeze aimed to provide to its guests. It highlights the notion that visitors could escape from their daily routines and enjoy a peaceful and enjoyable experience during their stay at the auto court and trailer park.

Today, the Pacific City shopping center occupies the area where the Sea Breeze Auto Court and Trailer Park once thrived, marking a significant change in the landscape of Huntington Beach.

Ski Villa
Near 5700 Carbon Canyon Road
Chino Hills

Ski Villa, a unique and short-lived ski venture, emerged in the picturesque setting of Carbon Canyon, near Chino Hills, during the years 1966 to 1967. It was an ambitious project that aimed to bring winter sports enthusiasts a taste of skiing and snowboarding in a region that lacked natural snowfall. Despite its brief existence, Ski Villa left an indelible mark on the local landscape and holds a fascinating place in the annals of recreational history.

Situated off Carbon Canyon Road and Canyon Hills Drive, Ski Villa was characterized by a striking 1,300-foot concrete slope adorned with approximately 1.3 million interlocking plastic tiles. These tiles were equipped with bristles to simulate the feeling of skiing on snow. The slope, although lacking the natural beauty of a snow-covered mountain, presented an intriguing and alternative skiing experience.

The ski slope was surrounded by cabins, which added to the charm of the Ski Villa complex. Visitors could rent equipment from the on-site shop and enjoy a meal at the restaurant, creating a complete recreational destination. The cabins provided a cozy retreat for skiers, offering respite from a day on the slope and the opportunity to immerse themselves in the alpine atmosphere.

The grand unveiling of Ski Villa took place on June 25, 1966, attracting curious locals and adventure seekers alike. The novelty of the concept generated excitement, and for a year, Ski Villa thrived as a hub of winter sports activity in an unexpected location. Skiers and snowboarders flocked to this unconventional destination, eager to experience the thrill of gliding down the artificial slope.

In addition to the unique features of Ski Villa, such as the plastic bristle tiles and the cabins, there were several other amenities and facilities that enhanced the skiing experience for visitors. The owner/developer of Ski Villa also acquired part or all of the former Camp Kinder Ring, which had been operated by the Workmen's Circle, a Jewish organization in Los Angeles, from 1928 to 1958. The camp buildings at Ski Villa were repurposed to accommodate various ski-related services. One of the notable additions was a skiing school, where beginners and enthusiasts could receive instruction and improve their skills on the artificial slope. The presence of a skiing school indicates that Ski Villa aimed to cater to individuals of all experience levels, fostering a welcoming environment for novices and seasoned skiers alike.

An equipment shop was also available on-site, providing visitors with the necessary gear and equipment for their skiing adventures. This convenience allowed skiers to access everything they needed without having to travel far from the slope. Having an equipment shop on the premises ensured that visitors could make the most of their time at Ski Villa without any unnecessary delays or inconveniences.

To cater to the culinary needs of guests, Ski Villa boasted a restaurant and lounge where visitors could relax and refuel after a thrilling day on the slope. The restaurant offered a range of dining options, allowing skiers to indulge in hearty meals and warm beverages while enjoying the ambiance of the ski resort.

Safety was also a priority at Ski Villa. The presence of a ski patrol office and a first-aid station ensured that any accidents or injuries could be promptly addressed. While the surface of the slope was touted as being comparable to midmorning spring snow on Mammoth Mountain, it is reasonable to assume that falls and mishaps still occurred. The ski patrol and first-aid station were equipped to handle such incidents, providing necessary medical attention to those in need.

It is worth noting that even with the efforts made to create a safe and enjoyable skiing experience, Ski Villa acknowledged the differences between skiing on plastic bristles and natural snow. An executive from Randazzo Plastic, the manufacturer of the bristle tile, admitted that falling on plastic bristles lacked the softness associated with falling on snow. As a result, Ski Villa advised visitors to have full coverage of their clothing to minimize any potential discomfort or injuries.

Despite its initial success, Ski Villa's existence was fleeting. The venture's peculiar nature and the challenges associated with maintaining an artificial ski slope eventually led to its demise. The absence of natural snowfall, coupled with the logistical hurdles of maintaining a large-scale operation, ultimately proved insurmountable. After just one year, Ski Villa closed its doors, leaving behind a peculiar concrete scar on the hillside.

Today, the remnants of Ski Villa stand as a testament to an audacious and unconventional endeavor. The gray concrete slope, now overgrown with stubbly weeds, serves as a reminder of a time when people dared to dream and challenge the limitations of nature. While Ski Villa may be viewed as a crackpot scheme gone wrong, it remains an intriguing part of local history, sparking curiosity and conversation among those who stumble upon its abandoned remains.

SOME NEON COMES BACK TO LIFE

The neon signs that once adorned certain Orange County motels were symbols of a vibrant and bustling hospitality industry. Anaheim officials initially considered the signs to have "outlived their usefulness" and lacked the necessary funding to restore them to their former glory. As a result, they were consigned to storage, where they remained untouched for up to 20 years. Fortunately, the fate of the neon signs from the Silver Moon Motel, the Sandman Motel, and the Americana Motel took a positive turn. Instead of languishing in a city yard, they were wrapped up and transported to a warehouse belonging to the Museum of Neon Art in Glendale. Here, these relics of Southern California's illuminated past will find a new home among other preserved neon signs.

Preserving these neon signs is not only a testament to the history of Orange County and Southern California but also an acknowledgment of the cultural significance of these illuminated landmarks. They serve as reminders of a bygone era and the vibrant motel culture that once thrived in the region. Through the efforts of the Museum of Neon Art, these signs will be showcased and appreciated for their artistic, historical, and nostalgic value, providing visitors with a glimpse into a unique chapter of Orange County's past. The collaboration between the museum and the city of Anaheim represents a positive

example of how cultural institutions and local authorities can work together to preserve and showcase the heritage of a community. By recognizing the value of these neon signs and providing them with a new home, the city ensures that future generations can appreciate and learn from these lost landmarks, allowing their stories to continue illuminating the history of Orange County.

Submerged Dam
Santiago Oaks Regional Park
Orange

The "Submerged Dam" was an innovative project that aimed to harness groundwater for irrigation and domestic purposes. The initial dam was constructed using clay in 1879, but due to flood damage, it was reconstructed using rock and concrete in 1892.

The construction of the dam involved reaching down to the bedrock, creating a barrier that forced the groundwater to rise to the surface. Once the groundwater was brought to the surface, it was redirected for various uses, primarily irrigation and domestic water supply.

The project was a collaborative effort between the Serrano Water Association, the Carpenter Water Company, and the Jotham Bixby Company. These organizations worked together to design and build the submerged dam, showcasing a combination of efficiency and cost-effectiveness.

The Submerged Dam played a significant role in the development of local agriculture by providing a reliable water source for irrigation. It also contributed to the growth of the community by ensuring a sustainable domestic water supply.

The Tabernacle Auditorium
Orange Avenue and 12th Street
Huntington Beach

Let's travel back in time to the early 1900s when this iconic structure stood tall in the heart of the old Methodist tent camp. From

1905 until its unfortunate demise in the 1930s, the Tabernacle Auditorium served as a vibrant hub of social gatherings, religious revivals, services, and various community events, shaping the spirit and memories of Orange County.

The Tabernacle Auditorium was a sight to behold. Its grand

presence commanded attention and drew people from far and wide. Located between 11th Street, 13th Street, Acacia Avenue, and Orange Avenue, it stood as a testament to the strong community ties and religious devotion of the time.

The auditorium's primary purpose was to foster a sense of togetherness and spiritual growth. It was a place where people gathered for worship, finding solace in their faith and seeking guidance from impassioned preachers. The air would be filled with heartfelt hymns and fervent prayers, creating an atmosphere of reverence and devotion.

Beyond religious services, the Tabernacle Auditorium played host to a multitude of events that brought the community together. Social gatherings, concerts, lectures, and cultural celebrations found their home within its walls. The auditorium buzzed with excitement as people mingled, shared stories, and forged lasting friendships. It was a melting pot of ideas, beliefs, and traditions, enriching the lives of all who stepped through its doors.

The Tabernacle Auditorium's central location made it easily accessible to residents and visitors alike. Its presence became a symbol of unity and a focal point of the town. The surrounding streets, such as Acacia Avenue and Orange Avenue, bustled with activity as people made their way to the auditorium, their anticipation building with each step. Sadly, the Tabernacle Auditorium met a tragic fate in the 1930s when it was ravaged by fire. The loss was deeply felt by the community, and the charred remains stood as a testament to the memories and moments shared within its walls.

Treasure Island Mobile Home Park
30801 Coast Highway
Laguna Beach

Back in the late 1930s, a new trailer park development emerged on the bluffs over Goff Island in Laguna Beach. Inspired by the popularity of the 1934 Hollywood film based on Robert Louis Stevenson's book, the development was named Treasure Island. It's interesting to note that despite the name, none of the *Treasure Island* movies filmed in 1934, 1950, 1990, or 2012 were actually shot there.

From 1939 through 1947, the trailer park experienced rapid growth as it offered motorists with trailers affordable accommodations and breathtaking coastal views. One unique aspect of the trailer park was its private beach, accessible only to residents of the locked community. The pristine beaches below were off-limits to the general public.

Throughout its existence, the trailer park also served as a popular filming location. It witnessed the production of numerous silent movies, adding to its allure. Notably, in 1946, Bette Davis filmed *Stolen Life* there, leaving behind a piece of cinematic history. The most famous film associated with the trailer park was the 1953 comedy blockbuster *The Long Long Trailer*, starring Lucille Ball and Desi Arnaz. The movie showcased the adventures of a couple traveling in their trailer. Interestingly, the actual trailer used in the film was kept on the property until the trailer park's closure in the 1990s, serving as a reminder of its storied past.

The presence of these film productions and the unique charm of the trailer park contributed to its allure and reputation over the years. Today, the location that was once the Treasure Island trailer park has been transformed into a stunning and exclusive resort known as the Montage. The resort stands as a testament to luxury and elegance, offering guests a memorable and indulgent experience.

While the Montage has undergone significant changes since its trailer park days, it still pays homage to *The Long Long Trailer*. As a tribute to the film, the resort features a plaque positioned next to two prominent palm trees that were showcased in the movie. These two palm trees hold special significance as they were captured on film and became symbolic of the adventures and humor depicted in *The Long Long Trailer*. To honor the legacies of Lucille Ball and Desi Arnaz, the trees have been affectionately named Lucy and Desi, respectively. This nod to the film and its beloved stars adds a touch of nostalgia and Hollywood glamour to the Montage resort.

Westfair Shopping Center
Intersection of Springdale Street and Warner Avenue
Huntington Beach

The year was 1969 when renowned architect Frank Lloyd Wright Jr., son of the esteemed Frank Lloyd Wright, bestowed his creative genius upon the shopping center. It was to be his final masterpiece, the culmination of a legacy of architectural brilliance. Little did he know that fate would soon cast its somber shadow upon his work.

Amongst his ambitious plans, Frank Lloyd Wright Jr. envisioned a towering structure that would pierce the heavens, a beacon of progress and innovation. Rising 92 feet into the sky, this architectural marvel would have taken the shape of a futuristic oil well, a symbol of the city's rich history and its inexorable ties to the petroleum industry. It was a vision that dared to challenge the ordinary and embrace the extraordinary.

The people of Huntington Beach, in their shortsightedness, rejected this audacious vision. They rose up against the towering structure, their voices echoing with fervor, and ultimately drove the visionary architect away from their town. Frank Lloyd Wright Jr., who had poured his heart and soul into his final creation, was forced to abandon his dream, leaving behind a void that could never be filled.

Yet, even in defeat, the spirit of Frank Lloyd Wright Jr. prevailed.

The developers, recognizing the indisputable brilliance of his plans, chose to honor his legacy by implementing the rest of his designs for the shopping center. And so, amidst the sprawling complex, behind the Arco gas station, stands a solemn testament to what could have been—a black granite "tombstone" that encapsulates the tale of the 92-foot tower that never graced the city's skyline.

Today, as visitors and passersby gaze upon this enigmatic monument, their imagination sparks with wonder. They ponder the grandeur that might have been, the awe-inspiring presence that might have drawn gazes from miles away. They reflect upon the clash between artistic vision and the constraints of public opinion, recognizing the delicate balancing act that often determines the fate of architectural marvels.

ACKNOWLEDGMENTS

WHEN I MOVED TO Orange County in 1999, my children were still young, around eight and five years old. We settled in Huntington Beach, and over the years, we witnessed the changes that took place in the area. Many of the places I wanted to include in this book had already vanished before our arrival. However, I was fortunate to connect with incredible individuals who had firsthand experience with these locations. They became invaluable resources, offering their knowledge and stories, helping me piece together the history of Orange County.

I want to express my heartfelt gratitude to the people who generously shared their insights. Bill Kettler, Phil Brigandi, Rick Blake, Dave Reynolds, and countless others along the way, thank you for your contributions. Your firsthand accounts and memories have truly enriched this book. Chris Jepsen at the Orange County Archives is not just a great historian, but the many photos he makes available through the archive certainly helped this book. Thank you, Chris!

As always, thank you as well to my family and friends for their patience through projects like this; to my good friend and publisher, Jeffrey Goldman; and everyone at Santa Monica Press, especially Jessica Ballardo and Amy Inouye.

PHOTO CREDITS

Tamara Asaki: 4

Courtesy of the Orange County Archives: 30, 32, 33, 36, 37, 38, 39, 43, 50, 54, 58, 60, 61, 62, 69, 70, 84, 92, 104, 110, 112, 113, 159, 160, 167, 178, 191, 232, 235, 253, 254, 260, 276, 279, 284, 292

Diane Valott: 259

All other images from Author's Personal Collection.